Asylum to Anarchy

WITHDRAWN

This is a study of democratic tyranny, a tyranny of the therapeutic, in which naked power replaced the ideals of a therapeutic community designed to eliminate hierarchy and bureaucracy. It is a detailed study of a day hospital in London, a model community for psychoanalytic treatment in a democratic setting, which went badly wrong in its attempt to capture the momentum of de-institutionalization in mental health care. It is also a critique of power for our time, as it moves well beyond a case study to analyse the shift of social control from overtly authoritarian oppression to a more punitive erosion of selfhood beneath an egalitarian mantle.

Claire Baron argues that Erving Goffman's classic work on asylums, as well as anti-psychiatry texts such as the writings of Laing and Szasz, were appropriate to the anti-establishment spirit of the 1960s and early 70s. But the democratic rhetoric of the New Right of the 1980s speaks of individual freedom and the overthrow of burdensome bureaucracy, and this new form of power calls for a new critique. This the author has provided.

Her analysis is based on an intensive participant observation. It will interest mental health and related workers in both out-patient and in-patient settings, especially those involved in community mental health, and indeed anyone concerned with the dynamics of institutions. It will also interest social scientists, political theorists and students of culture who want to refine the understanding of power in a post-Goffman epoch.

Claire Baron studied at the London School of Economics and gained her doctorate there in 1984. She has taught and done research at Brunel University and Bedford College, London; she is currently Health Policy Adviser to the Social Democratic Party.

CLAIRE BARON

ASYLUM TO ANARCHY

*'an association in which the free development of each
is the condition of the free development of all'*

FREE ASSOCIATION BOOKS / LONDON / 1987

First published in Great Britain in 1987 by
Free Association Books
26 Freegrove Road
London N7 9RQ

British Library Cataloguing in Publication Data

Baron, Claire
  Asylum to anarchy.
  1.   Mental health services—Social aspects
  I. Title
  362.2'042   RA790.5
ISBN 0 946960 61 5
ISBN 0 946960 62 3 Pbk

Typeset by Input Typesetting Ltd, SW19
Printed and bound in Great Britain by
Short Run Press, Exeter

To the patients and staff
of the day hospital

Contents

Acknowledgements

The writing of this book took many years from the first stumbling draft of my PhD thesis to the present book, and during that time I had an enormous amount of help from many quarters.

First and foremost, I would like to thank the patients and staff of the day hospital for allowing me to share their daily life for nearly three years. I feel deeply indebted to them, as I am acutely aware that what caused them anguish gave me material for firstly my PhD, and later my book. Their generosity in letting me participate freely in the day hospital, treating me as one of them and always being open to questions, gave me a uniquely fortunate research experience. I was excluded from no situation or activity and could pursue any line of interest I desired. Dr Peter Reder and Mary Hall were particularly kind and helpful.

I would also like to thank the staff of the rest of the institute who allowed me access to the communal staffroom and to the Professional Staff Committee meetings. The openness of the members of the institute in their dealings with each other and in allowing a sociologist such free access to their communications, especially in a time of crisis, is a tribute to the profession of psychotherapy and specifically to the institute as a whole. I would like to mention in particular Dr Lionel Kreeger, who first welcomed me to the institute and who encouraged me all the way along.

Professor Paul Rock, who was my supervisor at the London School of Economics, nursed me along from my first tentative steps as a PhD student to the completion of the thesis in 1984.

Acknowledgements

He believed in the project from the beginning and was always stimulating, encouraging, kind and forbearing.

I would like to thank my publishers, in particular Karl Figlio, who helped me in so many ways in the many months it took me to find the book in the thesis. He was inspiring and endlessly patient and resourceful, and gave the kind of help every author would wish to have from their publisher. I would also like to thank Selina O'Grady for her painstaking and imaginative work during the many stages of the publishing process.

I would also like to mention those people who in their different ways supported me during the whole of this period: Professor Keith Hopkins, Juliet Hopkins, David Rosenberg, Dr David Billis and Professor Percy Cohen.

I am particularly grateful to all those who struggled with my difficult handwriting and typed the manuscript at one stage or another, including Michael Shak, Jenny Bagley and Patricia Stroud. Ellen Sutton not only typed but painstakingly edited a large part of the work, which flew back and forth across Europe to and from her home on a Greek island.

As well as typing, Michael Shak meticulously organized the notes and references, and he and Dr Sophie Botros gave me unfailing and inestimable moral support and understanding, as did my family, especially my father and my two sisters, Rosemary and Margaret. They were all always there when I needed them.

I would like to express my gratitude to Dr Alexandra Mancia, my analyst through my postgraduate years. The experience of my analysis not only helped me in my work and in my relationships but deeply enriched my life.

Finally, to Nicos Mouzelis I owe the fact of both thesis and book. He gave me great inspiration and intellectual stimulation and guidance, as well as the support, love and encouragement I needed to complete my task, which, without him, would have been impossible.

Preface

This book is the story of a psychiatric day hospital in London which was for a while the model therapeutic community of its time. But this is not just an ethnography or a history of an institution: it has, I believe, much wider implications. For it is first and foremost an exploration of power and its nature and relationships within an organization. Although the day hospital was a libertarian institution – indeed, in conception it was the very opposite of an authoritarian institution – within it grew up an oppressiveness in some ways more tyrannical and dehumanizing than any that direct control could have produced. The unimaginable outcome – the tyranny of the anti-institution – is what this book is really about.

By focusing on the coercive nature of democracy, my exploration of a therapeutic anti-institution incorporates the anti-establishment currents of the late 1950s, the 1960s and the early 1970s. For the power underlying the anti-authoritarian movement took on a stark form in an institution based upon a democratic, egalitarian rhetoric. The story of the day hospital points out the potential for oppression in that rhetoric, and by so doing provides an added dimension to the critical social theory of that period.

But it is also – and importantly – a story of the potential for tyranny that lies within therapy. Indeed, it shows how the combination of democracy and unbridled therapy can produce a nightmare situation of hidden and not-so-hidden controls. Whereas Goffman describes the degradation that is part and parcel of treatment in a total institution, my analysis of a more free therapeutic context shows the manipulation that emerges

Preface

in the service of therapy when formal controls have been removed. In the day hospital we see the staff conducting collusive 'Laingian' games of smiles and double-binds and the patients' attempts to free themselves from the control of the therapy that they desperately needed.

By focusing on the naked power that is masked by an appeal to democratic values, my case study illustrates how the power relationships of treatment and care can become a tyranny of the weakest. It shows how punitive and degrading the rhetoric of democracy can become when it is cut free from social structuring and when psychoanalytic treatment replaces formal control processes. The story of the day hospital and the crisis that ensued when the patients challenged the manipulation they detected in the therapy gives, I hope, an understanding of power that, with its emphasis on individual responsibility and when pursued relentlessly, falls in line with the move to the right of the late 1970s and 1980s, which under the guise of egalitarian democratic rhetoric results in an unfreedom that is the more pernicious because of its hidden nature. Just as Mrs Thatcher's emphasis upon the individual's right to participate in the marketplace masks the lack of freedom imposed on a large minority by small wages and unemployment, so the notion of equal participation in the organization and the therapeutic control of a therapeutic community results in paralysis and oppression for the most confused.

Asylum to Anarchy

1

The asylum and the anti-institution

The depersonalizing environment of traditional psychiatric hospitals became the target of Erving Goffman's now classic study of inmate life in total institutions, and a generation of sociologists, psychiatrists, therapists, nurses and other paramedics have worked with the conceptual tools he has provided. Indeed, his work influenced many people who turned against the asylum and who finally brought this mass institutional treatment to an end. This process was aided by the introduction of the major tranquillizers which so effectively controlled the more acute symptoms of mental illness that long-term incarceration in a mental hospital became unnecessary for most people. They could usually be sent home in a matter of weeks rather than months or years as before. Although in the public sector psychotherapy was available to National Health Service (NHS) patients only in the context of a few newly emerging therapeutic communities, private psychotherapy started to provide alternative modes of treatment.

Alternative treatment was further extended in the 1960s by the growth of day centres and other non-residential organizations providing care for psychiatric patients. Much of this alternative treatment adopted the anti-institutional views that were beginning to be popular as a result largely of the works of Laing (1967) and Goffman (1968). Gradually more and more people involved in psychiatry, either as carers or on the receiving end of treatment, were beginning to reject the control dimension in much of modern psychiatry.

It was in this context that the day hospital which is the main focus of this book came to be regarded as *the* therapeutic community of its generation. In its very nature it embodied the complete renunciation not just of the treatment methods of the asylum but of its entire structure and procedures. It was to be the realization of the anti-institution: it believed in patient participation and equality between staff and patients, and its well-publicized ideological strictures against rules and clear-cut roles gave it the reputation of being, *par excellence*, the antithesis of the hierarchical institution.[1]

Before the drugs revolution and the decarceration movement of the 1960s, mental hospitals were as much concerned with containing aberrant behaviour as with treating the sufferer. *Asylums*, Erving Goffman's important book about inmate life in a psychiatric hospital, detailed this control process. His book presented for the first time a truly empathic view of the role of the patient and his passage through the treatment system. Mental patients who had until then been incarcerated for years in long-stay wards and treated as outcasts were at last being given a human form. Goffman shocked us out of our complacent acceptance of psychiatric treatment by deliberately giving a partisan view of the hospital as experienced by the patient. Rather than describing the problems and methods of treatment from the viewpoint of the staff in the organization and talking in terms of the control aspect of disturbed behaviour, he told the world what it was actually like to be a patient in a mental hospital governed by highly detailed rules, excluded by 'normal' society, stripped of individual identity and seen in terms exclusively of his or her deviant role, the 'master status' of madness.

By describing in detail from a participant observer's viewpoint the daily interaction between patient and patient, patient and staff, and patient and relatives, he outlined the process of social exclusion, social control and alienation experienced by inmates of highly bureaucratized psychiatric institutions. He showed us exactly how oppressive and damaging the experience of hospitalization can be and how, indeed, the very processes of care and treatment can in themselves 'produce' the so-called mad behaviour that in its turn legitimates hospitalization. The peculiar gait of an inmate, for instance, can no longer be seen as a symptom of his or her illness, nor can the apparently regressive behaviour of the old man hidden under a blanket on the floor. These must both be seen in terms of the pressures of the

2

The asylum and the anti-institution

institution, and attempts by the individual to express himself or gain privacy in a context that denies the right to personal space. In other terms, in a situation where the institution details every area of the inmate's life, odd behaviour may be seen as a rational way of meeting personal needs.

Describing the stages in the process of being hospitalized, Goffman showed how the enforced role of mental patient has more to do with the dynamics of interaction between members of an institution than with so-called symptoms. Disturbance can, therefore, be seen as the normal reaction to treatment that is disturbing. He made the reader feel how frightening it is to lose personal belongings, to be herded about against your will with a large group of strangers, to have all your actions dictated by others, to be given treatment involuntarily, to be inspected and judged according to a 'diagnostic' label – indeed, to have your every action regarded as odd rather than natural and at the same time to be estranged from the family and loved ones who have usually initiated the hospitalization. The new entrant into any institution flounders until he or she has learnt the rules, and how to produce some congruence between personal feelings and the role laid down by others. Goffman showed us how difficult it must be when the only role available in an institution is that of a 'mad' persona and where therefore only acts of conformity are regarded as signs of health.

Goffman's frame of reference was extremely radical and very controversial because it forced us to re-examine our assumptions about madness and normality. Because his work was based on first-hand experience it could not be rejected as 'pie in the sky' theorizing, and it appealed to those who did not believe that mental illness really existed.[2] To less radical students of psychiatry he gave a perspective on the problem that could only add to our understanding. By making more accessible the experience and suffering of the mental patient, Goffman made a major contribution to our appreciation of mental illness and its treatment. He made questionable the assumption that the authoritarian nature of mental hospitals was either necessary or always helpful, and indirectly encouraged new approaches such as those adopted by the therapeutic-community movement. Following Goffman's well-documented experience, many voices

3

joined the criticism of the asylum. It was now felt that perhaps after all there was no need for such strict rules and clear role demarcation in the treatment of mental patients – indeed, that therapeutic communities should replace such institutions and restore a sense of responsibility and identity to the disenfranchised patient. It was surely this perspective that influenced the decision to de-institutionalize the day hospital which I shall describe.

Whereas the therapeutic-community movement offered the patients the opportunity to take control of their feelings and lives in the contained and safe context of a supportive community, the day hospital believed it was handing over the control entirely to the patients themselves.

The day hospital itself was quite unlike Goffman's hierarchical hospital and was in many ways an extraordinary institution: it was regarded as a leading therapeutic community in the 1970s because somehow it had managed to capture the essence of the enthusiasm at that time for organizations that had been created by and for the people they were supposed to serve, yet it was committed to psychoanalysis; it rejected the bureaucratic hierarchy of the traditional hospital, yet was dependent upon the specialized knowledge of therapy; it treated quite severely disturbed NHS patients, yet was offering them the kind of therapy for which people would normally have to pay enormous sums. It appealed therefore to patients, staff, and general practitioners because it was attempting to provide humane treatment in a 'democratic' context to those people who would normally be regarded as untreatable and relegated to the margins of society. It also went one step further than most other therapeutic communities by turning itself to the task of trying to build a natural anti-authoritarian community.

This was what particularly intrigued me, so I was very baffled when I started to sense the degree to which this post-Goffman libertarian anti-institution exercised power over its members. I had – perhaps naively – assumed that an institution that had abolished rules would be liberal and open and leave members a high degree of manoeuvre, but I discovered a very far-reaching exercise of power underlying the surface liberality.

This discovery did not, however, contradict Goffman's

4

The asylum and the anti-institution

findings;[3] rather it has led to the description of an additional type of manipulation to those he described. Whereas Goffman focuses on the constraints imposed by rules and rigid structures, my research focuses on the relationship between a lack of rules and manipulation. In the day hospital I discovered that the deliberate abandonment of formal hierarchical structure led to more subtle and therefore perhaps more invidious mechanisms of control. The lacunae left by the rules and roles that had been rejected were filled with attempts to control behaviour through the therapy itself. Expressions of independence on the part of a patient, for example, were quickly identified as pathological and the behaviour controlled under the guise of therapeutic enlightenment and understanding.

The stripping of identity through rituals and obedience to rules that Goffman describes is paralleled in my case study by the psychological invasion that occurs when the individual is publicly described as unknowingly motivated by a pathological unconscious. In a situation where the staff are seen as the exclusive purveyors of knowledge about the unconscious the patients are deemed to be vessels empty of all but their pathological unconscious, and feel robbed of their power in the process of believing they are being enabled and given insight. It is the closeness of healing and evil that had such a profound effect on day hospital members, as it threatened them with a deep sense of loss of identity. The attack was on the individual's social role as a patient, as well as on the more internal matter of his or her identity.

Because Goffman's analysis of power was limited to overt mechanisms of control, I turned to Foucault for a more general analysis of power. Indeed, his concept of 'power-knowledge' seemed more relevant to the more subtle forms of control through expertise that were apparent in the day hospital.

Foucault (1965) argues that the sciences have themselves instituted a new regime of power that is exercised by control mechanisms and by the assertion of norms of human behaviour. We all have concepts of what it is to be a 'normal' woman, a 'mature' person, a 'healthy' body, and these are reproduced through the practices of teachers, sociologists, psychiatrists, doctors, policemen and judges. By defining what is normal, the

5

human sciences outline the borders beyond which deviance occurs.

Foucault makes an important distinction between two types of power. There is power that is related to knowledge, in the sense that knowledge of *how* a car works gives one certain powers, and there is the kind of power one has when one knows not only how a car works but how to *make* a car. It is this *creative* power that the social sciences possess. They have the power to set the rules within which games of power are played out.

Foucault describes these processes of power as 'totalizing discourses' that tyrannize the human subject. He shows how transparent is our conception of ourselves as subjects. We are both the subject of study and subjected to the rules of the state. We assume we are subjects with the capacity to choose and act freely, but in these terms what we take to be our 'real selves' is really a sham. For Foucault there is no room for doubts, deviance, disease and irrationality. Only our conforming selves are allowed to be real, so that we reflect the social order and, by internalizing this order, ourselves cast out that which does not fit the mould. In this way, in the guise of science, political order penetrates to our inner selves.

According to Foucault psychiatry is, *par excellence*, a regime of power where knowledge is synonymous with power. In a hospital where only conformity will lead to the lessening of constraints, we can see how the power to define normality is derived from expert knowledge or is, indeed, synonymous with knowledge. For Foucault, as power is an inherent feature of all social relations, the only way in which it can be opposed is by 'local opposition'. This is typified by the recalcitrance of individuals who resist the subjugating effects of power. For example, there are those who resist religious, ideological or ethnic domination or who refuse to accept the professional's claim to superiority through expert knowledge. This 'localized resistance', which he sees as the only method of stemming subjugation, is well illustrated by the patients at the day hospital. Once they had identified the control being exercised over them in the name of therapy, they resisted all attempts to define them or their actions in unconscious terms. They would insist that their problems had nothing to do with the psyche, that they had no problems or that they were social in origin, and ridiculed the staff's sexualized interpretations as being the product of 'one-track minds'. Indeed, one could argue that it was the power of the 'localized opposition' of the patients that finally unseated the medical director. Without the patients' rebellion and insistence that they were being abused, it is unlikely that a single inquiry, let alone two, would have taken place.

The story of the day hospital, from the early days of the experimental use of psychoanalysis in a community setting and the abandonment of rules to the inquiries and the sacking of the medical director, can thus be seen as an illustration of a type of manipulation and resistance against it that goes beyond the scope of Goffman's theory. Indeed, I see my work as taking up where Goffman left off, explaining an area he could not have known about at the time of writing. For history has thrown up from the antithesis of the asylum another form of power, which bears lessons just as did Goffman's.

None the less, I would argue that these theories of Goffman and Foucault set the parameters of my material, and I will return to them in the conclusion. For the time being, however, I shall ask the reader to enter the world of the day hospital and relate that to what they know or have experienced of psychiatric treatment. For my focus upon the inner workings of a marginal institution will, I believe, bear a psychopolitical lesson that is relevant to policy-makers, health-care professionals, sociologists, patients and relatives alike. It is an intimate account of a particular institutional approach to the treatment of mental illness, and as such gives the reader an idea of the member's experience, whether treater or treated, and exposes some of the weaknesses and problems of therapeutic-community care. For the sociologist, not only do we see the institutional world as experienced by the participant observer but also, unusually, it is an account of *crisis*.

For my account is of an ordinary day psychiatric hospital that was exposed to a radical type of therapy – institutional psychoanalysis – whose extreme application provoked the patients to complain and request a public inquiry. The idea behind the treatment was that the community itself was the equivalent of

7

the analyst's consulting room. Everything that went on in it was seen in terms of the unconscious. This approach was combined with the so-called 'democratization' of the hospital by the removal of formal rules. Despite this 'debureaucratization', the day hospital still had to cope with organizational factors lacking in the traditional one-to-one psychoanalytic relationship. Transposing individual psychoanalysis to an organizational setting without taking into account the context of treatment (the number and conditions of patients, the statutory requirements of an NHS hospital, the relationship with other departments, etc.) was bound to create problems. Practical problems necessary to the running of an NHS hospital – medical certificates, meal and fare reimbursements and domestic services, etc. – were seen exclusively in psychoanalytical terms.

Indeed, these practical matters threw up the main problem with the day hospital's method of treatment. By making the community itself the consulting room, it became a totalizing and over-inclusive therapy. Whereas the psychoanalyst's consulting room is an environment which attempts to exclude as much of the 'real' world as possible in order to focus upon phantasies without the complication of their being reflected in the real world, the day hospital precisely encompassed as much of the external world as was possible in a day-care context, with the resultant confusion between inner meaning and outer reality. So, for example, a patient's request for a medical certificate for the Department of Health and Social Security (DHSS) office, which was a bureaucratic requirement, was always regarded by the staff as a demand at a deeper level for help. In this way these daily practical arrangements became foci for discussions about unconscious needs, and the patients seemed willing to accept this view as long as it did not touch them practically; but when, for example, meals and fare reimbursements were stopped, they complained to the authorities, thus sparking off a lengthy crisis.

From the time of this complaint to the sacking of the medical director, the already strong feelings on all sides were intensified and as the problem of the treatment and the patients' rejection of it was discussed daily, the organization remained in a heightened state of emotionality that amounted to a crisis.

The asylum and the anti-institution

Were the basic tenets of the therapy justified? Were the patients 'acting out' by complaining? How valid was their complaint? How threatened was the future of the day hospital? Would it and its members survive the inquiry? What would happen to staff and patients if it did not survive?

During this prolonged phase of ferment I (as a sociologist) was lucky enough to be on the spot. At the time I was living in the Little Venice area of London, sharing a flat with three friends. The house was a large white Regency building in a tree-lined road running along the side of the canal, quite close to the 'Basin' with its small tree-covered island in the middle. My room on the ground floor looked directly on to the canal and the brightly coloured barges and houseboats lined up tip to tail down its length. The road was full of similar large white houses but few of them were divided into flats though many, like ours, were owned by the Church Commissioners.

Some of the more beautiful houses were owned by the rich and famous (Barbra Streisand and Edward Fox, for example); ours was the only one filled with academics and, unlike the others, needed a lick of paint on its crumbling if magnificent exterior. But its high ceilings, tiled corridors and well-proportioned rooms retained an elegance and spaciousness of a past age that had not needed to make money out of every square inch of space. It was difficult and expensive to heat my large room, with its huge sash windows, and usually I would be roasted on the side next to the bare electric bar and icy on the other. But the feeling of space lent a sense of luxury to my habitat after the tiny Hampstead bedsitter I had had previously, and I also had the company of fellow-academics, all of whom had been or were still in psychoanalysis.

So it was a sympathetic environment to be in when I was working, and sitting at my desk I could watch the barges passing slowly by, the boys casting their lines and sometimes neighbours chatting to our road-sweeper, our spy who would warn us if a traffic warden were on the warpath.

It was all very urban – Paddington Station was just around the corner and Edgware Road at the end of the street – but between the two was Little Venice, an oasis of greenery, quiet roads and picturesque boats. Only half a mile away was the Psychotherapy Institute which, lying under the flyover, could not have been in starker contrast. Every day I would leave my house, cross the bridge over the canal, pass the leafy Basin and enter the 'park' of a new housing estate. Already the atmosphere changed from lush picturesque, genteel Georgian beauty to an open space of freshly sown grass and stubby young trees with high- and low-rise concrete buildings plonked down arbitrarily, it seemed, and set in no relation to each other or to the rest of the environment. Beyond the tower blocks was the dual carriageway running underneath the motorway. It was a windy, unprotected space edged by modern breeze-block shops with plastic signs – a cobbler, a fish and chip shop, a newsagent. The desolate newness and brashness of it all, as well as its proximity to the noise and dirt of the flyover, deprived these so-called 'local' shops of their community feeling. They seemed unconnected with the flats and there was no sign of people knowing each other or sharing daily life.

Opposite, across the traffic island, was a three-storey building made up of squares of dirty blue plastic and concrete interspersed with equal-sized squares of window. I was crossing the big divide between the hospital's nearest shops and the institute. Lying in the shadow of the M40 flyover, with only one dead-looking Victorian building for a neighbour and the dual carriageway as a gulf between it and the inhospitable shops and flats opposite, the institute was psychologically isolated from the rest of the neighbourhood.

The front door hung a little open, and inside the stairs led up to the Adult Department on the first floor and the Children's Department above that; down the stairs in the semi-basement was the day hospital. There was a familiar smell of cigarettes and staleness. The grey lino was stained and the brick wall daubed with a rust-coloured paint covering some badly disguised graffiti. Each day I would make my way down the darkened corridor past the lavatories and the so-called library (usually fuller of empty bottles than of books or readers), past the two small-group rooms on the left, and into the large-group room. I would take off my coat in the tiny boxroom which, cut out of the larger room and bulging with filing cabinets, served

10

The asylum and the anti-institution

as a staffroom at the time. Saying hello to whoever was there, I would grab a coffee from the canteen across the corridor and return with other patients and staff to the large-group room to wait and wait with coffee steaming for whatever would happen – for the interpretations, the cigarettes to be exchanged, the sardonic remarks, the grimaces and sighs, the angry atmosphere or the depressed air, the restlessness, the rebellion, the feeling of at-seaness, the shouting, the whispers, the cold words, the mockery, the discomfort of it all. But also the stimulation. Because at times, especially at first when I, like many of the other members of the day hospital, was still hopeful of what the experiment could do, I would sometimes go home after a large-group session rejoicing over I know not what – the courage of the patients to be honest and the courage of the staff to tolerate odd and sometimes disturbed behaviour in their joint attempt to get at the 'truth'? Rejoicing that I could sit through such disturbance and come out alive and not too frightened? Perhaps I was simply happy that *someone* was attempting to offer an alternative to the 'chemical straitjackets' that many of the patients had experienced elsewhere? For these patients were not herded about as a group, they were not stripped of their identity nor 'deprived of air and liberty'; they were trusted not to kill themselves but to look after themselves in their squats and lodgings. They were regarded as 'persons' in their own right. Above all, they were individuals. This was quite different from my first contact with a traditional psychiatric hospital when, as a teenager, I worked as a volunteer in the Women's Royal Voluntary Service (WRVS) canteen in the local mental hospital.

Brought up in the socially concerned atmosphere of a vicarage, I had some – if rather limited – experience of people suffering from mental illness (several people came to stay to recover from breakdowns), but even so my first exposure to the inside of a psychiatric hospital was quite a jolt. Apart from observing some bizarre behaviour (one woman thought herself a chicken and kept pecking with her beak-like fingers at the ground), I also noticed that nearly all the patients had burnt their fingertips by smoking their cigarettes to the very end. Since some of the wards had as many as eighty beds it was the WRVS canteen selling cups of tea, sweets and cigarettes which

11

constituted the patients' main leisure area. It was there that they were free to spend what little money they had just like any other citizen.

With the other facilities that were available – a hairdresser, films, music – it seemed almost understandable when it was said that patients often did not want to go home, which usually meant back to loneliness and responsibilities with which they could not cope. Despite these attractions, life in the hospital was dictated from morning to night by endless rules. Even the more pleasurable events, such as social occasions or entertainments, were officially organized and hence out of the patients' hands.

Those Saturdays I spent in the hospital canteen left me wondering about the treatment of the mentally ill. Was it possible that the free films and hairdressing helped to make the patients as dependent on the institution as did the formal rules that bounded their daily life there? Why was it that the apparently purposeless but pleasurable occupation of smoking seemed to have taken on quite a particular importance in the patients' lives and was enjoyed in itself as a limited expression of freedom? A possibility occurred to me that the institution itself might be engendering the kind of behaviour for which its patients were being treated.

When in later years I heard about the new therapeutic-community movement, I asked myself whether this would perhaps prevent the effects of institutionalization and the need for behaviour to counteract the oppressive nature of the traditional, rule-bound psychiatric hospitals. Neither compliance with the rules of the hospital nor the 'underlife' that emerged in some cases as a protection of the individual against its authority seemed likely to lead to 'health'. Having seen for myself the adverse effects of such institutions, I hoped that the advocates of the therapeutic-community movement would be able to utilize the impact of this new type of institution positively to help the individual patient recover.

This, indeed, was the aim: on the social level the individual would be encouraged to use and participate in the organization, try himself out, discover through open discussion where he 'went wrong', and so prepare himself for a more satisfactory and beneficial participation in life outside the hospital. On the

The asylum and the anti-institution

psychological level, the therapeutic staff would attempt to make the patient aware of how his psychological problems manifested themselves in his interactions with other people in the institution.

Indeed, other patients and their reactions would be particularly beneficial. Whereas individual therapy often remains at a highly abstract level of discussion, a therapeutic community sets out to afford the individual an opportunity to express his concepts of the world (his attitudes, hopes, fears and phantasies) through the process of expressing them in the community itself. The therapist is then able to trace out for the patient how his psyche affects the way he sees the world, show how he often distorts it, and analyse the extent and meaning of that distortion. It is hoped that the individual will feel encouraged to take on as much responsibility for himself as he is able to manage. Such independence is considered preferable to being made more dependent on the highly bureaucratized life of an institution, while in a defenceless position.

At this point I would like to re-emphasize that the day hospital was *the* therapeutic community *par excellence* during the early 1970s. Its history is not merely a story of the breakdown of any therapeutic institution; at the time the eyes of the therapeutic as well as the psychiatric world were upon this *enfant terrible* that had the nerve to extend certain therapeutic-community ideas and actually put them into practice. By going out on a limb and exaggerating these precepts, the day hospital was in a sense enacting the phantasies of many therapists, psychiatrists and budding therapeutic communities. This was why so much excitement was engendered by its exploits.

The general feeling was that if the day hospital succeeded in providing psychoanalysis to large groups, it would have forged a new direction in the treatment of the mentally ill. Psychoanalysis was more or less exclusively practised in the private domain, NHS patients being largely treated by quicker and more crude methods that often entailed short or long periods in residential care. Psychotherapy had hardly developed in the public sector. As the day hospital patients were fairly typical of NHS patients in residential hospitals, if the experiment worked it would prove that disturbed NHS patients could benefit from

13

psychoanalysis and did not necessarily need in-patient care and drug treatment, which had been the assumption for so long.

Because the day hospital was in the public eye, any new development could not remain private for long. For instance, in 1975 it was the day hospital's turn to house the annual conference of the Association of Therapeutic Communities (ATC). The experiment was at its height at that time and was being largely supported by the rest of the institute. Being, therefore, full of optimism for the new approach, the medical director decided to run the conference along day hospital lines. This meant the minimum of organization, merely dividing the day up into two sessions of small and large groups. In the morning the ATC members found themselves sitting in a large group with day hospital staff and a few patients, having their reactions analysed in terms of the unconscious motivation of the large group. Many of the participants, including myself, broke away from this and formed informal small groups in other parts of the hospital, in which they could express their annoyance or amusement at this eccentric annual conference.

Certainly the day hospital succeeded, by making delegates participate in their experiment, in giving them an idea of the new approach. There were long silences and outbursts of annoyance or frustration, attempts to analyse the analysts and finally so-called 'acting out' by those who could not or would not tolerate the experiment within the experiment in which they found themselves to be unwitting participants. Each delegate could taste for him- or herself the experience of large-group analysis. This unusual hosting of the conference may in fact have provided bad publicity for the day hospital, as many members went home feeling sore if not outraged and cheated. They had expected to receive the usual presentation of the work of the host hospital, not to be part of the show themselves. None the less, the unusual day went down in the annals of the ATC as one of the most original annual conferences.

Just as the therapeutic world had focused upon the day hospital to see how this novel approach would work out, I too, when I heard that they were experimenting with a new therapeutic-community method and had deliberately abolished all rules, wondered whether this might indeed be an answer to

14

The asylum and the anti-institution

my doubts about the role of the institution in the treatment
of psychiatric patients. I decided to follow the day hospital
experiment as a participant observer, hoping to understand the
institution by sharing the experience of its daily life. While I
had no preconceived idea of what I was likely to find, and
intended simply to record whatever I could, I did enter into
the situation with a number of hunches.

Firstly, I suspected that the opposite of being rule-bound is
not to be without rules altogether. As institutionalization has
such a profound effect on inmates, I felt it could not be counteracted by simply removing all the establishment's rules. In any
case, an institution is not expressed merely through its formal
rules and regulations. It also has an informal side even though
the informal is strongly influenced by its formal aspect. (For
example, in institutions where the possession of money is
forbidden, tobacco, if it is permitted, often takes its place as
currency and tobacco kings (Goffman, 1968) emerge who domi-
nate the 'market'.) Furthermore, inmates may form groupings
and friendships which stem from personal interaction and are
not necessarily the consequence of or reaction to formal regulations. Such groupings remain informal in the sense that they
are not part of the formally ordained world of the institution.
This retains its impact – rules or no rules. And these aspects of
informal institutional life may themselves under certain circumstances develop a rule-like and compelling nature, so that
beneath the surface chaos a consistent patterning of behaviour
can be observed.

I was interested in seeing whether a rule-less organization
would really be as liberating for its members as the day hospital
ideology maintained. I had a hunch that psychiatric patients,
whose inner worlds were likely to be insecure and fragmented,
needed not only understanding but a firm and consistent framework, so that their external world would not reflect their
disturbingly uncertain inner world. I frankly doubted whether
an organization could survive at all without some deliberate
ordering of affairs or whether, if it did, it could do so without
some new type of management or control replacing the earlier
regime. Following Goffman's (1968) analysis of the informal
strategies patients developed to preserve their identity in the

15

face of the regimentation of traditional psychiatric hospitals, I was curious to see if similar structures would emerge in a context where formal authority had officially been jettisoned. I also wondered to what extent Scull (1977) was right in arguing that the move to decarcerate patients from traditional hospitals to community treatment was really merely a way of cutting costs rather than a beneficent reform.

The balance of power in the NHS was another aspect I wanted to examine. Doctors seemed to be so very powerful and I wondered how this fitted in with the idea of democracy in therapeutic communities. Would some staff still be 'more equal than others' no matter what their position might be in theory? No matter how much they might disclaim power in a particular context, as Freidson argues in *The Profession of Medicine* (1970), their position in society is such that they can be relatively free of external bureaucratic control. What impact would this fact have upon the experiment in the day hospital?

These ideas concerning rule-lessness and power were the vague hunches I had concerning the drama I was about to witness when I became an ethnographer in the day hospital for nearly three years. I attended the hospital two or three times a week and then daily for six months and, in the process, experienced much of the confusion and the breaking-down of assumptions which any new member would have felt. It was a world of unreliable clues and signposts, where one's everyday assumptions were continually challenged. Eventually I was able to discern a clear power structure which curiously grew increasingly strong as time passed, but at first it was extremely difficult to differentiate between staff and patients. This was not due to the absence of white jackets or uniforms, but rather because staff members uttered their psychoanalytic interpretations in a language so allegorical that they sometimes defied comprehension and seemed like the typical incoherent wanderings of an unbalanced mind.

I believe that had I simply entered as a sociologist with a structured questionnaire, I would not have seen the hidden 'political' activity in the day hospital and would not have been able to distinguish the various groups of patients from staff. As a participant–observer, however, I could look beneath the surface

16

The asylum and the anti-institution

and, to a large extent, experience membership myself. Like the others I felt bored, nervous and sometimes frightened in groups when nobody spoke for an hour or more, or when patients shouted and tried to intimidate the other people in the room. I often disliked the physical discomfort and dirt of the place. I feared being challenged by staff or patients. Sometimes I was depressed and angered by what I had witnessed and at other times I was intrigued by the unscripted drama I found myself both participating in and observing.

During the initial phase – about a year before the patients' complaint – the very fluidity and amorphous nature of the place made it impossible to erect any set of hypotheses about institutional functioning and change. The central issues I eventually uncovered were simply not yet apparent. Initially, all that could be said was that the day hospital seemed to be an institution using an already quite radical approach (that of a therapeutic community) and was in the process of becoming continually more extreme, particularly in its rejection of any structuring of daily activities. Although staff and patients seemed fairly cohesive in their joint experience of being outside the traditional psychiatric system and apparently enjoyed being 'different', it was as though an ill-defined constraint lay on the behaviour of all participants.

During this period I felt I could not get at the root of the organization, but that I should observe and write up my notes at the end of each day. At some staffroom discussions I was able to take notes verbatim. At that time there was a relative lack of written material on therapeutic communities[4] and the hospital's unique structure was so intangible that the theoretical inferences had to be left to arise out of the material acquired by participant observation. This meant that carefully planned questionnaires and interviews were both impractical and irrelevant.[5]

Gradually, as I became familiar with the daily life at the hospital, certain impressions came to the fore. I began to feel that the *anomos* and anarchy of the organization were more apparent than real, and that beneath the blurring of roles there did lie a kind of power structure – albeit unacknowledged: there was a script that mapped the apparently extemporized drama of interaction. As a participant, I too experienced a sense of

17

being compelled to act in some particular way. I felt, for instance, that individual conversations with patients were frowned upon and that any direct approach to me by a patient in a large-group session should be evaded or ignored.

This feeling of constraint was in contrast to the *laissez-faire* attitude to my participation as a researcher. The almost unquestioning acceptance of this was a reflection of the prevalent ideology. My introduction to the institute of which the hospital was part had been through a consultant at the adult out-patient department. Although interested in research into the experimental methods of the day hospital, the consultant referred me to the hospital's medical director as the appropriate locus for any decision concerning my research. As the day hospital had dispensed with bureaucratic machinery and the medical director had apparently delegated formal power to what was known as the large group, I had no formal meeting with him to discuss my role or research objectives; instead, I was simply advised to 'come to the large group'. As a result there was no open discussion about whether or not I should be allowed to do my research or how I should conduct it, and my long-term participation seemed to be legitimated by the very fact that I, as a 'problem', had been brought to the large group at all.[6]

This form of legitimation was used continually to replace formal hierarchical bureaucratic rules. The idea was that if 'we', the large group, bore witness to everything that happened in the day hospital, we then *ipso facto* had control over the situation. That everything should be seen by the large group was regarded as a democratic mechanism in itself and, it was argued, the use of democratic methods implied that the group as a whole was in control. What actually happened was that any person or issue introduced to the large group was thereby exposed to the process of psychoanalytic reductionism, an exposure which reduced any threat they or it might have posed. As there were no formal channels for direct control and no power of veto, the fact that a problem had been put before the large group meant that it had pretty well been accepted before anyone could disagree. Democratic power was therefore more apparent than real, especially since any doubts or queries were seen as part of the individual's psychopathological condition.

18

The asylum and the anti-institution

So, one patient's doubts about the usefulness of my participation were interpreted as 'envy of the new baby' – in psychoanalytic terms, sibling rivalry similar to that experienced by the patient as a child.

While being to all intents and purposes accepted by the large group, I knew none the less that in order to avoid the only negative sanctions available to day hospital members in lieu of formal refusal – that is, indirect hostility – I would have to conduct myself as unobtrusively as possible, participating but rarely (if ever) taking notes. Furthermore, I did not want my presence as a researcher to affect the people and the situation I was researching. Some effect would be inevitable, of course, as the mere presence of a new person always provides an extra dynamic, but I wished to keep this to an absolute minimum. As matters became more dramatic, day hospital members increasingly wanted to draw me out, to see which 'side of the fence' I was on, and it was with difficulty and sometimes with reluctance that I failed to declare my own position.

In fact, this position changed over time. I started out feeling, as I have said, delighted at the attempt to reverse the ills of the old asylums by removing rules and trying to give psychoanalysis to largely poor and quite ill NHS patients. However, as the so-called 'experiment' became more entrenched, my sympathy decreased. For the staff's inflexible adherence to a specific theoretical approach meant that the abolition of bureaucratic control structures did not result in the freedom it was meant to promote, but in unintended control structures which did little to advance organizational goals. It is with these *unintended control structures* that I am primarily concerned in this book. Much has been said about formal rules and the informal reactions they inspire. What is more unusual about this case study is the possibility my method of research (participant observation) allowed of exploring the kind of hidden power structure that emerges when formal rules are abolished and, further, the group reactions to that control.

In the radical therapeutic-community context of the day hospital the lack of formal rules meant that control was exercised through psychoanalytic interpretations, as any independent opinion became defined as evidence of pathological thinking.

The attempt to reduce all other meanings and interpretations of reality to the level of the unconscious I call psychoanalytic reductionism. This form of control was particularly pervasive because it was not circumscribed by any externally imposed definition, since society sanctions doctors to delineate for themselves the area over which they have clinical autonomy. In other words, if a doctor takes it upon himself to define his area of responsibility very widely, there are no external sanctions that can be applied to stop the control from being very far-reaching. Apart from the drastic action of a public inquiry, neither administrators nor other health workers can impinge upon the doctor's 'professional autonomy'.

In this particular case study it was the patients themselves who defined the therapeutic control as illegitimate, when even basic facilities such as meals and financial reimbursements were looked at in analytic terms and eventually withdrawn because they were regarded as redundant. The official complaint they made sparked off a crisis in the day hospital as inquiry followed inquiry and culminated first in the dismissal of the medical director and ultimately in the closure of the hospital (though the rest of the institute still flourishes). My research encompasses this critical period and the preceding year when the experiment was developing, but I have also included a history of the overall organization so that the meaning of the later developments may be apparent.

Before I embark upon the specific theoretical and ideological background, I shall set the case study within the broader societal context of social climate and research into the treatment of the mentally ill.

At this point I would like to say that I have been at pains to protect the identity of the day hospital members by giving them numbers and letters, which I have altered in each example. I have given a fictional name – Adrian – to the only person who, because of his role as medical director, cannot be disguised in this way.

A brief synopsis of the events leading to the closure of the day hospital is given in the Appendix.

PART
1

THE THERAPEUTIC CONTEXT

2
The historical background

This book is the story of an institution – a unique institution caught up in a crisis that divided staff from patients and staff from staff. It tells the story of a psychiatric institution that aimed to provide therapeutic care for even the most disturbed NHS patients. Inspired by a zeal to provide the kind of treatment normally provided only privately to the well-off, the experiment in the end went horribly wrong, finally damaging the very people whom the staff wanted to help and who had most need of care. For by mistakenly attempting to provide psychoanalysis for the community in a context bereft of formal controls, the treatment itself was quickly adopted to fill the vacuum left by the abolition of formal rules and roles.

In this chapter I shall outline the history of the day hospital from its inception in 1962 to the time of my research there, when the staff had been experimenting with new therapeutic methods and organizational structure for about a year. I shall trace the developmental changes during this period from the hospital's classical rehabilitation function when it was founded to the unique type of therapeutic-community approach it adopted from 1973 onwards. This historical account will be followed in the next chapter by a description of the day hospital experiment and a typical day in its life. I shall look at the meaning members gave to the idea of 'democracy' and the importance of the medical director's charismatic leadership, as well as describing the types of problem that arose as a result of the hidden control structure that emerged to replace the bureaucratic rules and roles abandoned as part of the experiment.

In this way I hope to set the scene for the description and

analysis of the events that led to the crisis depicted in the remaining chapters. For the experiment that ended in crisis could not, I would argue, have been initiated, let alone taken root for as long as it did, if it had not been for the earlier crisis in the history of the day hospital when staff and patients together defended psychotherapy against more traditional psychiatric methods that were being bureaucratically imposed upon them.

This earlier crisis arose in 1971 when the local hospital board proposed replacing the therapeutic-community approach of the day hospital with a reversion to short-term, high-turnover and predominantly physical methods of treatment. This was regarded as a return to traditional psychiatric methods. Indeed, it was proposed that the day hospital should become an out-patient department of a local traditional psychiatric hospital.

The medical director's role as the clinic's saviour during this first crisis contributed to his growing charismatic attraction as leader. However, despite the day hospital members' commitment to the ideals he symbolized, his charisma was not sufficient to protect him against ultimate resistance from the patients once they had perceived the control element underlying his psychoanalytical interpretations. Neither could it withstand the formal institutional controls that, after two inquiries, found his approach wanting and resulted in his removal from his post. The Area Health Authority's exercise of these controls reversed the situation; now the controller was being controlled, and the definer of the situation was himself defined by others as deviant. Both the experience of the 1971 crisis and the charismatic personality of the medical director contributed to the climate that produced the day hospital's unique approach.

Social and theoretical context

Since the 1930s, when Freud and many of his colleagues settled there, north-west London had become the psychoanalytic centre of Europe, producing in time the Institute of Psycho-Analysis, the Anna Freud Clinic and the Tavistock Institute.

Inevitably, as a result of theoretical developments and empirical experience of cases, new ideas arose that diverged from established psychoanalysis. These dissenting ideas consoli-

The historical background

dated into different psychoanalytic 'schools' such as the Ego Psychology School which was founded in this country by Anna Freud, as well as the Object Relations School which was pioneered by W.R.D. Fairbairn and D.W. Winnicott, with the Jungian and Kleinian Schools remaining the two most important alternative rivals to classical Freudianism. So radical are the differences of opinion even within the Freudian fold that they are reflected in the structure of psychoanalytic institutions. In Great Britain, for example, great effort has been made to ensure that each of the three main schools (Freudian, Jungian and Kleinian) are represented in the organization of the British Psycho-Analytical Society.

The feeling of attachment to a particular set of analytic ideas is so strong that it is quite usual for an analyst's analytic ancestry to be regarded as almost as important as his or her own skills or training. One acquires status by being able to show how one's analyst is linked analytically to major figures in the analytic world, and ultimately to Freud.

None the less these earlier theoretical disagreements and allegiances existed more or less within the psychoanalytic establishment. Klein, for instance, emphasized Freud's concept of the death instinct, even though she rejected the concept of stages of development and fixation-points in favour of a theory of positions and attributed greater importance to the first year of life than to childhood in general. The Tavistock Institute has become the major centre for Kleinian thought; here both Henry Ezriel[1] and the medical director worked, and the latter trained.

Existential psychoanalysis which is perhaps closer to the day hospital's approach, represented a criticism of Freudian thought from outside the establishment. Existential analysts criticize classical psychoanalysis for neglecting 'ontology', or the study of being. These ideas were taken up in this country primarily by R.D. Laing (1960), who emphasized the importance of 'primary ontological security'. For him this is the existential position of a person with a 'centrally firm sense of his own and other people's reality and identity', a position which he argues the psychotic cannot attain.

These existential ideas in psychiatry were part of a more general social movement present in the middle and late 1960s

25

and early 1970s, of which the day hospital experiment formed a part. During this period a radical, libertarian and existential perspective was adopted by a wide variety of people: philosophers, writers, poets, hippies, academics and so on. Becaus of their concern with the development of the individual self. which was regarded as essentially crushed by traditional or conventional institutions, new 'alternative' theories and institutions were set up. The existential philosophy and therapy of R.D. Laing and the therapeutic-community movement offered alternatives to traditional psychiatry. Alternative universities were created by students teaching themselves and conventional young business executives and bank employees 'dropped out' to live in hippie communes. In this context mental patients were linked with other minority groups such as the poor, blacks and women. Their cause was fervently championed and the movement culminated in 1967 in a massive conference entitled 'The Dialectics of Liberation' (Cooper, 1968), where the freedom and development of the individual were debated in a number of different contexts by, amongst others, R.D. Laing, David Cooper, Stokely Carmichael, Herbert Marcuse and Lucien Goldmann.

It is important to see the development of the day hospital not only within the context of the 'hothouse' society of psychoanalysis, with Henry Ezriel and the medical director being key followers of the Kleinian schism, but also as part of the more general social turbulence that R.D. Laing represented. (The crisis in the day hospital was only seven years after the May 1968 upheaval in Europe.)

Certainly within the professional context the day hospital experiment was seen as a challenge to traditional psychiatry. As the first non-residential therapeutic community in Britain it had already been a pioneer in the field, but the members still felt that the constraints of NHS rules marred the community development. The experiment thus represented a more radical departure from both the drug-orientated, highly regimented, traditional psychiatry and from conventional psychoanalysis, by providing psychoanalysis for large groups. As well as taking into account the wider social context of the day hospital experiment,

The historical background

it is important to relate its activities to the specific context and history of the centre itself.

The history of the institute

The day hospital was part of a larger organization, the institute, which was established in 1962. It was made up of three separate departments: (i) the child guidance department (a hospital for psychiatry and child guidance, itself originally the psychiatric department of a hospital for nervous diseases); (ii) the department for adult out-patients (which did not join the institute until 1965, and was staffed by Freudian-orientated psychoanalysts offering psychotherapy in an NHS setting); and (iii) the day clinic (newly founded in 1962 and at first chiefly responsible for rehabilitating patients discharged from a large psychiatric hospital). Although these three organizations found themselves under one roof (rented to them by the NHS), there was little interaction between them, and their links were limited to using a common administration and secretarial service.

This lack of cohesion was quite marked. It was described in the 1971 report of the institute's medical committee (to the local hospital group's medical committee) as being 'an uncoordinated juxtaposition of three units with dissimilar backgrounds and aims, its function yet undefined in relation to the provision of distinct psychiatric services'. Better collaboration was achieved with the appointment of a senior registrar working with both the mother hospital and the unit, and the medical committee felt that by 1971 there had gradually evolved an

> *integrated community-based clinical, consultative and teaching service related largely to the Branch Catchment Area but also to other parts of the country. The Unit is now able to offer a unique family and community-orientated service through its child guidance Clinic, adult out-patient and day hospital sections.*

The adult out-patients' department, which offered individual or group therapy, occupied the ground floor of the modern block that houses the institute as a whole. The child guidance section

27

on the top floor treated children and parents, and the day hospital in the basement offered psychotherapy to individuals, referred by consultants within and outside the institute, who would not sufficiently benefit from, or were unsuitable for once-weekly psychotherapy.

The adult and child guidance departments were staffed by consultant psychiatrists qualified in psychotherapy, as well as by social workers and psychologists trained in psychotherapeutic methods. There were some staff – a psychologist, a social worker and an occupational therapist – who were appointed to the institute as a whole as resource workers, and who divided their time between departments according to demand. Many of the day hospital staff were also full-time employees of the institute, dividing their time between the day hospital and the adult out-patients' department where, under a consultant's supervision, they took on individual patients for psychotherapy.

In addition to the administration, based in an office on the first floor, the three departments shared the use of the art department, as well as the kitchen and canteen which were housed in the day hospital.

The organization of the institute: the 'management' of therapists

Despite the fact that, unlike the employees of most other NHS psychiatric units, the institute staff regarded themselves as primarily psychotherapists, in terms of the NHS bureaucracy they were employed as members of their own disciplines. In most hospitals it is usual for nurses and occupational therapists to work only in the field in which they have qualified. However, in some psychiatric hospitals, and especially in therapeutic communties, there is a tendency for this original training to take second place in favour of most staff working psychodynam-ically as therapists.

Since the NHS has few formal psychotherapy appointments, in organizations that want to help patients understand them-selves psychologically rather than provide care only, it is usually necessary to employ staff qualified in other disciplines and train them in the organization itself (if they have not already completed psychotherapy training). This is because the NHS psychiatric sector, dominated by traditional psychiatry with its emphasis on biochemical causes of mental illness, is not yet ready to accept the various training bodies as meeting the required standard for psychotherapy roles. In fact, psychotherapists are themselves divided on this issue; there is no register yet of psychotherapists within the profession itself.

Because of the formal hierarchies to which the nurses in the day hospital had been attached, they felt that their work in the institute was and should be exclusively that of psychotherapists; nevertheless they were still managed as members of the nursing hierarchy, and ultimately by the district nursing officer. Similarly, occupational therapy came under the management of the local authority occupational therapy hierarchy, even though the occupational therapists considered that they had developed specialist psychotherapy skills well beyond traditional occupational therapy work. The hierarchy of the local authority's social services department presented the social workers at the institute with the same problem, as they continued to be managed by social workers outside the institute. Even within medicine itself there is a managerial relationship between consultants and junior medical staff, and the former also manage trainees from all disciplines and departments.

Despite this complex interweaving of hierarchies – and perhaps because it was recognized that certain psychotherapists had reached the stage for independent practice and could provide psychotherapy cover – the institute strongly resisted any form of hierarchical organization, arguing that all its therapists were colleagues working on an equal basis.

The medical committee and the Professional Staff Committee

The gradual integration of the institute, the various departments of which treated different sections of the population but were united in their espousal of psychotherapy, was reflected in the demand for a central committee to represent all the professions working in the institute. It was suggested that such a professional committee should replace the medical committee which had decided on policy and shaped the form of the institute between 1962 and 1970.

The medical committee was made up of all the institute's consultants, who had voting rights;[2] registrars and locum (temporary) doctors were entitled to attend meetings, but not to vote. It was a decision-making body which deliberated on medical policy and liaised with the management committee of the local group of hospitals (in the reorganization of 1974 this was replaced by the District Health Authority structure). Under this arrangement non-medical staff had little influence on decision-making. Although they might be consulted in their own departments, it was the medical staff member among them who was regarded as their representative, and they had no right to expound their views otherwise.

Some of the institute staff regarded this as unsatisfactory, arguing that doctors, as an interest group of their own, were bound to place their professional concerns over their representative role for the department. This was felt especially strongly in 1970–1 when the day hospital was threatened with closure. There were then only three consultants responsible for the future of the unit, because the rest of the medical members (more sympathetic to the day hospital's plight) were either in locum positions or registrars – that is, without voting rights on the medical committee, and hence powerless to influence decisions.

In these circumstances the professional staff demanded the creation of their own multidisciplinary committee to consider all policy matters. Everyone holding a professional staff position could automatically become a member. But whilst most of the non-medical staff joined this Professional Staff Committee (PSC), which was chaired by an occupational therapist, the medical staff kept to the previous arrangement until 1972, when the locum in the day hospital and two other consultants became members of the PSC.

When, in 1973, another permanent consultant was appointed who wished to be part of the PSC rather than the medical committee, the institute finally voted to have a combined committee under the chairmanship of a medical member.

The PSC meetings took place on Wednesday afternoons and

The historical background

usually all the staff, professional and therapeutic, attended. Because the PSC had been an issue for so many years, its meeting was of central importance in the institute. It symbolized the move away from medical domination towards the idea of a collectivity of therapists. Staff were eager to attend and quick to detect overly dominant medical participation. On Wednesdays there was always an expectant air in the staffroom, more staff were present in the building and there was more generally a feeling of everyone belonging to an overall community. An agenda and the minutes of the previous meeting would be distributed and eagerly read.

For the day hospital staff, participation on the PSC represented another more autonomous role in relation to the other members of the institute. Whether working in the day hospital or the Adult Department, as trainee or as therapist, in this context they had equal status to the other participants. Whenever serious matters such as the patients' demand for an inquiry was raised, the PSC meeting, being the only place where all the staff met, would often become a focus for conflict. In this setting problems and criticisms could be brought out into the open, for there was an emphasis upon openness and sharing – the staff's conception of democracy in the making. However, it remained more of a concept than a fact, as professional hierarchies remained. The medical assistants, for instance, were still answerable to the consultants, who were ultimately responsible for renewing their contracts.

For example, following the sacking of the medical director the consultants decided they wanted to renew for only three months the contract of the fully qualified therapist employed as clinical assistant to both the medical director and the consultants in the Adult Department (or, as it was called, 'on the adult floor'). It can be seen in the following exchange how the notion of democracy was in conflict with the very real power the consultants had over their medical subordinates. And yet, as the excerpt indicates, the day hospital staff persisted in trying to assert their definition of the situation – that it was a democratic committee.

When the clinical assistant psychotherapist complained that the annual renewal of her contract had previously been automatic and that she was a psychotherapist and did not see why she should be treated like this, one of the consultants reminded her: 'You are a psychotherapist but you are also a clinical assistant.'

Clinical assistant of day hospital: But why will my contract be renewed for only three months – I've worked satisfactorily for seven years?
Day hospital member A: Yes, it's very mysterious.
Consultant in Adult Dept: We are concerned about the day hospital and don't know if you'll fit in with the new medical director.
Clinical assistant: *You* determine whether I fit in, not me?
Consultant: You can refuse to take the contract we're offering you, if you like.
Clinical assistant: I have worked satisfactorily.
Consultant: That's open to question.
Day hospital member A: How can *you* know? *She's* satisfied.
Day hospital member B: I can second that. You just want to get rid of 'old hats'. This is supposed to be a democratic body, you know.
Consultant: If we did want to get rid of 'old hats' we wouldn't have renewed the contract at all.
Day hospital member A: You have to say *why*!
Consultant: I don't have to. That's a function of consultants.
Day hospital member A: To get rid of other people?
Consultant: If they want to, yes.
Day hospital member A: It's persecution.

The history of the day hospital

When the day hospital first opened, it was used mainly to receive patients who had been discharged from a local psychiatric hospital. As these patients were inclined to attend for only a short time, generally a matter of days, there was a high turnover. Typically, a patient would be referred by consultant psychiatrists at the local residential psychiatric hospital and given a first interview by a day hospital psychiatrist who would prescribe treatment, normally conventional. The patient would

The historical background

then attend the hospital daily, as a kind of halfway house between full in-patient treatment and discharge into the community.

The day hospital's main concern was to rehabilitate the patient to ensure as smooth a return to normal status as possible. At that time the accent was on ability to adapt to the social setting, whereas the later emphasis on psychodynamic work meant concern with the individual's development. Gradually the day hospital started to move towards an approach resembling that of the therapeutic communities. This implied the use of 'group techniques to help the patient understand and control his own emotional impasses' (Cummings, 1969).

Now the traditional psychiatric approach, which emphasizes social adaptation, requires skills and ideologies on the part of the staff very different from that where emphasis is given to self-realization on the therapeutic-community model. For example, a nurse trained in a traditional psychiatric hospital expects to see that the patient takes his drugs, provides him with sympathy and takes care to order his environment. Here the patient is in a dependent position, whereas in a psychotherapeutic setting he is called upon to take greater responsibility for himself, and the nurse's role is to encourage him to strive actively for greater self-understanding. In this case the importance of the physical and social setting lies mainly in the fact that it is through interaction with his environment that the patient gains a better understanding of himself.

In the first context the patient is regarded as a passive, childlike creature who cannot be given responsibility because he cannot help himself and who therefore needs nurturing; in the second he is regarded to some extent as capable of choice, change and action. Here the staff member has an educational role – in the sense that through his own knowledge, theoretical as well as personal, he may lead the patient to a greater understanding of his psyche. This difference is more than a change of emphasis; it actually requires and utilizes different skills and ideologies. Many of the day hospital staff initially resisted the therapeutic-community approach, feeling that they lacked the appropriate skills and training and sensing that their own professional training was being undervalued.

Meanwhile the newly formed PSC met fortnightly, with every member of the professional staff a member and decisions taken by consensus. It was an unwieldy body, however, and the rules for decision-making were unclear. When it was felt that a particular action should be taken, the chairman would inquire if all were in agreement, dissenting voices would be heard and, if they requested it, their statements were minuted. If the majority of the members approved the decision, most of these objections were ignored thereafter.

This somewhat ambiguous decision-making was reflected in the committee's role *vis-à-vis* outside bodies. Because it was the creation of the members of the institute and deviated from the more usual medical committee structure, the PSC had no such formal links with the district management team as the medical committee enjoyed. As a result, although it was sent the policy edicts of the Area Health Authority, in formal terms it could function only as a 'talk shop' and as the mouthpiece of the institute. When the medical committee was dissolved and there was no overall head of the institute, official bodies had to address themselves either to the PSC or to individual consultants. Conversely, there was no constraint on official bodies to respond to any request from the PSC, since it had no formal standing. While the committee *qua* committee could express an opinion, action was more readily taken if individual members contacted the next managerial level of their particular discipline. During the 1976 crisis, for instance, complaints by staff members about the running of the day clinic (for example, about medical cover during holidays) were taken up with the local Cogwheel committee of the Division of Psychiatry[3] in the area.

The development and structure of the PSC is a point of some importance – as will be seen especially in Chapter 7 on the crisis – because after the patients' complaint it became increasingly necessary for the institute to liaise with outside bodies. Although the PSC was the major forum for discussion among the staff, decided on policies and tried to influence the behaviour of its members, the fact that it had no formal constitution and no formal rights over its members or in respect of the NHS managerial hierarchy meant that it lacked bite. In fact, the ambiguous role of the PSC reflected the institute's fuzzy overall organiz-

The historical background

ation. The idea of all departments wanting most of their staff to work as colleagues on a democratic basis was translated in this instance into a refusal to formalize and 'bureaucratize' this committee. This in turn meant that in the absence of a constitution accepted both internally and by external bodies, no formal channels of communication could be set up.

Therapy groups

At the beginning, the day at the hospital was sharply divided into work by small and large groups, occupational therapy and art work. There were two large groups a day, three small groups a week and a once-weekly business meeting. It was not until 1965, when a senior nurse and a registrar from another well-known therapeutic community were appointed to the day hospital, that it became a therapeutic community proper. This approach meant the flattening of the authority structure, a blurring of roles, and an egalitarian value system: the therapeutic community proper

> is distinctive among other comparable treatment centres in the way the institution's total resources, both staff and patients, are self-consciously pooled in furthering treatment.
> (Jones, 1962, p. 46)

With the appointment of two new staff members, who came from the Henderson Hospital (a residential therapeutic community using sociotherapy[4]), the day hospital adopted that institution's approach. Henceforth, emphasis was on the manipulation of social situations to facilitate the individual's greater understanding of himself. For example, work groups were set up and patients allocated to groups specializing in some activity such as sewing, general maintenance or research into, for instance, patients' attitudes. The objective was to give the patients experience of working at certain tasks within the community, and stress was laid on discussion of work difficulties. At that time the staff members – although all were therapists in that they were trying to help patients learn to improve their skills in interpersonal relationships – were also encouraged to use the particular skills of their professional training to create a supportive environment where the patient felt free eventually to express his difficulties, where he felt secure and safe from hostility.

Admission groups

By 1968, two other types of group had developed in the day hospital. As new patients were referred from a number of agencies (varying from general practitioners to psychiatrists, social workers, student health services, or probation officers), current patients were invited to attend what was known as an 'admission group'. This consisted of five or six staff members, four patients and two, three or four fellow-referrals. It had to elicit enough information about the new patient to decide whether or not it was advisable to admit him to the day hospital. If the group felt that the patient might be violent or otherwise express 'inner difficulties' in a nonverbal way, or if he refused to see that he had a psychological problem at all, then he would be rejected. This group had full authority to decide on the day hospital intake, and its decisions were generally adhered to. Every patient who was accepted was then allocated to a small-therapy group. The current patients were thereby given 'a chance to identify with the admission procedure and to deal with their feelings over new patients' (Gregory, 1967). Patients were not bound to participate in the admission groups; it was more that they were given the opportunity voluntarily to take on what was in fact part of the responsibility of the psychiatrist as the person who would normally decide about admissions.

Assessment groups

Another part of the psychiatrist's work was passed on to the patients when assessment groups were set up. In a group comprising staff members and patients and with a patient as chairman, individual patients would give an account of their own progress; this was followed by opinions from the staff and patients present, focusing on attendance and participation in the small and large groups and making recommendations for the future. For example, it might be suggested that the patient remain a day patient, or become an out-patient (visiting two or three times a week for therapy) and start to work at a regular job.

By introducing the concept that patients should become involved in each other's assessments, the day hospital was already deviating considerably from normal hospital practice under its first consultant/medical director. The patients were already being invited to assume some of the psychiatrist's role in assessing each other's behaviour and development. Although they were not asked to sit in judgement on themselves, they were having to switch roles from definer and controller one day to being defined and controlled the next. The fact that this control emanated in part from their peers provided an additional source of conflict. Given this role conflict as the result of contradictory sets of expectations according to their different roles and role partners, it is not surprising that, as Lemlij et al. (1981) report, the patients' rules about attendance and progress became 'harsher and harsher'.

Even at this stage (1969), when the day hospital was more highly structured than it was later to become, there was no formal discharge procedure such as is normally found in hospital units. It was simply that a two-year limit was set for all patients, with the possibility afterwards of out-patients' group therapy three times a week.

Staff meetings

Until 1968 the staff met on their own twice a day in order to discuss patients, groups and events, but patients, as a result of their own requests, were soon allowed to attend the once-weekly formal staff group meetings. The medical director regarded this patient participation favourably as 'genuine staff–patient cooperation in running the day hospital' (Gregory, 1967).

Despite this cooperation and tendency to blur roles between staff and patients, under the influence of one staff member there were strict rules until 1969 about attendance at the day hospital. At the weekly business group meeting matters of attendance were brought up regularly, and patients who had fallen short were encouraged to attend more often. If someone had come to the hospital only fifty per cent of the week, for instance, he would be enjoined to attend at least sixty per cent the following week. However, the only sanction was a negative assessment in the assessment group,[5] and it was never clear whether in the final analysis the staff would go as far as discharging a patient for ignoring such suggestions.

In 1970 the first medical director left, to be replaced by a locum medical director who had already worked at the day hospital for a year as registrar. For a while the approach remained largely within the old format, but with greater emphasis on psychotherapy rather than sociotherapy and a gradually increasing flexibility in the application of rules. Both processes were aided by a certain polarization of attitudes which developed during the first crisis in 1971, when patients and staff united in battle against the employing authority to prevent the hospital's closure.

The protest

In 1971 it was proposed by the management committee of the local hospital group that the day hospital should be closed down; a new psychiatric unit with day places was then being created at the mother hospital, in response to a request in 1970 from the Secretary of State.

At the day hospital both staff and patients felt that this ignored the hospital's specific contribution of long-term therapy in a therapeutic-community environment, as compared to the hospital's short-term day treatment mainly through physical means (drugs, etc.). The decision had been made over the heads of those most intimately concerned, and the medical director was simply told to wind down his psychotherapeutic programme in preparation for the change.

There followed a year of uncertainty about the future, and of solidarity against the higher administration. The patients for their part were afraid: they no more wanted the hospital as they knew it to disappear than they wanted to have to return to the older methods of treatment that many of them had received in the past in more traditional hospitals. The staff wished to protect an organization that allowed them to practise psychotherapy in an NHS setting – a rare, if not unique, situation. Many of them (for example, the occupational therapists and the nurses), lacking formal qualifications in psychotherapy, would have found it difficult to run a private therapy practice, and in most other NHS environments would have been required to work more traditionally and more strictly within their field of training.

Given this joint apprehension, once it was established that it was really intended to stop the day hospital from functioning as a therapeutic community, staff and patients formed an action committee to contact the press, radio and television, local Members of Parliament and general practitioners. They also canvassed support from other groups. For example they called a public meeting, as a result of which local GPs, about eighty of them, requested that the hospital be kept in its present form since it was very useful to them for the referral of 'revolving-door patients'[6] in particular. The day hospital patients and staff, together with friends and supporters, demonstrated outside the Hospital Board, and their actions were given some publicity in the local and, to a limited extent, national press. Twenty-two MPs signed their petition to the Secretary of State.

Because the day hospital patients were the only coherent group in the institute with common interests, they were more active than patients in the other departments who mostly attended as individuals and rather infrequently; no one knew anyone else and none identified with the institute to the same extent. Also, the patients at the day hospital had greater liberty than the staff to voice their protest: apart from the locum (later to become the permanent) medical director, whose professional freedom allowed him to give interviews to the press, the rest of the staff had been advised, as employees of the local hospital group, not to participate in demonstrations. Many feared they would lose their jobs if they did so. It was again a matter of dual accountability: these staff members could not just follow their medical director but were subject also to the opinions of their manager within their own discipline, who could reprimand or sanction them.

In the end the protest, led mainly by the day hospital, succeeded in keeping the centre open in its original form. The episode as a whole had a considerable effect on the hospital and its members – both structurally (in terms of its organization) and therapeutically (the outside opposition uniting staff and patients in a way they would not have thought possible before). They had fought, protested and acted together; gone was the sharp dividing line between those in authority who made decisions and those who were affected by them. The inevitable polarization in that time of crisis had created a feeling of 'us against them', pitting the day hospital against what lay outside it. This division even put the rest of the institute into the category of 'them', because the day hospital members felt that the institute staff had left 'most of the fighting to us'. Furthermore, the events of that time had also encouraged the relaxation of rules; partly as the result of the egalitarian camaraderie of canvassing for the protest and partly because of the re-emphasis on psychotherapy rather than the more traditional methods of treatment.

'Social adaptation' or 'self-realization'?

In their fight against being replaced by traditional psychiatric methods of treatment, the day hospital staff and patients had to convince their adversaries of the overwhelming importance of their own treatment – psychotherapy in a therapeutic-community context. To understand the full significance of that fight, which concerned ideological positions as well as treatment methods, one must look at the therapies offered in different treatment settings.

An insight into the history of the day hospital helps one understand how the experiment of dispensing with all rules and simultaneously focusing on psychoanalytic interpretations of all that happened not only managed to emerge but also to take firm root: it was the protest of 1971–2 which had a radicalizing effect on the day hospital and provided a fertile ground for so extreme an approach. The exclusive emphasis upon the psyche of patients was a mode of treatment that could take hold only when, through that polarization, the participants had come to idealize the psychoanalytic reality of the unconscious. From this perspective all other more mundane facts of life, such as

The historical background

organizational matters or the patient's relationship to his home or social environment, became of secondary importance. It was therefore as an indirect result of the events related above that a shedding could occur of the more conventional ideas accepted in most psychiatric institutions.

On the other hand, having mobilized so much and such varied outside support, it is possible that the day hospital could have derived greater profit from these connections by becoming more involved with other agencies, thereby helping its patients to build up relationships with outsiders. This indeed was the direction the head occupational therapist wanted to take, but instead she found her medical director 'turned inwards', having 'turned his back on people who had supported us and kept us going' (from a discussion with a staff member).

Many of the staff felt that most of the patients had undoubtedly benefited from the involvement excited by the protest, but everybody now considered it time to get back to the business of therapy, their prime objective. Although the majority of the staff believed that participation in the fight had been therapeutic for the patients, they now began to argue that it was much easier for patients to fight the external aggressor than to understand their own intangible inner conflicts. At this time the staff were a more homogeneous group than they were later to become. Also, as they had witnessed and themselves benefited from the patients' ability to take on responsibility, the rather rule-bound regime was greatly relaxed.

The 'new broom'

Apart from the change in emphasis from sociotherapy to psychotherapy, the new medical director also stimulated a greater interest in small groups. Under the regime of the first consultant/medical director two large groups had met daily, but the three small groups only once a week; now two small groups and one large group met every day. Also, the large group was no longer regarded as the central forum for information feedback from other activities in the day hospital, but became a therapy group for interpreting the unconscious.

Although the medical director himself did become rather

inward-looking after the protest and began to focus more on intrapsychic matters, for a couple of years many of his staff continued their attempt to foster links with the outside world. For instance, they started a once-weekly out-patient group for isolated people in the community; then they organized the day patients to help this (mainly elderly) group with practical matters such as window-cleaning, while other patients helped in local youth clubs. In 1972 some of the staff set up a patients' commune, managing to acquire a house from a housing association by raising money from a stall in Portobello Road antique market. A good number of patients lived in this house in a self-managing fashion, with the possibility of calling in day hospital staff whenever matters could not be resolved by the residents themselves.

However, such efforts on the part of the staff were neither encouraged nor supported by the medical director. When some of his staff arranged a meeting with the social services department to set up further links with social workers, the medical director failed to attend and the staff began to feel disheartened. When later – in addition to discarding any admission and discharge procedures – he started to decry small groups and focus on the daily large group as the central interpretative forum, some staff even argued that this was based less on theoretical considerations than on his personal convenience, as he would therefore be needed in the hospital for less time. In fact, at this time he was attending only the large group in the morning and no longer participated in the afternoon meetings of the small groups.

The end of staff meetings

At the beginning of these changes in 1972 many of the staff started to attend the seminars run by H. Ezriel, the psychoanalyst whose theories were being followed by the medical director. As a result of learning the Ezriel theory and method, more and more staff began to do interpretative work in the therapy groups by providing explanations of a patient's unconscious motivation. Gradually, over the next two years, some staff members lost all interest in activities involving outsiders.

The historical background

For example, the monthly evening socials and the domiciliary visits to the patients' families were now deemed to be interfering with interpretative work. The weekly business meeting also came to be used as a forum for interpretations of unconscious material. As the medical director argued that any business discussions the staff had should be conducted in front of the patients, he himself preferred to 'bring it to the large group' and to drop more private discussions with his staff. This meant, as one staff member said, 'We had no contact with him . . . no way of discussing with him.'

This approach was not helpful in attaining the various specific objectives of groups or activities. Some staff felt that they needed exclusive staff discussions on, among other things, the particular needs of individual patients as well as policy decisions concerning the whole hospital, and that these could not take place satisfactorily in front of the patients. (The psychoanalytic justification for dropping the staff meetings had been that if staff expressed both inter- and intrapersonal problems in public, the patients would be given a useful model of parents tolerating conflict.) Being untrained in psychotherapy, many staff also felt they needed the support in their work of a fully trained specialist such as the medical director. The exclusive focus on the psychological element in business discussions meant ignoring the fact that material and social matters were distinct from the unconscious motivation of patients and should indeed be treated as such.

The new venture

By 1974, although the work of the day hospital was still divided up into small and large groups, patients were no longer formally requested to attend the hospital at a particular time. This growing flexibility meant the gradual phasing out of the admission and assessment groups. No newly made rules decreed that this should happen; it was rather that as neither staff nor patients were compelled to attend, and with the ideology turning against any type of small group as a dilution of the large-group transference relationship, the necessary number of people to form these groups attended less and less, and so they simply faded away.

In any case, once the medical director had adopted his open-door policy, neither admission nor assessment groups were needed. If it was not clear who was and who was not formally a patient, then attempts at evaluating a given stage in his treatment became meaningless.

In the years following the successful protest against closure, more emphasis was placed on psychotherapy as the primary aim of all groups. The importance of the large group kept growing until, by 1974, it was regarded as the most important locus in the therapeutic setting. All other groups became subordinate to it, and any noteworthy knowledge or experience from other settings was expected to be relayed back to it. For example, if in the large group a member referred to an incident that had arisen or been discussed in art work or in a small group, he was urged to bring the matter into the open there and then and was told, moreover, that it should have been brought to the large group in any case. This attitude denuded any knowledge gained elsewhere of intrinsic value and deprived the less oppressive, more intimate setting of the small group of any inherent advantage. Everything was useful only in so far as it embellished the knowledge and functioning of the large group.

The streamlined day hospital

What had started out after the 1971 protest as a move towards greater flexibility, endorsed by most members of the hospital, had by the end of 1975 become an almost complete restructuring, or rather de-structuring. Previously the clearly defined staff roles and goals of rehabilitation meant that the daily life of the hospital could be formally organized into specific times for specific activities, with specific, specially skilled personnel for each. Under the new regime such formal organization, along with all formal rules, were abandoned. One rule only remained: that everyone and every matter happening in the hospital should be brought to the large group, which met in the large-group room and was theoretically in operation whenever people were present. By 1975 even the small groups had ceased to function, although they had always been popular since they allowed more junior staff greater autonomy in their work away

The historical background

from the control of their superiors and were less intimidating places for patients to express themselves. In the small groups there had been about eight patients with two staff members and the membership of these groups was always known. Going to attend the large group, on the other hand, meant being uncertain about the number or composition (ratio of staff to patients) of the participants from one time to the next.

The new structure was so streamlined by 1975 that it was almost unrecognizable. In its reduced form it had lost all variability. Previously there had been a number of different kinds of help available, enough to meet the needs of any number and type of patients. A large group is often felt to promote primitive, amorphous 'at sea' feelings which some individuals find hard to tolerate, preferring instead the relative security of small groups. Other patients, in a state of mental collapse, might want to give up for a while and allow themselves to be held, metaphorically speaking. The idea of such support was anathema to many of the day hospital staff who saw psychotherapy as the promotion of self-responsibility; they rejected all forms of help they thought traditional hospitals could offer, because they objected to the suppression of antisocial behaviour by drugs and electroconvulsive therapy (ECT). This apparently exclusive emphasis on social adaptation and social control was mirrored in the day hospital by exclusive emphasis on psychoanalysis and self-realization and individual self-responsibility.

Around this time, formal selection procedures were also abandoned.[7] In his comments on the article by Lemlij et al. (1981) Stuart Whitely (1981) – no doubt referring to practices at the Henderson Hospital, where he works – argued that it makes sense for patients and staff together to decide on the admission of new patients, since it is the patients who have to live and work with each other twenty-four hours a day. However, in his experience, senior staff would already have filtered out unsuitable patients. In other words, the patient/staff group considering new admissions would not be fulfilling a psychiatric role by assessing the patient's condition; they would rather be exercising their personal tastes and preferences in respect of what kind of person they would like to live with. Stuart Whitely argues that the day hospital staff's failure to select suitable

patients implied a denial of their expertise, and that this in turn
resulted in a feeling of being 'deskilled'. Ultimately there was
no selection procedure at the day hospital at all and the patients
became self-selected: only those who could tolerate the lack of
structure, the dirt, and the type of treatment given remained.
By 1976 this had resulted in an almost complete absence of
women patients.

Even though the staff themselves had rejected their more
traditional roles – and although at first many of them were
excited by the idea of having therapist status and participating
in an experiment – as time passed many of them admitted to
feeling deskilled and demoralized. Whereas previously, under
the more conventional regime, they had been able to use their
original professional skills in work groups and other established
settings, these skills now had no legitimate place. The caring
skills of nurses and the activity-orientated skills of occupational
therapists were rejected in favour of interpretative work. Since
most of the staff had little training in analytic work, however,
they felt incapacitated in their newly defined or, rather, their
undefined roles.

Despite the abandonment of social activities, out-patient
admission and assessment groups as well as small-group therapy,
the apparent absence of any compulsion to attend did not mean
an entirely free atmosphere, the open-door principle notwithstanding. Regulations about attendance and timing may have
been dropped to allow patients to 'bring themselves to the
group' (as the medical director put it) when *they* felt they could
come, but one all-dominating rule remained: in all situations
the unconscious level of reality was the prime and single focus
of attention, any other level of discussion being deemed illegitimate and, indeed, irrelevant.

This gradual organizational change was based chiefly on the
belief that external social realities were of secondary importance
to internal psychic factors, and that the former could only interfere with the process of reaching an understanding of the most
basic and deep-rooted primitive phantasies and fears that give
rise to neurosis and psychosis. At one time the efforts of patients
to discuss and take action concerning such matters as renting a
house had occasioned feelings of pride among staff members;

The historical background

now such discussions were regarded as red herrings and as an avoidance of more vital, central issues.

To explain how the day hospital came to adopt such a radical stance in the treatment of its patients, I shall outline in the next chapter the theoretical underpinnings of the experiment. This will be followed by a description of a day in the life of the hospital, showing how theory and ideology were expressed in practice.

3

The theoretical and ideological background

Following the discussion in the preceding chapters of the wider social, theoretical and historical contexts of the approach adopted in the day hospital, I shall now describe how the experiment came about in terms of the changes that emerged and its ideological antecedents. For although the medical director, the instigator of the experiment, did announce one day in 1974 that a new venture was about to take place in the hospital, the move towards greater and greater flexibility of rules, the blurring of roles and the psychoanalysis of the large community group had already begun. The experiment as such was not a consciously designed affair but was put in train quite gradually.

I was a relative newcomer to the therapeutic community and it was not clear to me for some time exactly what the experiment was. Gradually, however, I became aware of the value placed by various community members upon such matters as the staff's participation in the Ezriel training seminars which many of them attended. In fact, the influence of Ezriel's theory (see p. 50) was far-reaching indeed, legitimating and supporting the staff's attempt to use psychoanalysis for large groups.

The emergence of the large group itself as the key therapeutic vehicle seems to have been largely an effect of the historical events in the day hospital (outlined in the preceding chapter) when the conflict between psychotherapy and physical therapy polarized attitudes.[1] Moreover, after a year-long political battle when little psychotherapy was given, it is likely that a greater need for it was felt. By that time, any form of treatment even vaguely related to non-psychoanalytical methods received little sympathy. So for instance therapies which provide relief simply

The theoretical and ideological background

by allowing a person to talk ('getting it off his chest') or offer advice or help to the patient by getting him to re-enact problems through psychodrama or sublimate them through occupational therapy were now regarded as palliatives in comparison with the painful work of learning to understand how and why negative feelings have arisen. Not only were such methods seen to be tangential to core problems, they were regarded as actually deflecting or displacing attention away from them, hence representing an 'avoided relationship'.[2]

Small groups run by staff members were considered as collusion on their part with patients opting for such 'avoided' relationships. It was held that they tended to dilute the intensity of the patient's childlike feelings towards the large group, which therapy had earlier revealed.[3] This position gradually became so extreme that all activities (including table tennis, drinking, the eating of meals, reimbursement of transport fares, as well as requests for the medical certificates which patients needed to collect their NHS sick pay) were regarded as mechanisms for avoiding the real issue of looking at the inner psychic self. It followed that nothing was allowed to be pursued on its own terms as an external reality or as separate from the all-embracing psychoanalytic interpretation. Eventually all but one small group was abandoned. It is hard to say how much this was with the full agreement of the therapists involved or whether it was more a matter of acquiescent deference to those more qualified and more powerful. Admission groups and clinical records were equally phased out during this period.

The ideas underlying the experiment, therefore, were developed and implemented in parallel as the medical director's thinking became more clear-cut. Trained originally as a traditional psychiatrist, he underwent personal psychoanalysis whilst training to become a psychoanalyst himself. Before his appointment to the day hospital he was a member of the Tavistock Institute, where he came under the influence of Henry Ezriel. He was, therefore, already impressed with Ezriel's adaptation of Freudian therapy when he first came to the day hospital. But as time passed he developed his own ideas of how to adapt this theory and apply it directly to the hospital's organizational structure, so that it eventually became a control mechanism itself, to be used by those holding ultimate, though not immediately apparent, power. In order to understand how such a radical approach was adopted as a legitimate mode of treatment, I shall now outline the therapeutic theory on which it was based and describe how the therapy actually worked in practice.

The theory of Henry Ezriel

From Freud onwards, psychoanalysis has been concerned not only with digging up events lying in the past but also with discovering their residue in the unconscious structures still active in the present. Reactivated in psychoanalysis these unconscious conflicts make it impossible for the patient to regard the analyst as a detached observer, a fellow-investigator helping to study his, the patient's, problems. During analysis, therefore, a *transference relationship* develops, whereby the patient transfers to the analyst feelings and ideas appropriate to significant figures in his childhood and, by extension, to all feelings experienced by the patient in relation to the therapist. The patient develops feelings of love and hate and imagines various attributes and impulses in the relationship which are out of keeping with the objective patient/analyst status. During each session the relationship changes according to which subjective feeling (love, hate, envy, and so on) is temporarily dominant in the patient's unconscious, and so the relationship itself becomes the focus of analytic study and therapy.

According to Ezriel (1959), unconscious phantasies are the structures that operate in the patient's mind in the 'here and now'. They set up a tension and concomitantly a need for its relief through the establishment of a certain form of relationship with the therapist(s). This need is said to determine the content and sequence of the patient's remarks and behaviour in a therapeutic session. If the analyst accedes to the patient's unconscious phantasy and meets his need for a benevolent relationship with as much as a reassuring smile or word (or, as might be argued in the day hospital, with a medical certificate for sick pay), then he is 'colluding' with the patient's neurotic needs. Although the patient may gain relief from such non-interpretative acts, it is

The theoretical and ideological background

usually only temporary and may actually interfere with the deeper task of interpreting to the patient the underlying cause of his need for the colluding relationship, a task which would have removed that particular need at that particular time. Thus at the day hospital the medical director interpreted Ezriel's approach to psychoanalysis to mean that, for example, meals, fare restitution, medical certificates, and so on, were to be seen in terms of such non-interpretative interference.

In the large-group situation, according to Ezriel, one finds an unconscious common group tension, built up through a progressive accumulation of the apparently unrelated remarks and behaviour of individual patients. These remarks can be seen as dynamically related if they are considered in context – that is, in conjunction with all other members of the group: patients may unwittingly support each other's unconscious phantasies, individual remarks on a given subject may feed the unconscious phantasy of another patient, then feed that of a third and so on. Gradually a subject becomes the 'unconsciously determined topic' of the group. As the group situation develops, each member is held to try to take up a role and push the others into roles that accord with his own personality structure. In other words there is an unconscious selection, rejection and distortion of others' remarks until the group arrives at the common denominator of the dominant unconscious phantasies of all its members. In the end, the group is structured so that what Ezriel calls the object relationships in it (that is, the transference relationships) correspond in some way to what is required by the various unconscious object relationships of each individual member.

The treatment rests in the analyst analysing the whole group in a given session, as well as the roles various members have taken within the group, so that he can show each his particular defence mechanisms. The analyst must know which particular roles certain individuals will be driven into. Ezriel (1959) quotes an example of a group session where he knew it was characteristic of one patient to become the group's leading figure by manoeuvring himself into the scapegoat position, and equally characteristic of the others to cope with their own desires to be leader by attacking this scapegoat member.

51

This process can also be illustrated by an empirical example from the day hospital. For some time patient S had dominated the group by continually talking and not letting anyone else speak. This brought angry and frustrated attacks on him, and one member referred to S's 'domineering and threatening ways'. The hostility upset S so much that when patient M said to him one morning, 'You just go on talking and talking without feeling anything', S replied: 'M has no right to insult me – he's provoking me – I *can* feel things – I can feel with these!' He showed his clenched fists and continued: 'If you want violence, I'll show you I'm a man – come outside with me!' He got up and started to take his jacket off. M evaded the issue by saying it was lunchtime. Another patient, J, argued: 'People don't just come here to be insulted, you know.' A further patient, R, replied: 'But sometimes when you tell a person the truth he just sees it as an insult.' Patient S left the room. Patient R and his friend B continued to call S a nuisance. They felt they could do no therapy with him around, and wished he could be discharged.

S's need for the particular relationship with the group in which he played the scapegoat was subsequently met. When he could no longer contain his conflicting feelings and acted them out in a show of violence with two other patients, he was eventually referred to a residential hospital. A few days later, his leadership/scapegoat position was being taken over by patient R, who had been most emphatically hostile about S's aggressiveness. R assumed his new role after a fight with B. Thereafter, B continued to attack R verbally, and between them they gained the centre of attention – they became the new leaders, in Ezriel's sense.

The therapists at the day hospital afterwards maintained that the violence had been the result of the correct interpretation having been missed. For Ezriel, this correct interpretation is the all-important crux of the treatment (see Chapter 5). It implies the 'correct description of the forces operating in the patient's mind at that particular moment'; any other comment or action constitutes 'non-interpretative intervention'. Firstly, everything the patient says or does is treated by the analyst as the *idiom* through which he expresses his need at that time

The theoretical and ideological background

for a particular relationship with the analyst. Secondly, the interpretation must give a rational explanation of the patient's irrational behaviour. It is important to show him why he is behaving as he is, rather than just pointing out to him that he is behaving in a particular way.

In fact, the analyst has to show the patient the three types of relationship he is trying to establish with him in one session. The first of these is what the patient is supposed to need (the *required relationship*) so as to avoid another which, while he unconsciously also desires it, he fears even more (the *avoided relationship*) because it would inevitably lead to a calamity (the *calamitous relationship*).

For example: a patient's murderous anger towards his parent/therapist could be interpreted as the avoided relationship. While deeply desiring to kill his therapist the patient may behave especially considerately towards him – this being the required relationship. The argument would be that this good behaviour stems from his fear of being attacked by the parent/therapist should he realize how the patient really feels, and this would be the calamitous relationship he is trying to avoid.

For Ezriel this process, which involves *reality testing*, is the essence of psychoanalytic therapy. The avoided relationship emerges as the required relationship and is interpreted. The patient can then test out his fears and finally compare the situation where the calamity has not happened with his unconsciously expected calamity phantasy. With the removal of the need for the required relationship, he can express the avoided behaviour patterns in external reality in a less disguised fashion. As a result he will often be able to link these feelings not only with external experience but also with early childhood experiences that may now come to mind.

An example of this occurred at one of the large-group sessions at the day hospital when an interpretation was made about someone feeling penis envy and a concomitant rivalry with the father-figure of the consultant who gave such potent interpretations. It was argued that it was the fear of retaliation (calamity) which prevented any direct confrontation with the consultant over his female staff. This interpretation about potency brought

53

one patient to remember a childhood experience: 'I was about seven when my father got me out of bed to watch a boxing match with him on television. He was only wearing a vest, and I remember wishing that I had a penis his size.'

Ezriel's emphasis on the here-and-now interpretation does not necessarily mean that he neglects the historical-genetic viewpoint of psychoanalysis. He simply holds that the former is a way of dealing with 'the unconscious precipitates in the patient's mind of unresolved infantile conflicts as they manifest themselves in interaction with the psychoanalyst'. (Ezriel, 1959).

Application of Ezrielian theory at the day hospital

The application of Ezriel's version of psychoanalysis to concrete factors of the environment (meals, cleaning, and so on) was the distinctive feature of the experimental approach adopted by the day hospital medical director. In most therapeutic communities, discussions of practical matters and the consideration of their unconscious meanings are kept separate. Thus a therapist in another day hospital told me that if at any time in a discussion of practical matters it seemed important to deal with the unconscious level of the patient's motivation, he would do so. A patient might be upset and it would be particularly helpful to interpret this to him at that moment. But the discussion of the practical matter at a conscious, surface level of reality would be postponed for separate attention later.

The Ezriel technique rested on an unstructured situation when it was applied in the day hospital.[4] Had the rules required for running an organization been permitted, their autonomy would have negated the therapists' attempt to reduce their importance to one of purely psychic interest. In other words, the theory was reflected in the very fabric of the hospital.

This theory was espoused so completely that everything pertaining to external daily reality, including staff's and patients' suggestions and criticisms of the approach and its repercussions on the organization, was regarded as unproductive 'non-interpretative intervention' (see Chapter 5). All actions or statements came under the control of those most expert at making interpretations. Whether or not they were relevant was seen solely in relation to the therapeutic process that was the prime objective of work in the day hospital. Nothing was allowed to stand in its own right and apart from its psychological interest. Given the power and extent of influence ascribed to the unconscious, of course, everything may be argued to have a psychic meaning. But the day hospital staff denied that the psychic element had an importance *relative* to that of other levels of reality. Which reality is of dominant importance at any one moment depends on the context in which it happens. So for instance, if a patient does not arrive in time for his fifty-minute psychoanalysis session, the unconscious meaning of being late is more important to the analyst than the material reality of a normal traffic jam.

Although most staff adopted the newly adapted Ezrielian group therapy, not all did so in a completely unquestioning way. The constant reduction to unconscious meanings at the heart of the type of therapy adopted meant that out of the chaos of an unstructured situation emerged quite a formidable power structure. Far from being democratically free, this was an almost total and encompassing world-view with important organizational implications. From the seeds of a democratic impulse grew a rather authoritarian regime, even though – or because – it was hidden.

Extremism in the application of a psychoanalytic theory that pervaded all aspects of life eventually offended members of the other departments of the institute. They called the experiment an abuse of psychoanalysis, and were particularly disturbed by it because they put such value on psychotherapy. They felt that the exclusive focus on the unconscious was inappropriate in a hospital which operated on the basis of being open a mere eight hours a day and where material aspects of life like meals and transport fares had to be taken into account. In their own work in the adult and child guidance departments they were all helping their patients and clients understand the relevance of the unconscious, but they felt that the medical director was making the discipline seem foolish by flying in the face of what was commonly understood as reality.

In a way it was the staff's vagueness about the democracy on which they put such a high premium that prevented them from controlling the undesirable developments in the day hospital. And, of course, except in serious cases of neglect or threat to life, consultants can be controlled only by colleague pressure, and the medical director simply resisted such pressure. But also, the control that might have been exerted through organizational structures could not be brought to bear, since these structures had been deliberately dismantled. The PSC had no constitution and so no formal authority to curb the actions of a member. At this impasse the committee could only – and at a much later stage – resort to the even more 'unequal' mechanism of the Medical Executive Committee which was, however, considered unrepresentative of the staff as a whole inasmuch as it consisted of exclusively medical members.

For the medical director, his modification of Ezriel's theory was simply the logical extension of Ezriel's own work. His argument that anything coming up within the boundaries of the therapeutic work should be similarly interpreted was not in itself unusual: within individual sessions, all matters arising during those fifty minutes are looked at for their unconscious significance. The same is true for group therapy sessions, but while these usually last about an hour and a half, the medical director's innovation was to stretch Ezriel's idea over the whole of the eight hours the hospital was open each day and to treat anything that arose during the day as part of the large-group session.

If anything other than psychoanalytic interpretation is regarded as interference with the therapeutic progress of the group, then it follows that bureaucratic procedures such as those of admission, discharge and clinical notes, as well as additional group activities such as small-group therapy, art, drama and yoga must also be seen as interference. Thus when such things came up as a problem for discussion in the day hospital it was decided that they should be abandoned. For instance, the question of a cleaner was ignored until she had left leaving no successor, when it was implied by the interpretations that no new cleaner was required. The patients, it was argued, must clean up their own 'internal mess' with the implication that the same applied to external reality. This was by no means the only example of such confusions and the way it affected the staff is illustrated in the following exchange. Therapist A (a nurse) was very unsure about the day hospital not employing a cleaner.

Therapist A: I told the divisional nursing officer about my conflict between being a nurse, concerned with standards of hygiene, and my role as therapist, who knows that if you chuck out the shit you may chuck out the good shit as well. But I could see how hopeless it was to try to explain that to administration people.
Therapist B: The real mess is in how these people live, and they're bringing it to the day hospital so as to reduce the split between their two worlds, external and internal. We don't treat these people as mad but simply as people. We go out and buy our own lunches when it's lunchtime, so if they had no meals provided for them, they'd have to be responsible too and make a choice about how they want to spend their money. It's true, they don't have much money, but the canteen food is so cheap, it wouldn't ruin them but give them some self-respect, and they'd feel less like babies with food laid on at regular hours.

In brief, the common-sense suggestion that it would, for example, be appropriate to employ a cleaner when the hospital was dirty was not considered on practical criteria – the reality of filthy carpets was ignored in favour of an explanation in terms of the patient's rejection of the 'bad' or 'dirty' part of his mind.

'Democracy' and psychoanalytic control

Although it was imagined that true democracy would naturally come about at the day hospital once bureaucratic rules and hierarchical roles had been jettisoned, in fact the lack of definition of the limits on freedom to act merely meant that people's power of discretion in respect of their actions stood on even less solid ground than before. Given the ultimate legal responsibility for patients which was vested in the consultant medical director, he had *de facto* power to veto all decisions concerning policy questions as well as practical arrangements such as medical certificates, or art therapy. The exercise of his veto, however, related to the prevention of action rather than to taking positive action.

By reducing all matters to the level of the unconscious, th medical director was not deliberately and hypocritically tryin to manipulate psychoanalysis for his own ends instead of for therapeutic purposes. The monopolistic control inherent in his approach, together with his superior ability (albeit denied) to prevent actions or decisions, acted as a constraint on attempts by members to deviate. So he did not actually refuse to sign a medical certificate; he simply queried analytically the need for it to be signed and evaded the practical issue by not being available to sign it.

Through the process of debureaucratization, the lines of responsibility and accountability became unclear.[5] Although the various disciplines had their own line of accountability with managers outside the hospital the psychodynamic skills they were learning in the day hospital went beyond the traditional work of their own disciplines and made them feel, quite plausibly, that their managers could not manage work they did not understand. In addition, because democracy was regarded as synonymous with debureaucratization, the staff saw no need to clarify the internal structure of the day hospital in the belief that, formal rules and roles having been abandoned, everyone had the same status and was free to do as he or she liked.

This anti-authoritarian ideology was an attempt to 'capture the absence of constraint' through avoiding the 'deleterious consequences of a personal social structure' in a formal organization (Punch, 1974). Hierarchy and bureaucracy were being equated with authoritarianism, even though it can be argued that the flattening of hierarchies does not automatically lead to freedom and democracy. On the contrary, removing formally vested discretion may actually reduce an individual's authority by allowing a less controlled power structure to emerge from such factors as strength of personality (for example, charismatic leadership) and control over knowledge.

When a power structure did develop in the day hospital it proved pretty well immutable because its strength lay in its lack of formal control by allocated position and discretion, and

The theoretical and ideological background

because it remained concealed.[6] When the whole institute –
and especially the day hospital – was emphasizing the rightness
of their democratic style and organization, it would be hard for
staff or patients to say exactly why this appeared to be a myth
rather than reality.

To give some idea of what it was like to be in a debureaucratized community, it may be helpful to describe the day hospital
as it was at the height of the experiment in 1974 and 1975.

Everyday routine

During this period the patients – numbering approximately
forty-five on the books, with about twenty-five regular participants – were free to come and go as they liked during the hours
the hospital was open (9.30 a.m. to 5.30 p.m.). Until about
eleven o'clock in the morning there was no formal therapy, so
this was mainly a social period when patients would meet and
talk over coffee. Except for one or two junior members, few
staff were available at this time. It was not until eleven o'clock,
when the large group usually started, that most staff members
entered the hospital section of the institute.

Although even this was not part of any official timetable
there were strong informal expectations that staff and patients
attended this one meeting, which was regarded as the major
event of the day and embodied most of the therapy done in the
hospital. Whenever staff were present all activities were seen
to be part of the therapeutic process and, in theory, any
communications between staff and patients – as indeed between
patient and patient – at any time of the day in any part of the
building was deemed to be of therapeutic interest and value and
thus to be fed back into the large group as the main therapeutic
vehicle.

In practice, it was quite evident that certain junior staff
members would discard their therapeutic role a little when on
their own with the patients in an informal setting. None the
less, there was virtually complete retention of therapeutic
distance. Over lunch, for example, such staff members might
chat with patients on a 'social' level about films, housing and so
on, and express their own opinions freely. However, if the

59

patient seemed too curious, or if the focus of attention shifted to the therapists personally, they would immediately don their therapist's mask and employ strategies such as a 'silent non-response'. So when, over lunch one day, a staff member and a group of patients were discussing a film together, and a patient asked (*à propos* of part of the film) whether she too was living with her boyfriend, the staff member immediately fell silent and concentrated on eating her meal. Although subsequent questions were less directly personal she withdrew from the conversation and left almost at once. The contact was ended abruptly.

Before the small therapy groups were disbanded lunch was followed by the patients breaking up into small groups in different rooms, each group being run by two therapists. While these groups were operating, they were the only arrangements in the day hospital's programme that were rigidly adhered to. If no patients attended the group within ten minutes of the appointed time, the staff would leave. Such stringency did not and could not apply to the large group and there were many sessions where only one or two patients joined the staff in the latter part of the morning. If the staff had walked off after waiting a short time this would have belied the idea that the patients would eventually wish on their own volition to participate in therapy.

The large group was held in the largest room in the day hospital. There was no exact time for it to begin; staff and patients would attend between eleven and one o'clock, bringing their coffees with them. The form of interaction was not prescribed, and varied from day to day. Patients were simply expected to say what they felt like saying during the session and staff would attempt to interpret whatever had been verbally expressed in terms of the patient's unconscious desires and feelings.

An account of a random large-group session is perhaps the best way of giving an idea of the experience, as the groups were unstructured and at times seemed quite chaotic.

A large-group session

Unlike the previous day, when only two patients attended the large group, the room is full, with about nine staff members

The theoretical and ideological background

and twelve patients. Since the last group, which had been dominated by an hour-long silence, the first patient had written a poem on the wall in large, flowery handwriting:

There are sometimes moments
When you feel you can't go on
The Joy of life has faded
And the will to live has gone,
Nothing seems worth doing,
As you plod from day to day
The thing that kept you ticking
Like a clock has died away.
While it lasts you think it's forever
But it goes
There's a turning of the tides
And once again life flows
Reaching out to every hidden part
Back into the hollows of your empty heart.

The large room – with numerous chairs, some old and broken, others new, leather 'dentist's' chairs – is untidy and dirty. The floor is littered with cigarette ends, plastic cups and sweet-wrappers, the carpet is blotchy with stains. Most of the chairs are pushed roughly into two rows facing each other: the rest are dotted around haphazardly. Not altogether typically, the staff are ranged largely on one side of the room and the patients on the other. The atmosphere is thick with cigarette smoke while patients sit 'rolling their own', a necessary economy when living on social security. The discussion is interspersed with the sharing of cigarettes (some even made from others' butt ends) and the fairly frequent comings and goings as people fetch themselves tea or make phone calls in the patients' phone box just outside the room. Once in a while a staff member disappears to answer the staff telephone in a tiny boxroom housing filing cabinets for old medical records, constructed in a corner of the large-group room itself.

Patient 1: What the hell is group therapy anyway? I still don't know after six months of coming here.

61

Patient 2: Yes, are we supposed to tell you our problems? You don't take much notice when we do.
Therapist A: Animals in a zoo are watched and looked after, fed regularly and given an audience, aren't they? [He is suggesting the patient feels little better than an animal.]
Patient 1: I'm not an animal. Why are you talking about zoos?
Patient 2: Yes, we're people, you know, not animals.

[From this moment until the end of the session, patients and staff leave one by one to go to lunch.]

Patient 1: Patient A told you about his problem with exhibitionism two days ago, and it took him six months to bring himself to do so – that shows you what kind of place this is. He's very disappointed at the lack of help he's getting, and he doesn't know what to do. He doesn't want to go back 'inside'.
Therapist A: All this patient is being offered in her cage is cabbages and not good nourishing food. [Implying that she wants something better than the interpretations being offered.]
Patient 1: I wish you'd shut up about zoos and cabbages.
Therapist B: This zoo analogy *is* being stretched rather far, I think.
Therapist A: What's wrong with animals?
Therapist C: At least animals are given a human response. [Implying that the patients are being treated in a less than human way.]
Therapist B: I think it's a language problem.
Therapist A: No. It's preverbal.
New patient: I'm sick of all this. What are you all trying to say? I don't understand!
Therapist A: It's just that he's new and doesn't know the rules yet.
New patient: Well, I know that I'm not an animal. Even when I've been treated like one. In the hospital where I was they had locked wards, they drugged people and gave them ECT, so much that they didn't know where they were. What are

you supposed to do here? Do you just talk or do you have
ECT and drugs?

[No one answers him, and in the ensuing silence the remaining
few people gradually leave to have their lunch.]

These rather bizarre exchanges are difficult to explain, and it
should not be assumed that everyone in the large group could
understand what was meant by the zoo analogy. Not only are
complaints about treatment here interpreted analytically but it
seems as if the attempt to explain the (first) patient to herself
is made more for the sake of communicating with other staff
members than for the patient's own enlightenment.

These kinds of communication, which at times involved quite
complex strategies, provided the situation with an underlying
structure. For what appears on the surface to be at times chaotic
and undefined may, on closer inspection, reveal itself as structured by regularly repeated patterns of behaviour. Leaving a
discussion of specific strategies for Chapters 4–5, where a more
phenomenological account of the day hospital is presented, I
shall mention here only the less hidden elements that structured
conduct in the large group.

The main expectation was that patients should say whatever
came into their minds but many found this hard to comply with,
as the group's membership was changing from day to day and
even within a given morning as people came and went. At times
there would be large numbers of people in the group, and few
people were accustomed to what amounted to public speaking.
In addition, the groups were frequently dominated by one or
two apparently fearless patients who often seemed unsympath-
etically confident and oblivious to the reticence of the others.
There were also times when groups would pass an hour or more
in complete silence. The atmosphere then became oppressive
as each person, often wishing for communication, was left to
wander in his own mind. Large groups are renowned for stirring
up an 'oceanic feeling' (Skynner, 1974), a strangely amorphous
sensation which is at no time more strongly felt than when a
large group is gathered together and yet all remain mute.

'Democracy' and the therapeutic community

Although the term 'democracy' was often employed at the day hospital to assuage fears of social control or the suppression of opinions, the place could hardly be described as democratic except in the loosest sense of the word. It was not a direct democracy in that it was not directed by the decisions made by either the whole body or the majority of the community members, even if problems were brought to the large group for airing. Usually, once the matter had been referred to the large group, it was left in the air and no decision or action resulted from the discussion. Neither were the members' rights exercised through representation. The day hospital could be described as democratic only in the sense that there was an express attempt to minimize social and economic differences by asserting that all members (staff and patients) had the same status and could exercise the same psychoanalytically interpretative role. Although members of staff were differentially paid according to their rank in the hierarchy and the particular discipline in which they were initially employed and despite the fact that the patients were NHS employees, differences in expertise – that is, differences in people's ability to understand psychological needs – were ignored.

Whenever a problem or conflict arose, the matter was never discussed on its own terms but referred to the large group, which examined exclusively its psychological underpinning.

This emphasis on 'bringing it to the group' and the constant reduction of all matters to aspects of the individual's psychopathological condition meant that the experiment went one step further than work in most therapeutic communities. In the latter there is usually an emphasis on sharing experiences and information about the self, in order for the individual to feel himself part of the community and to provide information about the self.

Wooton (1977), for example, in his research in a therapeutic community, points out the underlying rules attached to sharing and shows how knowledge gained about another person, or the recounting of one's own experience in another context such as small-group therapy, would be relayed to the big group of his community. This became a rule of 'descriptive adequacy' whereby statements unrelated to an affective state would not be counted as 'sharing'. Similarly, contributions should not be too disparate as a lack of 'topic coherence' would also be regarded as 'not-sharing'. On the other hand, when a certain event such as a suicide attempt had occurred, it was necessary to focus on one individual and other members had to learn to 'not-share' and to hold back on their own problems. There were also certain legitimate ways in which a patient could exclude himself from sharing by stating, for instance, that his own particular problem was different. These rules were not, of course, formalized; Wooton found that by connecting different pieces of interaction he could effectively make up a body of rules for participation.

However, whereas in Wooton's therapeutic community the idea of sharing was made explicit, in the day hospital it was not. So for instance in Wooton's hospital the patients were told they were 'not-sharing' when they were jumping from topic to topic. It was held that this implied the expression of anger. This type of remark, which could be construed as reducing the surface discussion to a question of hidden aggression, differs from the psychoanalytic reductionism in the day hospital in that there is the connecting concept of sharing, which was a term explicitly used implying a known rule of interaction. Making the problem part of the concept of sharing in Wooton's community encouraged understanding by linking it to the assumption that such sharing would be therapeutic – and thereby legitimated the rule.

At the day hospital the ruling out of court of certain patients' remarks, or the insistence that any question (such as a researcher's participation) should not be discussed on its own terms but that it (and the researcher) should be brought to the large group, was not linked openly to any clear rule of participation such as sharing. This lack of such a link often left members mystified and, as only some people appeared to understand, it fostered a real sense of unequal access to psychoanalytic knowledge. It was not clear to some patients – or indeed staff members who lacked training in psychoanalytic theory – why a subject was ruled taboo and what it meant analytically.

This non-understanding was not recognized openly, however, as the day hospital ideology maintained that all members could participate equally well in interpretative work.

In this way the apparently democratic mechanism of 'bringing it to the group' worked effectively to suppress deviant opinion – particularly as, according to this ideology, all opinions were welcome for discussion (if not resolution).[7]

Without any positive or negative guidelines, the limits of acceptable independent behaviour were indicated in a rather vague fashion. In response to a complaint or a worry a staff member might remain silent instead of saying: 'So you don't think you can do so and so'; or 'Why do you feel you can't do so and so? What's stopping you?' The patients would have to interpret the staff's silence on the matter as encouragement or prohibition. This vagueness reflects the 'uncommitted' stance of the stereotype psychoanalyst.

A new patient at the hospital, who had not yet learnt which activities were acceptable, assumed from the lack of formal rules that there was general encouragement of mutual participation, and that therefore he could suggest they have some Gestalt therapy for the long and empty afternoons. Rather than decry the idea the staff simply would not discuss the matter, and remained silent even when approached by the Gestalt therapist himself who, fearing the possible repercussions of a private practitioner practising in an NHS hospital, dropped the idea when the day hospital staff would not commit themselves.

Thus all aspects of the treatment method relied on implication rather than overt rules. The existence of clear rules allows criticism and disagreements, but control may be very much more potent when, for instance, it is generally assumed that people know what is being referred to in an oblique fashion rather than said straight out. Implicit rules leave decisions about action to the individual's conscience and make open discussion amongst a group who may all, mutually but unknown to each other, be rebelling against the rule much more difficult, since the individual in it assumes that he is the only person who does not understand or the only one who disagrees with the rule. In this way the mechanism of bringing it all to the group (see Chapter 5) did not further democratic ideals and practices at

The theoretical and ideological background

all; on the contrary, it served to control deviance from the official ideology.

The humanistic rationale behind the therapeutic-community approach that centres on 'democratic participation, sharing of responsiblity, equality and mutuality of respect' has often led, according to Skynner (1974), to the naive idea that 'equality, permissiveness and abolition of the authority structure are in themselves curative principles.' Rather than regard such organizational changes as providing the kind of environment where it is easier for the patient to effect his psychological changes and adjustments, it all too often happens that this 'facilitating environment' (Morrice, 1979) is considered a form of therapy in itself. This was the case at the day hospital, with its emphasis on large-group therapy.

Therapeutic communities in general take for granted the concepts of communication, democratization, permissiveness and reality confrontation as ideal organizing principles which are rarely queried or more closely defined. At the day hospital this tendency was taken to an extreme, and any questioning in the large group of these basic tenets was actively discouraged by being reduced to individuals' psychopathological symptoms rather than referred for appraisal in business or staff meetings. In fact these concepts, especially that of democracy, became 'over-used slogans of an ideology' (Morrice, 1979) which were simply re-affirmed rather than re-examined. Few people dare to question what they assume to be the subject of consensus, especially when any attempt to query what is taken for granted is treated as deviant behaviour.

The therapeutic community's failure to clarify these terms is due perhaps to the fact that, as Morrice argues, such concepts have a strong appeal to the liberally minded:

This term [democracy], like the word 'therapeutic' itself, tends to disarm any disagreement. It is not only a principle, but also possesses the characteristic of a humane and liberal attitude which all 'right-thinking' people must surely accept and strive to implement.

(Morrice, 1979, p. 50)

The term 'democracy' (literally 'rule by the people') is used in a very general sense in this context to mean not rule by a few from above (the consultant) but authority dispensed at all levels so that staff and patients can have a say in how their work and treatment is conducted. As Morrice notes, democracy has often been confused with equality, resulting in the belief that everyone has a right to speak on every subject, and he points out that this produces slow and inefficient decision-making. It also fails to distinguish between situations where the right to a greater say belongs to specialists (for example in the treatment situation) and those where anyone's views count (in this setting, business decisions about concrete and material reality). On the one hand, the therapeutic-community specialists will define all problems as being central to their specialization and in consequence as falling outside democratic debate; on the other there is a refusal to accept anyone's claim to specialized knowledge and an insistence that all problems are amenable to democratic discussion.

At the time of the complaint, these were indeed the two dominant views: the staff adopted the former (as a specialist concern) through their psychoanalytic interpretation of all political statements while putting up a false front of democratic ideology. The patients, by later repudiating the staff's specialist knowledge, adopted the wholly political position which at its most extreme denies the very existence of any internal problems. This polarization came about because business and psychological discussions were not kept distinct. Day hospital members adopted wholly either one or the other of two definitions: everything is completely political or everything is linked with psychopathology. Both views entailed a reduction of one level of reality to the other.

Rather than accept either of these positions, Morrice argues that democracy is relative and will vary according to the constraints and goals of the community. If one knows what these goals and values are, one can locate the decision-making centre. If, however, there is a big gap between the community's ideals and its practice, he sees 'myth' becoming part of the process, for myth tends to develop in difficult situations where concepts are vague and operate as a 'defence against anxiety'.

The theoretical and ideological background

Although the day hospital professed the vague overall aim of helping all types of patient through psychoanalytic treatment, it was not at all clear how much help the patients were actually receiving – especially since psychoanalysis is such a lengthy and tenuous method of treatment, and given the impossibility of defining success or cure. Ezriel's approach as used by the medical director then became a kind of myth, not fully understood and remaining shrouded in mystery. At the same time, although rules had been abolished and no differences between staff and patients had been officially acknowledged, the members experienced an uncomfortable sense that the democratic organization was more of an ideal than something actually realized: the objective of removing constraints had not resulted in government from below; indeed at this stage no consistent policy emerged at all. True, there was some notion of democracy and power-sharing, but any possibility of this becoming fully realized was denied by psychoanalytic control. As psychoanalytic interpretation was the absolute currency of the situation a 'natural' hierarchy took over grounded in expertise in and control over the knowledge base.

The claim that people were equally free to have a say in the running and organization of the hospital added to the strength of the already powerful, although the claim was denied in practice. When the existence of hierarchical controls is denied, they become even more potent. If someone makes a suggestion or criticism and a psychoanalytic interpretation is used to quell the idea, he may still believe that he is free to have a say. In reality, however, the force of his statement has been neutralized and he is left wondering about his unconscious motivation for it. Those who have made the interpretation have defended themselves by attacking him in his already vulnerable position as the analysand, by ignoring the content of his statement and deflecting the arrow back to him. Indeed, such an approach is a useful defence mechanism and wards off counterattacks by those less expert.

Stanton and Schwartz (1954), in their study of a ward in a mental hospital, show the same kind of psychiatric reductionism at work. They remark how one of the most serious 'misunderstandings' in interaction would come about when individuals 'ignored the explicit meaning of a statement or action, and focused attention on the inferred meaning.' This was a habit of both psychiatrists and schizophrenics. Paranoid patients felt much at home in such an atmosphere, and the psychiatrists applied the same method of 'deep' interpretation to their colleagues' remarks. A protest by a junior staff member would be explained as a 'transference rebellion'. This created a situation where it was implied that if the staff member disagreed, he needed to see a psychiatrist. The actual cogency of the protest was not dealt with.

This mode of psychoanalytic control was well expressed by a disillusioned member of the day hospital staff in an informal interview:

Therapist: The day hospital had been a real disappointment to me. I'd so much idealized the MD [the medical director] that now I feel really let down. I've come to think that the day hospital is hopeless. The theory behind it is good, but this technique of laughing at people and saying that everything is just part of a person's pathology is enormously damaging. It muddles patients even further – it makes them lumps of jelly, doubting everything they do because they think it's determined by their unconscious. So they can't make any choices, and in consequence they have no self-respect. And making all interpretation in sexual terms is distorting. No reality is allowed at all. I felt like laughing out loud on Tuesday when [staff members] X and Y were madly interpreting, and the two patients just said 'Fuck off'. They were quite justified, because the analysts were completely ignoring the reality of the issue . . . Of course patients will reject analysis in total if there is no recognition of external realities . . . It was like the orchestra playing while the *Titanic* was going down. Until a month ago I was like everyone else, idealizing the MD [Adrian] and unable to sort out the confusion. Now I see that his idea of complete freedom is completely unrealistic; it simply permits him to do what *he* wants. He puts in half an hour instead of three-and-a-half, and his staff members are doing the same – not allowing their superegos to intervene and get them to work, but allowing

70

their neuroses to run riot and be projected on to the
patients . . . It would be a good thing if we could all meet up
here [in the staffroom] and sort out our difficulties, and then
we could feed the result back to the large group. Two years
ago the MD had a chance of doing what only he could do: to
define the boundaries of freedom for people at the hospital.
This would have given especially the patients a greater sense
of security. But he didn't do it, and the so-called freedom we
have now actually means that he and he alone is omnipotent.
That technique of mocking the patients is bad. But when I
challenge it, he reduces the issue to my father-figure problem
instead of taking it seriously as a reality. It's the same for me
as for the patients. I understood just how much of a mockery
the day hospital is after T's [an Adult Department consultant]
persecutory behaviour towards me. It was horrible, but I
realized it was like my past life experience – being torn
between two families – and that the time had come for me
to find out who I am, what I think and what my values are. I
felt particularly let down that Adrian wasn't there to support
me. He's never there even to talk to. He's putting everything
on his staff, and it is all a shambles and confusion. Some of
the things T was saying were quite true: Adrian *is*
irresponsible, psychopathic, and feels omnipotent, and the
patients do suffer as a result. There isn't enough care and time
put into helping patients sort out their muddles – just plenty
of freedom for the staff to display their neuroses in the large
group instead of helping the patients . . . It's quite unrealistic
to expect that all staff discussions can be held in the large
group, because we can't be really free there . . .

Open discussion and the grouping together of staff in opposition
to the experimental approach was effectively prevented by the
taboo against separate staff meetings. The mechanism that effectively controlled staff criticisms and paralysed their opposition
is a very well-known plebiscitarian technique adopted by, for
example, populist leaders. It implies a distrust of intermediary
bodies and allows the leader's direct appeal to the 'people', in
this case the patients. In this kind of situation, those at the
intermediate level (here the day hospital staff), who in a

bureaucracy might mediate between the highest echelon and the lower orders, are unable to gain autonomy from the populist leader as their power is derived solely from that leader's personal charisma. This produces an unstable and fluid organization where the only fixed reference point is the leader himself. In the day hospital, the idea of bringing everything to the group was an autocratic method of control adopted by a regime masquerading as a democracy. It was emphasized that *all* issues must be discussed with the 'people', but of course many problems could not, because of their nature, be discussed with the general populace. In consequence problems were not aired and, while appearing staunchly democratic, the leader had, it was said, his own way entirely.

Administrative authority is diminished

As the ideology of the day hospital became increasingly extreme, any administrative arrangement was regarded as bureaucratically authoritarian and therefore anti-democratic. Because administrators in other parts of the institute or in the higher echelons of particular disciplines were dealing directly with the social/economic/material dimensions and not merely looking for the psychological significance of such transactions, the day hospital staff regarded their activities as disruptive of therapy. Having carried the theory to such an extreme themselves, they saw normal administrative work (concerned, for example, with meals or fare reimbursement) as a form of opposition to their own perspective. The administrative staff meanwhile were not denying that the patients' activities had psychological significance; they simply went on working as usual within their own sphere of concern: mainly the material needs of patients. The day hospital staff – rather than emphasizing the psychological dimension of reality for therapeutic purposes in the context of the large group – asserted that this was the one and only reality that mattered, and refused categorically to acknowledge any other.

It is generally accepted by psychiatrists and therapists alike that in the context of the therapy administrative work makes a necessary and useful contribution as back-up support to their

The theoretical and ideological background

own work. In the day hospital however – except for occasional concern about hygiene or records, shown by nurses higher up in the administration – administrative interference in the processes of therapy was kept to an absolute minimum to provide merely, as far as it was allowed, the hospital's physical requirements. Administrative influence was much less pronounced than in other hospitals because the medical director's professional autonomy gave him the right to question the authorities' administrative scope.

The problem of the limits of consultants' clinical autonomy is nowhere outlined with any precision, but rarely in practice is it confused with administration. After all, the administration exists to help the doctor while he is treating his patients. Conversely, it is because he must be free to treat each patient in the way he thinks best that he has no overall manager; if he were being managed, the patient's right to negotiate his treatment with his doctor would be undermined and the doctor's decisions about treatment would be open to change without the participation and agreement of the patient. If the administrative situation does not please the doctor, he can simply withdraw patients from the hospital on the argument that he cannot treat them there as, in his expert opinion, he thinks he should. This means that consultants have a particular power legitimated by the implied contract they have with their patients, to whom they are answerable.

The emphasis on the importance of this relationship, which is the legitimation of clinical autonomy, must have confused the institute's administrative staff when the day hospital's consultant made their responsiblities his own prerogative. When he used his right to clinical autonomy to further the aims of his experiment, he was merely exercising a traditional right of consultants; but when he applied psychoanalytic theory to organizational structure he was making a radical break with tradition. The result was an anarchic championing of the removal of structures.

By overtly denying the legitimacy of the administration by ignoring its role in the running of the day hospital, and by emphasizing the staff's exclusively analytic roles, the medical director deprived the staff system of its administrative and social

73

aspects. Yet, however unlikely it would seem, this did not actually result in complete chaos. On the contrary, the organization was strongly underpinned in two interrelated ways: first, the reduction of the administrative role and the denial of social, economic and material elements resulted in a strongly one-sided monolithic system; second, the hospital was held together by a common ideology embracing democracy, debureaucratiz-ation and psychoanalytic reductionism and led by a medical director of considerable charismatic personality.

Charisma

Having had to overstate the case for psychotherapy in the protest of 1972 in order to make their point and influence the NHS administration accordingly, staff and patients at the day hospital had come to idealize it to such an extent that in the end they believed in psychotherapy as the only correct treatment for all patients, whatever their individual problems. From this position, staff and patients had no difficulty in accepting the medical director's more extreme approach when he began to reject all and any other forms of interaction as interference in the psychotherapeutic process. The application of Ezriel's theory, with its notions of democracy and rejection of administrative/bureaucratic authority, was transformed from theory into ideology as members came to believe that this approach was the definitive answer to mental illness. It was sincerely thought by staff and patients that if all patients were treated by psychotherapy, and given the right to act responsibly and to influence decisions, they would become better.

Behind this idea lay the belief that the day hospital had at last found the true secret of 'curing' mental illness. The ideological argument was that until then, with few exceptions, treatment had been in the hands of people who simply wanted to prevent the social deviation of the mentally ill. For instance drugs and ECT had been used to control behaviour and the only humane therapy available was psychoanalysis privately paid for by what the staff held to be well-off middle-class neurotics. Most of the patients at the day hospital were poor working-class 'borderline psychotic' cases,[8] and the idea that the day hospital was

74

The theoretical and ideological background

providing psychoanalytic treatment under the NHS – albeit in a community context – for very disturbed patients was very attractive. In the light of this the medical director, as the initiator of the experiment and the possessor of a rather charismatic personality, became a kind of saviour figure, a Messiah.

The danger of the therapeutic community becoming messianic is discussed by Hobson (1971). In his terms, the messianic leader develops a following who believe in what he symbolizes and experience a feeling of oneness in their shared belief. Differences between people are denied, and what Lemlij *et al.* (1981) call a 'pseudo-mutuality' is generated. As the movement develops it generates opposition and the leader is regarded as a dangerous radical by his adversaries. Hobson argues that this process – which he calls the 'therapeutic-community disease' – arises out of an idealization of the leader, and warns that if the members of the community do not recognize that they have idealized their leader, then catastrophic events may result which may culminate in the termination of the community – as indeed I outline in Chapter 7 on the crisis. Hobson's idea of the dangers of group phantasy stemming from a psychoanalytic perspective is allied to Weber's concept of charisma, whereby the leader's followers believe him to be endowed with magical powers which they will eventually inherit. This authority of charisma (literally 'gift of grace') 'transforms all values and breaks with tradition and rational norms: "It has been written . . . but *I* say unto you . . . ".'

Although the medical director's appointment was a bureaucratic one, the kind of authority he possessed did have charismatic overtones. Weber defined charismatic leaders as

> . . . *bearers of specific gifts of body and mind that were considered 'supernatural' (in the sense that not everybody could have access to them). As well as having no formal appointment and dismissal procedures, no career or salary, charismatic authority is self-determined and sets its own limits.*
>
> (Roth and Wittick, 1975, p. 89)

So it was exactly by setting its own limits that the charismatic

75

element in the medical director's authority reflected the bureaucratic rule that allows consultants to define their own area of
authority.

Under the experiment, the medical director gave his job and
work the widest possible definition – he was responsible for his
patients' unconscious and for all situations where this became a
salient feature. In other words, he saw himself as alone having
authority in every single situation in the day hospital, as well
as in respect of the institute's administration where patients
came into contact with personnel.

Given that in the matter of professional autonomy he was
entitled to define the area of his responsibility, his definition
remained unchallenged. This is an example of how charismatic
authority is not externally constrained. The bearer of charisma
is 'delimited from within, not by the external order' (Weber, in
Roth and Wittick, 1975). Charisma usually operates within specific social, political or ethnic groups and tends not to extend
beyond the group. However, in the NHS the group of mentally
ill patients is related to other specific groups, for example social
workers or the administrative staff who generally run the
material side of the hospital. There was therefore a clash in the
day hospital between the charismatic authority of the medical
director and the bureaucratic authority of the administrative or
managerial level.

It was during the protest of 1972–3, when the medical
director was leading the fight against the changes sought by the
NHS administration, that his charisma as a leader first became
apparent. Staff and patients both focused on him as the leader
who would save 'his people' from a reversion to more traditional,
primarily physical methods of treatment.[9] At least half of the
patients looked back with horror and distaste on the psychiatric
treatment they had received before attending the day hospital,
and the prevailing attitude among both staff and patients was a
very positive desire to be involved in an approach that offered
an alternative to conventional psychiatric methods. In this the
medical director was their spokesman, and by the time it was
clear that the protest had been successful he had come to
symbolize all that was good in more 'humane' and 'liberal' therapeutic methods. The successful campaign elevated him from a

The theoretical and ideological background

straightforward consultant in the NHS to a saviour leading his people to the promised land of sympathy, comfort and health.

Weber argues that charismatic authority is inherently unstable, however, because the holder has acquired it through repeated proofs of his power, rather than – as in the case of bureaucratic authority – through officially recognized competence. The medical director had of course achieved his formal position as a result of his 'officially recognized competence', yet he denied that he had any special abilities and expertise and argued that every member of the day hospital had therapeutic skills. As he rejected the formal acknowledgement of his specialist knowledge, his power was made to rest on repeated proofs of his extraordinary abilities in his daily work. Miracle-making took the form of the 'correct' psychoanalytic interpretation. Although anyone could interpret, invariably it was the medical director's words which were regarded as the really accurate description of the unconscious mechanisms at work in the group, uttered at a moment when the patients could make sense of them. Any other explanation, comment or interpretation was automatically wrong and an intervention in the therapeutic process. Whether or not the medical director really was accurate is beside the point: what mattered was that most day hospital members believed him to be.

His apparent omnipotence and omniscience seemed to appeal to many of the staff. He was both the delinquent schoolboy rebelling against authority (actually skipping with perverse glee when he had annoyed an officer higher up in the hierarchy) and a father-figure whose pronouncements were invariably right. His words and actions, like those of a religious martyr, were true simply by virtue of who he was, not because of what he said.

There was often much discussion about the 'father-figure' especially among the staff when they were trying to understand why it was that although they felt one way in opposition to some of the ideas behind the new approach in the day hospital, they acted in another way and 'despite themselves'.

Therapist A: Many of the staff are little Adrians. They've

77

internalized him as an authority figure, and that's so much more powerful than open authority.

Therapist B: The staff's been colluding with the patients to let this father-figure act for them. And how persuasive he is, too!

Medical director: Well, the power of the teacher depends on the acquiescence of the pupils.

Patient 1: But if it's a school, you have to have control of your pupils or else there's chaos and it can't work.

This was followed by a discussion among staff in the staffroom a few days later:

New therapist: What do *you* think about the idea that only group interpretations are useful in a large group? I must say I'm unsure about it myself.

Therapist A: Well, I do individual therapy. I don't go along with the group interpretation idea . . . I hate this hidden oppression. It's worse than open fascism, there at least you know what you're up against. We're all supposed to be able to make a valid contribution, but we don't – because of this hidden power.

New therapist: I'd like to be able to express something of my feelings about what's going on, but I daren't, because I think that's not the way things are done here.

Therapist B: The medical director says we're all free and not affected by the hierarchy with the consultant-in-charge as the boss. But we're not really free. He's the guru. There's this feeling that Adrian has some mystical power or hidden wisdom, and everyone wants to get some of this knowledge for himself. But I for one don't think he has it at all, and I'm disillusioned.

The prevalent ideology at the day hospital encouraged an idealization not only of the leader as a charismatic figure and of the efficacy of psychoanalysis, but even of the patients themselves. It was generally assumed that all patients (that is, in day hospital terms, anyone who joined the large group) could be 'cured' by the hospital's psychoanalytic psychotherapy.

78

The theoretical and ideological background

Eventually, however, the patients' simple belief in the medical director as charismatic wonder-worker needed to be reinforced by fact: they had to feel they were experiencing a sense of well-being from having become his disciples. When staff members threatened to stop the provision of meals, the patients started to have doubts as to what they had gained and wondered whether the medical director was really the 'God-sent master' they had believed him to be. Because they had so richly endowed him with special powers his fall from grace, when it came, was felt particularly strongly by his earlier admirers.

PART
2

STRATEGIC
INTERACTION

4

Debureaucratization and psychoanalytic reductionism

I want now to focus on the particular aspect of the day hospital experiment which emphasized the deliberate abandonment of rules and roles. Although the repudiation of bureaucratic procedures was at the heart of the overall experiment, and despite the fact that both staff and patients valued this innovation highly, this supposed move away from hierarchical organizational forms was more myth than reality.

Firstly, the day hospital was not independent but financed by the state, and even if the internal changes did lead to a somewhat flattened hierarchy the unit still remained part of the NHS hierarchical structure. With all the staff members except the medical consultants continuing to have external managers in their own disciplines, the unit had to keep within the broad guidelines laid down by the Area Health Authority which was employing the staff and which allocated the funds to maintain the hospital. Secondly, as long as a hospital requires the specific skills of medical personnel (in this case formally trained in psychiatry), such differentiation of skills does not permit a truly egalitarian system. Thirdly, no matter what the declared aims of a unit where exclusive emphasis and value are placed on psychoanalytic understanding, a 'hierarchy of analytic enlightenment' is likely to develop.

In this chapter I shall explore the ways in which the day hospital was structured despite the apparent lack of rules governing either staff or patients' behaviour, and will follow this with an examination of the role conflict of staff caught between the contradictory demands of their medical and professional managers. I relate this dual accountability to Coser (1979) and Merton and Barber's (1976) notion of 'sociological ambivalence', where the need for control in a therapeutic institution conflicts with the need to provide sufficient freedom for the development of the patients' inner dispositions.

My status as participant–observer enabled me to have considerable access to the behaviour patterns and rules of inter-action lying beneath the formal ideology. However, because of the unique approach to treatment the differentiation between appearance and reality, or overt and covert rules, becomes an unusually complex task, both easier and more difficult than it would have been in a more conventional organization. Where there are formal rules one may expect them to be evaded by informal means, and this would have to be accepted as part of the organization's life. Where there are no formal rules the alternative, informal communication network is more hidden and subtle and in crisis, particularly, it may come to replace formal controls.

The experiment's aim of debureaucratization implied a contempt for official reports and accounts, and this became part of the semi-official ideology. The staff emphasized that official versions presented a one-sided or even false account of reality, and maintained that only those directly involved could really know 'the truth'.

For example, it was argued that the label 'schizophrenia' (dealt out on a medical certificate, for instance) had nothing to do with the actual feelings, state, or potential of the patient. In parallel, it was asserted that it was impossible to make an assessment of a patient without taking into account the group, since taking the individual out of his group context would make nonsense of both his 'real' condition and the nature of the large group. Seen from this perspective, experience became a paramount factor, and gradually the ideology outlined above replaced the formal aspects of the day hospital *qua* hospital, as the strong norms and ethics developing out of it actually influenced behaviour.

In addition to the ideological replacement of a bureaucratic account with a collective and informal one, there is another level of interaction which is the informal version of the hospital's consciously created informal life: the actual groupings among both staff and patients that related to their group definitions of the situation, and the norms and values that these expressed.

Effectively, then, there were three levels of reality. Firstly, there is the formal level, which is outlined in this chapter as far as possible, given that formal rules and roles had been abandoned. Apart from my description of the different disciplines, this level is symbolized by the version of the day hospital encapsulated by the report of the first inquiry. Secondly, there was the quasi-official level of the experiment's ideology – the way in which staff and patients expected each other to behave. Thirdly, beneath these expectations, lay the 'underlife' of the day hospital – the way in which participants really experienced their situation and what actually happened in practice regardless of formal or ideological expectations.

Although the report of the inquiry instigated by the patients' complaints did manage to ascertain some of the ideological expectations, this third version of reality eluded it because the formal methods of inquiry excluded participant observation. The members of the inquiry team, for example, could not uncover the actual interaction in the day hospital: how the staff developed particular strategies for dealing with situations which, without formal rules, could be chaotic. Nor could they account for the way in which a group of patients, sometimes described as 'disturbed' and 'socially inadequate', had managed to organize themselves to make an official complaint.

In this chapter I shall focus upon the implied new 'rules' of the experiment and the types of problem that arose for the staff in particular – how, for example, the 'rule' to ignore bureaucratic procedures often conflicted with the expectations of senior staff in the NHS administration outside the day hospital.

Debureaucratization

Admission and discharge of patients

The process of debureaucratization involved abandoning attendance and medical records, patients' progress reports, referral letters to and from general practitioners and other agencies, and in general any formal rules governing both staff and patient behaviour. There were, however, two specific ways in which the medical director attempted to put debureaucratization into practice which I would like to explore in more detail. The first of these shows just how the admission and discharge procedures were abandoned, and how this move compounded the threat to the patients' identity inherent in psychotherapy as such; the second relates to how the medical director ignored the formal roles and training of his staff from the nursing and occupational therapy disciplines, and how this rejection of their original training left the latter without any formal authority for their psychotherapeutic roles.

In most day and residential hospitals, an individual obtains patient status through referral by a general practitioner, social worker or some related agency to a named psychiatrist in the hospital. In the day hospital admission procedures changed during the different stages of the hospital's life. In time, responsibility for this administrative and clinical decision passed from the psychiatrist to the patients themselves.

At an earlier stage in the hospital's history (before 1972) when it was more conventionally psychiatric in approach, admissions were left to the discretion of the psychiatrist to whom the patient had been referred. In the course of a one-to-one interview the psychiatrist would make a clinical diagnosis and assessment of the potential patient. On the basis of this he would determine whether his condition was appropriate for the kind of treatment the hospital was offering and whether or not he was likely to fit in with the other patients. Later, when the hospital became more therapeutic-community-minded, a similar kind of assessment would be made, less formally and without the use of a psychiatric diagnosis, by a group of patients and staff.[1] Through this experience in the group, the 'pre-patient'[2] could decide whether or not he wished to try the treatment offered by group therapy. (This choice was available to him anyway as there were no compulsory admissions, and the prime requirement for therapy was personal motivation.)

When this procedure was abandoned in turn, admission was decided entirely by the patient himself. Self-referred patients and those referred by some particular agency would usually receive a letter from a staff member, suggesting they visit the hospital for a therapy session to see for themselves whether they would like to join.[3] The idea behind this *laissez-faire* approach was that the patients needed to 'find their own way in their own time to bring themselves to therapy' and thereby begin to take responsibility for themselves. It was argued that it did not matter if patients did not attend the large group for quite some time after their arrival, since in the absence of any constraints they would eventually bring themselves into the therapeutic arena more effectively.

During the crisis, self-referrals increased in proportion over other new arrivals. Patients would often bring along friends and relatives for treatment, even though the organization was not designed for family therapy.[4] At this time referral agents were wary of sending patients to a unit that was gaining a reputation for being disorganized and, uncertain about the treatment offered, preferred to direct them elsewhere.[5] In any case, the decision whether or not to join or remain in the community was left almost entirely to the patient himself aside from the occasional use by staff of the ultimate veto of discharge, although this was not sanctioned by the medical director.

Leaving the therapeutic community again was also largely *ad hoc* during the experimental period. The staff never formed the opinion that a particular person was 'cured' or 'healthy' enough to leave. Patients would gradually become less and less involved and more irregular in attendance until they simply stayed away altogether or found themselves a job, often informing the day hospital only shortly before starting work. (The concrete reality of earning one's own living was rarely discussed directly and there was no working through to this major decision.) Occasionally a patient would come to the conclusion that he could no longer cope with being responsible for himself outside the hospital and, after talking it over with members, would opt for referral back to a residential hospital. When patients overdosed or became psychotic they would be taken to the emergency out-patients' department or the mother hospital and referred elsewhere from there. Alternatively they would seek help from that department if they could not cope outside the day hospital opening hours. As with admissions, therefore, responsibility for discharge passed largely to the patient himself,[6] though it was still used by some of the staff as a sanction against unacceptable behaviour.

The staff as therapists

The staff, composed of two medically trained psychotherapists, two occupational therapists, one registrar and two nurses, were all defined by the medical director as psychotherapists, even though they were employed as members of their respective disciplines and accountable to their superiors in their particular hierarchy. In fact, there are as yet few psychotherapist roles and no formal training for psychotherapists in the NHS, which employs people in terms of their original discipline and expects that if the job requires therapeutic skills they will learn as they go along. If such an employee has had formal training at one of the very few privately based training institutions, there is no official recognition of his qualification in terms of higher pay.[7]

Perhaps it was the fact that the majority of the staff (four out of seven) lacked formal training and qualification in psychotherapy which partly explains their uncritical acceptance of the medical director's experiment: they had neither the theoretical nor the personal judgement to assess the experiment in terms of its status, advantages or weaknesses.

As a rule – except for their supervised work in the adult department – their only training had been in the day hospital itself and at the weekly seminars held by Ezriel. These were a combination of group therapy sessions and case conferences where discussion of particular cases was the vehicle for learning Ezriel's approach. Every member of the staff was informally expected to attend these seminars for at least one year in order to come to understand the theory behind the new method used in the day hospital.[8] In the circumstances this was a very necessary socialization process, since without it the nursing and paramedical staff would have had a very different approach to the goal they held in common with the medical director – the psychological treatment of patients. Had they remained unschooled in Ezriel's theory, they might well have seen signs and behaviour, all of which the medical director related to deeper layers of the personality, in a much more common-sense light.

The theoretical approach aside, however, the fact that their original training and experience was considered irrelevant to their work in the day hospital (even though they received no formal training in psychotherapy) meant that many of the staff were left with no skills recognized as appropriate to their new roles. They were enjoined to regard themselves as an undifferentiated company of equals employing psychoanalytic methods of treatment, while their managers in their discipline of origin still respected the NHS hierarchy and related to them in hierarchical terms as their superiors. Despite attempts to debureaucratize the day hospital, therefore, the institute did not remain as undifferentiated and as rule-less as the medical director declared he intended it to be.[9]

The staff: control through interpretation

Once formal rules and roles had ceased to be acknowledged as points of reference, when patients or staff deviated from the line laid down by the medical director it was increasingly psychoanalytic interpretations that were marshalled to control behaviour.

As a participant–observer, I have personal experience of the powerful nature of control by psychoanalytic assumptions. After a large-group session, when a new patient had become very frustrated with the prevailing attitude and lack of help, I was called to her aid by another patient. She was in the cloakroom, retching and about to vomit. When I arrived she broke into tears and told me how annoyed she was, and how the medical director had upset her by, as she felt, making light of the problems and 'ignoring me as an individual'. She was diabetic and being upset, she said, often made her sick. I tried to calm her and we discussed why she was so upset. At this point one of the medical director's main supporters came in and, with a disapproving look at me for the way I was handling the situation, told the girl that she must put her objections to the group the next day.

This seemed a tough and crudely unimaginative approach to

89

someone who had just confided her not unnatural difficulties of speaking up in front of twenty or more people. Instead of the staff member trying to discover the individual needs and problems of this patient, she applied the universal dictum that 'everything must be brought to the group' – an impractical solution in this particular case. This therapist later informed me that I should simply have told the girl this, and she wondered what my own need had been to step in as I had.

After this I felt I would have to eschew such individual contacts if I wanted to protect myself personally and professionally. I was afraid the medical director might inhibit my access to the day hospital or rather, as he was not an overt rule-maker, create such an uncomfortable atmosphere for me that I would find it hard to continue. The ridiculing tone in which control was exercised through psychopathological interpretations could be personally humiliating and was not something to be suffered gladly. The therapy and organization did not allow for individual discussions, and although I suggested to the patient that she try to see a staff member individually if she found this easier than going to the group, she never managed to get this kind of attention even though I had myself relayed her wants and needs to other staff.[10]

Many of the day hospital staff members tried to protect themselves from this kind of dilemma by taking refuge in imitation of the medical director and apparent agreement with his theory, since deviation from the ideology that maintained the supremacy of psychoanalytic interpretation over all other forms of treatment and its appropriateness for all patients was strictly taboo.

When one member of staff informed the large group that she had not attended it the previous day because a violent patient, one of the ringleaders of the 'gangsters', was being allowed to remain in the large group and she thought the staff should support patients who felt frightened of his violence, she was told that she was setting up in competition with the medical director and was annoyed that the rest of the staff were following him rather than her. She was also told: 'That's the trouble with not having a penis' – implying that she was merely experiencing so-called typical female penis envy rather than making a valid organizational and therapeutic point. Such psychopathological interpretations left staff members reduced to the status of patient. The above was a typical 'double-bind' situation: if a staff member protested at such mocking statements this was seen only as proof of the interpretation having been correct, since 'people resist the truth more than anything'.

In the absence of formal rules with clearly defined rights and duties as well as any formal training in psychotherapy, staff members often quelled the doubts and criticisms they felt in respect of their colleagues by reflecting that these others, most of whom had been through analysis, had 'sorted themselves out' and being 'enlightened', would not really be ridiculing their fellow-staff or patients with an abuse of psychoanalysis. The fault was much more likely to lie in the person feeling such doubt. In mitigation of such unclear thinking it might be said that especially for those only partly analysed it was in the circumstances very difficult to decide who 'really knew' and who did not; and given that the unconscious is by definition unknown and largely unknowable, how can the individual say what is at the root of his own questioning?[11]

As to independent explanations of feelings and events, especially when they expressed an attitude of caring, these were liable to be regarded as collusion[12] since the medical director's approach denied validity to simple sympathetic caring and, further, labelled it intervention in the therapy. Those therapeutically untrained staff whose own profession was 'encompassed' by the medical director's often avoided such conflict by crudely imitating him in designating any signs of sympathy as collusion or intervention. Because it was only the qualified staff or those who had been in the day hospital for a long time who could attempt Ezrielian interpretations, other staff just showed their support of the experiment and their apparent understanding and acquiescence in the interpretations by exchanging knowing smiles, remarks and laughter. This tacit support was expressed frequently because – particularly for any new staff or patient member – the large group could seem quite unreal and often resembled a Beckett play with its non sequiturs and analytic/allegorical language which seemed quite unrelated to actual events, displays of emotion or the discussion of a problem during the session.

Although, therefore, formal roles and rules had been jettisoned, a hierarchy of power persisted based on expertise and personal experience in 'enlightenment' reflecting fairly accurately the staff roles in the formal NHS hierarchy. But because the day hospital ideology held the formal rights and duties of the NHS hierarchy in contempt, the nursing and occupational therapy staff experienced conflict because of the contradictory expectations and demands made on them by their two sets of managers. At first it was only the managers in their own hierarchy whom they openly queried and criticized. Later, opposition to the experiment in the public arena of the large group took the form mainly of vague questioning, with more direct disagreement being left to informal discussions in the privacy of the staffroom. Here the reductionism of the theory was indeed criticized, but no consistent line of opposition was ever clearly formulated and no concrete groups formed. Perhaps it was too dangerous to go out on a limb when the justification for one's position remained so vague in contrast to the wealth of argument and conviction put forward by the other side. So the contradiction between strong private feelings and lack of public expression was not resolved.

Indeed, the staff seemed never to be free of ambivalent feelings, which in turn led to contradictory statements and constantly changing views.[13] To begin with many felt they should be loyal to the day hospital, which was trying to maintain its independence as a unit and had to be protected from all outsiders, even the members of the Professional Staff Committee (PSC). If the staff were to support and hence legitimize intervention by the PSC, they were afraid they might lose the control over their work that they believed themselves to have. Secondly, allegiance to the PSC or the administration was regarded as defection from the day hospital's ideology; it could only lead to insecurity and discomfort in the individual's work since no support of his position would be forthcoming. Thirdly, it must be admitted that an organization without strict rules of attendance and responsibility allows a looseness of work not ordinarily encountered in most occupations, and this is not without its attraction. Sometimes staff would remark that they had better be careful of attacking their medical director or they might get someone who would do everything by the book and allow no flexibility.

The ambivalence of the staff's attitudes to the experiment emerged in a brief discussion between two staff members shortly before the patients' complaint was filed. One therapist felt that no work was being done:

Therapist A: The whole ethos is emanating from the charisma of Adrian. Everyone just takes his lead. Why aren't staff working in the day hospital in the afternoon when he's not there? I don't either, and I feel guilty about it but I can't get myself to do it. All the staff must feel uncomfortable that the hospital isn't really working, so why don't we discuss it and work out something more useful?

He was, however, against 'rigidity of time and place', and also the 'secret nature of small groups', and so implicitly supported the experimental view.

Therapist B: We oughtn't to be working because the contract says we should, but because we want to. I don't mean because we enjoy it, but because it's fulfilling some function, if only just to be there for the patients if they need us. Anyway, why *were* small groups just dropped, without any discussion?

This staff member could not reconcile himself to the view that small-group therapy interfered with the work in the large group. In fact, he had continued to run a well-attended small group for months after other staff had complied with the medical director's opinion in the matter.

Reactions to the process of debureaucratization rarely took the form of faithful adherence to any one particular line of thought but found expression in radical changes of opinion and response. This remained so until the concerted effort of a number of patients brought about the demand for an inquiry when, against all odds, this group closed its ranks and provided a solid breakwater against the flood of psychoanalytic control mechanisms.

In their rejection of the general approach adopted during the experiment, the patients found little support among the staff. Although the staff often (and usually secretly) concurred with the patients' feelings on many aspects of the work, the latter saw little evidence of this within the large group. Moral support from the PSC came only after it had received the patients' letter of complaint, copies of which had meanwhile also been sent to outsiders.[14] Isolated incidents and remarks were the only tangible support from the day hospital staff for the patients' increasing opposition to the experimental approach. Even staff who were in sympathy with the patients' complaint felt that such a challenge might mean a rejection not only of their own work but of therapy as a whole, and they could not, they felt, ally themselves with a potentially anti-therapeutic attitude.

Indeed, immediately after the letter of complaint had been written, support for the psychoanalytic method by some members of staff was even more emphatic than before, almost as if a restatement of loyalties had to be made at the moment when the patients sought to have those in agreement with them 'stand up and be counted'. However, the staff seemed to feel that at a time when feeling was running high, and when the patients' inner world might need greater support, therapy could not simply be dropped. Taking a stand meant being ready for the consequences, and the therapists felt they must help the patients understand the guilt they assumed they must be (or perhaps ought to be) suffering.

In terms of psychoanalytic theory, the staff were afraid that if they were openly to disagree among themselves the patients would see this as confirmation of the damage they imagined they had done to the staff by disrupting the fairly unified front usually presented to them, that is by having to acknowledge that their own destructive phantasies had become reality. Perhaps in an attempt to control a possibly explosive situation in the session following the complaint, one after another the therapists gave their psychoanalytic interpretations of why events had developed in this way:

Debureaucratization and psychoanalytic reductionism

—— Those with small pricks have been getting together in misery and hatred of the bastard who claims he's happy with his potent prick [implying that the patients were envious of the medical director's authority and strength].

—— Children see how adults cope with life and think that childhood will never end, that the process of growing up is too long and tedious, and it is far more exciting to act as an adult and bypass those immediately there by writing a letter to an impersonal higher authority.

—— The fear of a confrontation, and the necessity of looking at internal matters, have made the patients go to a third party.

—— It's easier to look at material things than at the shit inside.

In other words, instead of examining the content of the patients' complaint, the staff were putting forward explanations of the situation in terms of what they thought was the inner reason for, and the meaning of, this complaint. They argued that the patients were reluctant to look at their own inner confusion and were trying to bring in other people who would intervene in the therapeutic process which aimed at such self-examination, or perhaps simply to stir up some excitement. However, in private discussions among themselves some of these same staff members – especially the nurses, an occupational therapist and a therapist – did consider what the complaint might mean at the conscious level. They said, for example: 'There's subtle coercion going on. There's a lot of lip-service paid to freedom, but there's manipulation underneath all the time.'

In the months leading up to the inquiry, staff in sympathy with the patients' complaint gave short shrift to their colleagues who continued to analyse the patients' action in terms of the unconscious: 'Try giving the Minister for Health and Social Security psychotherapy!' (The Minister had been sent a copy of the complaint.) On the other hand, one staff member argued that the patients wanted to 'cut off the head', and compared their attack on the medical director (which might lead to his dismissal) to a child's rivalrous and castrating feeling towards his father.

Before the complaint, staff attitudes towards reducing administrative problems to internal ones had varied between members and over time. In the early stages more staff had supported the experimental method, but eventually some tired of the overworked issues that had dominated the large group for so long. Gradually more of them disagreed with the sole use of the Ezriel approach, recognizing that other types of interaction were equally relevant and arguing that communications need not be forced into a theoretical mould. In the course of the year leading up to the complaint, worries about the approach were occasionally sounded in staffroom discussions. Two staff members never admitted doubts throughout the whole three years of the experiment; others, although not taking a consistent line of opposition, would make such remarks as: 'I'm not sure that Adrian is right. All this emphasis on interpretations; there are times when patients need holding and caring.'

At the time of the complaint there were three main groups of staff opinion on the continuum between commitment to the approach and vocal opposition to it. The medical director had two disciples who never questioned the validity of his method. At the other extreme, three members of staff were quite critical of many of the aspects of the experiment but they did not really join forces until some time after the complaint; one in fact, despite his quietly consistent criticism, preferred not to commit himself openly. He did not contribute oral evidence at the inquiry and avoided much of the informal discussions (largely because he was working part-time). Of the remaining two staff members, one resigned from the part of the work that took him into the day hospital and undertook similar work at another day centre. Thus none of these groups exercised any collective action.

Dual accountability

The staff had little contact with their superiors in their own formal hierarchies outside the clinic. In the clinic they could regard themselves and their colleagues with equal authority and status, whereas their position in their own disciplines was based on a bureaucratic hierarchical model[15] of differential authority.[16]

In terms of the outside managers' responsibility for the work of their subordinates, the situation was particularly complicated because each staff member's manager was a generalist in his discipline and usually quite unacquainted with psychotherapy. For example, the district nursing hierarchy found that certain aspects of the day hospital's exercise of psychotherapy conflicted with the basic tenets of the nursing profession. One staff member, who found the accumulated dirt worrying to her nurse's conscience, occasionally did set to work on her own to clean up. This was quite in accordance with the unspoken directive contained in the medical director's decision that members should themselves keep the place clean. However, her doing so alone gave the act the appearance of the standard nurse's role in a traditional hospital: caring for and looking after the patients in a practical way.

The medical director remarked à propos of her cleaning, 'That's what I like to see', and commented on the fact that not only was she cleaning a lavatory, but that it was not labelled 'men' or 'women' and that he saw this as 'interestingly ambiguous'. The meaning of this comment (as of so many) was unclear, but he was probably referring to the nurse's unconscious motivation. Feeling accused of acting in a traditional way, the nurse answered: 'This is my kind of therapy', implying that she was espousing the material level that was always being reduced to psychopathological causes, and was indirectly spurning the kind of therapy where only interpretations of the unconscious were regarded as valid. When other staff applied directly to the administrator for a cleaner they met with refusal, because the administrator was afraid of contradicting the medical director and 'hindering therapy'.

When the nursing manager was officially informed by a sanitary inspector that the standards of hygiene were well below the acceptable level for the treatment of NHS patients, the nurses in the hospital were asked by the district nursing officer to explain how they could have allowed the situation to reach this point. The explanations they gave of the therapeutic reasons for the persistence of this insanitary state, and its significance in analytic terms, were met with blank incomprehension. The nursing world-view could not grasp the meaning of the therapeutic notions entertained by the medical director, who saw the external fact of dirt as symbolizing internal messing and considered that employing a cleaner was not the appropriate solution.

Nursing managers do not tolerate dirt, however, let alone the accumulation that had been permitted in the day hospital, and the inspector's report implied that the nurses had been professionally negligent in their tolerance of such a health risk. This is one example of how acceptance by the staff of their medical director's ideas meant directly contravening the regulations of their original discipline; and how, by directly opposing his beliefs, the senior nurse in the hospital found herself in the wrong – a classical double-bind.

The following extract from a staffroom discussion shows the nurses' problems in trying to reconcile dual accountability.

Therapist A: I'll have to give evidence at the inquiry about cleanliness. One of the nursing officers seems to think the inquiry will only mean a clean-up.
Therapist B: We can say that we did ask for a cleaner but that Adrian was against this. Or rather, that he said he wasn't against a cleaner but that it would work against the therapy.
Therapist A: The Administrator agreed, though, that we could order supplies for the cleaning group.

This was a group of patients and staff who, at the instigation of therapist A, had set up a group to clean the clinic. The medical director had accepted the existence of a cleaning group, but as always interpreted their action psychoanalytically, once more putting the participants into a double-bind.

Therapist C: If this place had a set membership we could clean for ourselves. But why should we clean up after dossers coming in from the Harrow Road?

With no rules and no clear definition of patient status, the

98

boundary between the outside world and the hospital had become very blurred. Since the focus was solely on the unconscious, anyone – staff, patient or outsider – was a patient by definition (by virtue of possessing an unconscious) as soon as he came into contact with those who were defining social reality, which in this case was synonymous with psychological reality.

The problems of multi-accountability are also well illustrated in a later staffroom exchange:

Therapist A: The divisional nursing officer was asking for information for the inquiry from full-time nurses. I think that's unfair, they should come to you [indicating the medical director].
Medical director: You should give her an interpretation.

He is almost stating outright that psychoanalytic interpretations are control mechanisms.

Therapist B: You can't interpret to her. I didn't ask for an inquiry, so why should I tell her anything? Why don't they ask you, Adrian, instead of the nurses?
Medical director: You should find out what they want the information for.
Therapist C [to B]: Why take the responsibility on your shoulders?
Therapist B: I have to keep up some liaison because I want some money for a course.

Not wishing to respond to an ordinary appeal to her sense of formal obligation, she puts forward self-interest as more legitimate.

Medical director: Why do you think they ask only the nurses? Because nurses are masochists.
Therapist C [a psychotherapist]: Yes, they haven't asked *me*. [to B]: Why accept that they put you in a position with Adrian to go and talk to these nursing officers? They can't put you in a spot unless you accept and go.

This exchange shows the staff split more clearly. While some staff are attempting to use the facts as proof of the interpretative explanation, others are more inclined to the requirements of formal obligations and external reality.

. . . and later . . .

Therapist A: I feel such conflict about my role as nurse. I want no part in the inquiry because I didn't ask for one. My role as nurse is to keep the place clean. That's what I was hired for, but I don't think that's my job. I work as a therapist.
Therapist B: Wait for the inquiry. They may be sufficiently tuned into therapy to understand the work we're doing, and the fact that you work as a therapist.
Therapist A: If we do get through this inquiry, then maybe we'll be free of interfering nursing officers and all their administrative books.

The nurses had recently been asked to keep a record of hours of work, days off and holidays. In their capacity as therapists they were alarmed and shocked to be thought accountable in this way, and considered that their work was qualitatively and sufficiently different from the traditional nursing role to be free from such rules of the nursing administrative hierarchy.

Therapist A: There's been a spin-off from the inquiry. The nursing officers have asked me to give evidence at a preliminary meeting on 1st June. I won't, because they want to split off one person from the rest, and I won't be involved in that. They can come here and learn a bit about therapy themselves if they want to know things.

This conspiracy theory entailing quasi-psychoanalytic explanations of outsiders' actions was frequent at this point in the crisis. Here the staff member is divided between the 'request' from her senior administration and the day hospital imperative of presenting a united front and not allowing others to interfere. If she acceded to the request she would be forced into discussing the situation in layman's terms at the concrete level, or fail to communicate and be seen to act perversely: insistence on the day hospital view that understanding of the situation is possible only through direct experience would be received as an assertion of independence she does not have in formal terms. And the argument that she was under the prescribing authority of the medical director is unlikely in view of his own supposed flattening of the hierarchy after democratization.

Violence and control

The verbal exchanges below will trace a gradual crystallization of opinion and show new alliances being formed among the staff group. In particular they show the emergence of the major division between staff who fervently supported the medical director's abandonment of rules and emphasis upon analytic interpretation, and those who had come to criticize such an exclusive belief in therapy and the exclusion of formal controls.

The part-time staff believed they could help all patients through interpretation alone; they supported the medical director. The more critical staff (who worked full-time), after trying to give psychoanalytic interpretations all day to a violent and frightening patient, came to the conclusion that such an aspiration, however laudable, was unrealistic. They also felt that to prove his own theory the medical director, who had been conspicuous by his absence all day, should help to show that treatment by interpretation was indeed suitable for patients of *all* conditions and possible to maintain continuously, whatever the circumstances. In one incident, four months after the patients had submitted their official complaint, three of them became involved in a violent fight in the course of which one patient was quite badly injured and two staff members were punched on the jaw.

The extracts below are from the group session held shortly after the violent incident; present were ten staff members and three patients, and one patient who came and went inter-mittently.

Therapist A: I'm quite clear about *my* boundaries and limits. I'm simply not prepared to work under the threat of violence, even if anyone else is.

101

She is arguing directly that there are limits to the extent to which psychoanalytic interpretations can be used to curb any and all eventualities in the day hospital, but rather than ask for a change of policy about rules she focuses on the staff's personal capacities for withstanding violence.

Medical director: Well, how unkind to the bad angry parts of ourselves! You can't stand the violence in others because of the violence in yourself. I suggest you give up practising therapy if you can't stand the bad part of yourself. There's a choice you have to make – work in an asylum, in the bad sense of that word, or be prepared to work therapeutically.

Trying to silence staff dissent by a psychopathological interpretation, the medical director says quite clearly that therapist A's refusal to work with violent patients is subjective, and invalid in that it merely reflects fear of her own subconscious. He even goes so far as suggesting that such evidence of psychopathological disequilibrium should make her change her career. At the same time, by appearing to be concerned with her inner development, he is obliquely attempting to control her openly critical attitude. He fails to acknowledge the actual, practical reality of the work being threatened.

Therapist B: You're faced with a piece of *reality* here. Yesterday someone was nearly killed and I and another member of staff were hit. I was frightened. I must have a secure environment in order to work therapeutically. You can't interpret when you get a fist pushed in your face. Murders do happen in mental hospitals.

Being one of the most fervent supporters of the experiment does not stop this therapist from pointing out its weaknesses.

Medical director: Yes, slow deaths in back wards.

He is reasserting the ideology of the therapeutic-community movement that therapy in a democratic setting, whatever risks this may involve, is better than the suppression of anger through drugs and patients being shut away in 'back wards'.

102

Debureaucratization and psychoanalytic reductionism

Patient 1: [who had been violent the day before, enters very angrily, making threatening gestures and shouting. He is holding a plate filled with earth, a bent fork on it.]: That registrar and his ideas about closing the canteen! I'm getting the kitchen staff unionized.

[He keeps opening and shutting the door, which he had repaired earlier.]

Eat your fucking food or you'll be . . .
Medical director: Were you breaking union rules by mending that door?
Patient 1: I'm no blacklegger! I've got my union card. What I don't know about electronics isn't worth knowing. I brought a psychiatrist friend of mine in here, and you should have seen the letter he wrote me about the place. It'll close, I tell you.
[He leaves.]
Therapist D: He's taking the piss off and on our Adrian's high-flown interpretations – so 'mature' and 'poetic'! This place may be free and facilitate people expressing their emotions, but I feel we're facilitating the destructive parts and not protecting the constructive ones.

He implies that the expression of destructive impulses seems to outweigh whatever the therapeutic gain from verbalizing feelings and phantasies. Then patient 1 returns. Staff member D tries to explain to him his behaviour in terms of his feeling persecuted, but the patient refuses to listen and keeps walking out.

Therapist D: I can't help you if you keep going away.
Patient 1: I don't need anybody's help. I'm okay. I only go pop if people goad me into it.
Patient 2: I agree with D. Some staff may think it's freedom, but really it's people taking liberties, which is a very different thing. If there'd been staff here in the afternoon, this wouldn't have happened.

Asylum to Anarchy

Most of the qualified staff worked in the hospital only in the morning, but as a result of the patient's remark they felt constrained to attend in the afternoon as well.

Therapist B: We all have our different limits of toleration. Adrian's may be very broad, and mine wider or narrower than those of other people here, but it's foolish to think we're all alike.

This so far enthusiastic supporter of the new therapy now implicitly rejects the notion that the day hospital can help every kind of patient and treat even violent patients through psychoanalytic interpretations. The idea that this was possible had been a seductive one. It made the therapists feel positively omnipotent when they could open their arms to all and sundry. By definition, omniscient and omnipotent postures recognize no limits (for example fear) and obscure the realization of one's true capabilities, and this is what the therapist is suggesting here. By way of answer, the medical director simply threw his theory back at her, comparing the potentiality of violence with the 'slow deaths in back wards'. He did, as a matter of fact, later win back her support, and she remained a committed ally until and beyond his demise as medical director of the clinic.

Therapist E: I draw the limit at physical violence.
Therapist B: I feel we should draw the line somewhere when such violence happens.

Five days later, in a staff discussion, staff member B (initially a fervent supporter of the medical director), who had been the first to insist on knowing the boundaries of one's personal limits, now starts to re-define the situation and her reaction to being hit by the violent patient.

Therapist A: The conflict seems to be about patient intake and that Adrian isn't giving enough care and attention.
Therapist B: Who says that?
Therapist C: It's because we've been over-confident that this thing happened. It may be okay to offer treatment to all and

104

sundry, but how do you stop them when they get violent and simply bring treatment to a standstill?

Therapist B: Proper sex can't take place without violence. If you don't accept that then you'll just get vegetables for patients.

'Sex' here is shorthand jargon for 'proper communication and development' in therapy which, in terms of primitive emotions, originally meant sex. Having asserted the need for boundaries when she was hurt while physically intervening in the quarrel, now that time has passed this staff member makes the rather strong statement that violence is a necessary part of communication and implies that to be really alive includes conflict and, apparently, even actual violence. This is a rephrasing of the medical director's argument that when too high a value is placed on nonviolence, people are locked up in back wards to die a slow death. Both he and therapist B polarized the argument to such extremes that they saw the repression to be found in traditional psychiatric hospitals as the only alternative to violence.

Therapist C: There was no disagreement about patient 1 when he first came. Adrian thought he could treat everyone, and I agreed at the times Adrian was here that 1 could come. But then he started coming every day.

Therapist B: This has nothing to do with 1, it's to do with the staff.

Therapist C: Why ask the staff to act on 1's behalf?

Therapist D: Exactly. It's we who must resolve it.

Therapist C: Yes, we're avoiding looking at ourselves.

C and D are regarding the issue of violence as obscuring the real phenomenon of the day hospital's inadequacies in general.

Therapist D: It's not just 1. There may be even more dangerous patients.

Therapist C: We must talk it out and see where we fall short. We're not gods. I for one won't take violence.

Therapist B: But that's control! You're just saying that if there's violence then the person must be kicked out!

She realizes with shocked consternation that her colleagues really want to bring in rules to regulate the patients' behaviour and that the discussion about rules, boundaries and structure has passed from the abstract to a more concrete level.

Therapist A: That's what a staff team is for. To decide what to do when some staff can take it and some can't.
Therapist B: What I did [in restraining the patients fighting] anyone could. I did get hit, but that was my fault. I could have avoided it. I was hit because I was frightened. If you can understand why you are afraid of violence you can cope. It's the violence in oneself that's so frightening.

She is reverting directly to the medical director's views.

Therapist C: Well, so we must see why some can work like this and others can't. If we all try together, we can discover it. It's fine for some people just to drop in and hand out an interpretation, but we must have a system and a boundary.

Neither this discussion nor any subsequent one ever discovered a generally acceptable 'system'. In any case discussions like this were rare, and if the medical director was present he would get up and leave, saying he had no time for such things. If the matter was aired in the forum of the large group the practical reality of it was smoothly transposed to the psychopathological level, so pre-empting any organizational change.

While behavioural control in a therapeutic institution concerned with its patients' self-realization is inevitably something of a paradox, at the O'Brien Hospital in the United States, where Rose Coser (1979) was doing her research, the problem of apparently contradictory mandates was resolved by differentiating the contexts in which each value system applied. On the one hand the treatment context was bounded by the fifty-minute individual psychotherapy session, carried out on the basis of the trust implicit in the therapeutic alliance; on the other the value

Debureaucratization and psychoanalytic reductionism

of behavioural control pertained to every activity on the ward outside the clearly defined therapy session.

By making a clean separation between the two types of context, each in charge of its own personnel, the hospital was able to meet these opposing needs. Such an organizational arrangement avoids the confrontation of conflicting mandates where one of them might be excluded or 'reduced' to the other – for example, the day hospital reduced the need for management, rules and social control to a question of the analysis of the individual in psychopathological terms whereas the traditional psychiatric model removes the problem of the patient's inner disposition by altering and 'normalizing' his mental state through drugs. At the O'Brien hospital the patient might talk of murderous feelings in his therapy session, but any such assertion made on the ward was treated as a potential threat.

In order to be capable psychologically of 'getting things off his chest', a person must be assured that within certain limits otherwise ordinary or possible sanctions will not operate.

(Parsons, 1954, p. 370)

The denial at the day hospital of any need for management and the medical director's reliance on the charisma of his personality, added to the fact that many of the patients frequently became disturbed, made it necessary to devise some way of controlling conflict and violence. Instead of differentiating between contexts of treatment and daily life arrangements, however, the medical director simply expanded the treatment context until it covered the whole hospital. Once the treatment setting was no longer confined to group sessions, the treatment alliance of trust was completely merged with the daily life of the hospital, that is with the context which came to require some control over anti-social behaviour. After her work at O'Brien, Coser argued cogently:

A system of social control that would put both the attitudes and the behaviour of patients under scrutiny by the same person, who has power to control their lives on the basis of knowledge of their innermost dispositions, would be a totalitarian institution in the most dramatic sense. The person who is in a position to observe the subordinate's behaviour would have access to the revelation of inner dispositions as well, and also have the power and authority to sanction both.

(1979, p. 41)

At the day hospital it may be seen that, as a direct consequence of the patients' attitudes and behaviour being under scrutiny by the same person, trust and freedom were destroyed until the hospital resembled the totalitarian system Coser warns against.[17]

The clear differentiation of administrative and therapeutic roles and contexts would seem to be one way in which limits can be set to the kind of therapeutic imperialism expressed by the reductionist approach adopted in the day hospital. The treatment triad of patient, therapist and the NHS (as represented by administrators in the different hierarchies) differed from that at the O'Brien Hospital in that the day hospital administrator was not medically qualified, and did not have the same status as the medical director. In fact, he was almost at the bottom of the administrative hierarchy in the District Health Authority.

Further, any intervention attempted by the higher administrative members in the district's nursing or occupational therapy hierarchies outside the hospital was limited to their authority over those hospital staff who were members of their own hierarchy. Where their opinions related to behavioural conformity (for example concerning violence) and thereby conflicted with those of the medical director, who denied the need for behavioural control, the medical director overruled them by virtue of his professional autonomy. The authority of these administrative representatives was not helped by the fact that they worked outside the hospital, so that their link with it via, for example, the senior nurse, was badly weakened when the latter supported the medical director's perspective and authority.[18]

Concluding remarks

This chapter has tried to show how, although there was a conscious effort to debureaucratize the day hospital, a hierarchy of enlightenment persisted once hierarchical roles and rules had been abandoned. This power structure was based on training, experience and ability to make interpretations of the patients' unconscious. Because formal rules had been rejected, psycho-analytic interpretations were used not only to enlighten the patients but also to control their behaviour. In this way the day hospital staff conflated the twin-pronged problem of control and self-development outlined by Coser.

Any institution that exclusively emphasizes *either* behavioural control *or* self-realization will provide only a partial treatment. The hospital which aims exclusively at self-realization will either dissolve into chaos or be indirectly constrained by hidden control mechanisms. So at the day hospital the jettisoning of rules and roles previously employed for controlling patients resulted in various staff strategies that served to emphasize their unity and to differentiate them from the patients – to whose status they themselves were reduced by psychoanalytic interpretations whenever they deviated from the official ideology.

Where self-realization is ignored, the hospital runs the risk of producing overdependent and institutionalized patients whose only hope of retaining a degree of personal autonomy is by asserting personal space, or 'playing the system'. The under-life that develops in a traditional psychiatric hospital is defined by Goffman as the way in which

a member of an organization employs unauthorized means to obtain unauthorized ends, or both, thus getting around the organization's assumption as to what he should do and get, and hence what he should be.

(1968, p. 172)

For Goffman, the so-called crazy behaviour of a new patient is a natural response to a deprived and frightening situation. Later, as the patient begins to get more used to his environment

109

and can see the constraints more clearly, he may learn ways of 'working' or getting round the system to meet his own personal needs. For example, psychiatrists may regard the behaviour of a man lying on the floor under a blanket as regressive, but it can make sense in a situation where other people and their rules intrude on the individual patient so continuously that this may be the only way he can obtain any privacy. Goffman notes that if such behaviour is defined and situated properly, it becomes meaningful. Similarly, an individual in a total institution may build his own 'empire', for example through trading in tobacco (which often serves as currency in such places) to become a 'tobacco king'. Methods such as these allow the person some individual expression of desires and needs in a situation where the organization demands only that he respond to rules – by either obeying or breaking them.

The day hospital staff were naive to assume that their approach would expressly create an environment where the whole community could become the equivalent of this 'personal space' and there would be no need for an informal world to develop. To begin with, no shared environment can possibly allow everyone to give full rein to his self-expression and exploration because the situation is always constrained by the desires and needs of others. Secondly, although the day hospital had abandoned formal rules and roles, certain constraints emanating from the NHS remained. So even if the medical director regarded his staff uniformly as therapists, the latter were still members of the discipline for which they had originally been trained *and* employed and paid as such, and their positions were subordinate to their managers in these disciplines.

Freidson (1970) points out that the formal position of workers does set limits to interaction and negotiation among staff, and between staff and patients, no matter how the informal side of the hospital develops. Although bureaucratic rules may depersonalize the service and produce rather distant relationships, there is no alternative to hierarchical differentiation as long as the hospital is dependent on expertise to attain the goal of therapy or cure. However, he is at pains to stress that it is wrong to assume that such limiting conditions must prevent satisfactory human relations in the organization. In fact, highly

110

productive interaction may result from clarity about limits imposed by the type of organizational structure and differences in expertise, whereas an apparent flattening of the hierarchy (when such differences actually remain) may, as I have shown in the example of the day hospital, result in hidden authoritarian control mechanisms which leave the patient feeling helpless without knowing why.

If patients are to be helped to survive in the world outside the hospital, their psychiatric treatment will have to include some measure of behavioural control and social adaptation. However, in order to prevent a patient from becoming institutionalized or hopelessly dependent on the organization and to avoid simply repressing the symptoms of faulty development by means of drugs, this behavioural control must be elastic enough for him to be able to take on as much responsibility for himself as he is capable of. This does not mean he should arbitrarily make all his own decisions, but rather that as he increases his understanding of his desires, needs and feelings he may become less of a victim of his drives and acquire a wider margin of self-control and choice. Although behavioural control is necessary, the organization must be flexible enough to let the patient discover his own inclinations and abilities. Psychologically, the staff must allow the patient enough rope to explore his phantasies and wishes, but not so much that he becomes entangled by it or enacts his phantasies and hangs himself.

5

Strategies of control

It became clear in the last chapter that in a situation where rules had been consciously rejected the need for control resulted in the staff using interpretations in such a way as to stem deviance and dissension.

Despite the fact that the day hospital's unique approach had arisen as a result of the anti-psychiatric perspective that developed during the 1960s, as time passed an increasing dependence upon interpretative control became apparent as the patients experienced once more in treatment the 'double-binds' and collusive behaviour that Laing (1967) had pointed to as the original cause of much illness. So the desire for democratic treatment started to turn into a devious search for control and eventually a tyranny over the feelings and actions of day hospital members.

This increasing emphasis upon the unconscious dimension evolved slowly but by January 1975 small-group therapy and practical arrangements such as cleaning, meals and fare reimbursements were already beginning to be seen in exclusively psychoanalytic terms. Whereas other hospitals and therapeutic communities accepted basic bureaucratic arrangements as necessary to the running of an institution, at the day hospital NHS provision of services to patients was regarded as an interference in the therapeutic work; the NHS intervention was like one parent indulging a child irrespective of the other parent's considerations of the child's emotional growth. Therapeutically such intervention further ran the risk, according to staff, of 'splitting the transference' the patient *qua* child was developing towards the therapist.

Thus when I started my research there was already a great

deal of discussion of the meaning of meals and fares, cleaning and medical certificates. In official terms these bureaucratic arrangements made up the institutional framework of the patients' lives. They needed medical certificates to receive their weekly benefits; they were allocated sick pay with the expectation that they would be provided with meals and reimbursed for journeys made to and from the hospital. As concern with unconscious motives increased such institutional support was regarded as unhelpful in being merely supportive. At this early stage this attitude put patients and staff in opposition to each other and these topics remained bones of contention throughout the first year of my research. In fact, it was the decision made by the staff to withdraw these facilities that threw the day hospital into crisis – a period I define as lasting from the patients' official complaint about their treatment to the medical director's sacking.

The question of the meaning of cleaning, meals, fares, medical certificates and small groups remained central to the whole argument about therapy, as the patients continued to need them in reality and the staff wanted to resist contributing to their provision. They were central issues as they raised the question of how far it was possible to talk exclusively in terms of unconscious meaning when other meanings, especially the practical level of reality, were bound to intrude. In the day hospital at the time the practical and the unconscious were dealt with as if they were mutually exclusive, rather than the staff accepting that dealing with actual practical reality did not preclude the examination of the unconscious meaning to participants in the object or activity.[1]

Having focused on the formal role level in the last chapter, I shall now analyse the actual strategies employed in the day hospital within and between different groups. Roles and status differences may throw up a framework of interaction, but we need to examine the complexity of interplay within that framework.

I have therefore striven to avoid the twin pitfalls of giving either an outsider's entirely static picture or offering a naive description of the situation based exclusively on the actors' own views. Neither is able by itself to explain satisfactorily the conflicts and constraints not immediately evident on the surface. Following a role analysis for staff and patients with a more specific report of interaction makes the formal and processual accounts complementary to each other. In this chapter I shall look at the day hospital as a negotiated order. Given the absence of formal rules, how did the unit avoid utter chaos? What was the actual process by which the order emerging from the ideology by way of a hidden power structure was created and maintained?

This chapter will therefore be concerned with outlining the strategies employed by the staff to counteract the threatened chaos. In the absence of formal rules and roles to set limits on behaviour, the therapeutic process itself arose to fill the vacuum left by the removal of formal controls and structures. Strategies of interaction developed that gave to the otherwise seemingly chaotic behaviour a degree of structure.

In the community room when the morning session was in train the lack of a formal starting and ending time, the comings and goings of staff and patients and the exchange of remarks, faint and muttered or fast and brilliant, could easily have portrayed at first glance the picture of acquaintances waiting more or less impatiently in a waiting room. But underneath the ebbing and flowing of this sea of movement and thought was a sense of a drama being enacted. Each member had to hold on to something – an idea, a desire, a need – in order not to drown unremarked by all. Amongst the staff certain patterns of behaviour became consolidated; once they were adopted as strategies in the game, they soon became rules of staff partici-pation in the large group. For example, it became a rule that so-called countertransference should be avoided. This translated into a stony non-response to patients' direct questions so that the person addressed did not become emotionally involved with the questioner and reproduced the stereotype of the blank-screen analyst. Or an esoteric game, in which staff communi-cated with each other through the use of psychoanalytic interpretations, was adopted at times when direct staff-to-staff communication in private staff meetings was vetoed. The staff game of 'collusion' was also employed as a means of defence, since mockery and communication through eye contact and

114

in-group communication could be effective in belittling open challenges from patients. This humorous contact was in marked contrast to the stereotyped cold-shoulder therapist role presented to patients at other times.

New staff also seemed to follow a particular pattern of behaviour as they learned to quell their enthusiasm to care for patients and became aware of well-established rules of staff behaviour. These staff 'games' came to be used increasingly as control processes as the staff felt more keenly the lack of the formal authority of which the experiment, with their support, had deprived them.

Having described the different types of staff 'games', I compare this development of informal control processes with the control exercised by other totalistic ideologies.

The blank screen: the stereotyped therapist role

When a discussion between staff members was interrupted by a patient, when patients pressed staff on personal matters or when a patient asked a question that demanded a straight answer on the conscious level, the staff would react by becoming completely silent and refusing to meet the questioner's eyes, even if he stood only a few inches away. As a result the patient would feel a sense of guilt for having infringed some rule or for having interrupted communication between staff.

This particular syndrome arose constantly in the large-group sessions. It was a highly marked feature, perhaps felt particularly strongly because it was a *lack of* response rather than a specific action. The silence[2] made the questioner feel as though he had not spoken, and the lack of eye contact virtually became a denial of his existence: he had become a 'non-person'. Thus exchanges in the day hospital would flow freely for a while and then be abruptly halted by a sudden lack of response from a therapist. This strategy was used so regularly that it became quite clear what kinds of question were taboo. For example, a person might have been describing how he was feeling and say: 'Do you know what I mean?', but would not expect to be answered. Or a patient might ask a staff member why he (or she) was working at the day hospital or express a liking for him or her. In a more ordinary analytic situation the therapist's reaction to this would vary according to what he saw as the meaning behind the words spoken (manipulation, threat, sympathy, etc.), but his response would include some kind of acknowledgement of what had been said. But the use of silence in the day hospital was a deliberate strategy and was the almost invariable reaction when anyone expressed his feelings directly.

The blank-screen syndrome was nicely exemplified by an angry repudiation of the 'myth of the inanimate therapist' when therapist A criticized another for having remained passive under verbal attack by a patient. This therapist had compared the patient to 'a cow that daren't say moo'. In response the patient had yelled 'Shut your fucking mouth!', to which the therapist replied that the patient was obviously responding to her interpretation by finally saying 'moo'. The two therapists met later the same day:

Therapist A: I've been psychoanalysed, but I feel I'd have been more vulnerable than you who haven't. Why didn't you respond to her? I don't mean by getting upset, but by explaining how she was trying to make you angry. Patients don't want inanimate objects to be angry at, they want to reach you. This distant interpretative stance only denies her anger, and her love, and her existence as a person. That's what's going on downstairs [in the day hospital]. But the inanimate, well-armoured object is an analytic myth, and such a lack of response is a way of defending yourself. You feel you've found the answer and have stuck to it. And if you say you're a staff member with 'work to do', that's a myth too. It's a defence against your own feelings. Everyone downstairs is a little Adrian . . . He can't reach out and we've all internalized him to protect ourselves.

This syndrome was particularly apparent when ordinary polite social conversation was required – for example, when there was a visitor. It became more marked as the hospital's approach became more extreme. When I first visited the day hospital, patients and staff still felt free to ask me questions about what I had been doing before, about my family and so on, but when

Strategies of control

six months later a psychoanalyst from the Adult Department brought a visiting psychiatrist, the polite introduction offered by the two men met with almost no response from those present. There was complete silence as people looked down or away, almost as if this courteous behaviour was embarrassing. A little later the conversation was resumed where the visitors' arrival had interrupted it, and their presence in no way acknowledged. The Adult Department analyst was utterly amazed, and later said the attitude had made him feel like 'a lump of shit'.[3]

In terms of the day hospital ideology, where anything or anyone extraneous to the psychoanalytic interpretations of the large-group sessions was irrelevant to and interfered with psychotherapy,[4] it was not only justified but actually required that such 'interventions' as the visitors should be ignored, or that they be shown how they were regarded in relation to the all-important analytic work going on. This meant that people felt they really had to treat visitors in this manner, and what looked like wanton discourtesy to the uninitiated was in fact based on ideological values. It was also a way in which untrained staff could counteract their feeling of vulnerability.

Collusive staff games

Within the overall game of the large group, the staff kept up another game between themselves which, despite apparent variations in allegiance, gave the impression that there were two separate teams: staff versus patients. Through the medium of highly analytical language, the staff pursued a dialogue of psychoanalytic interpretations of the unconscious. Only those initiated into the language could understand its jokes, and according to the letter of complaint (see Chapter 7) this 'fun' was experienced as mockery by those who were excluded from it.

Anyone not thoroughly coached in those terms found it very difficult to translate the analogous interpretations into statements appropriate to the individual to (or at) whom they were directed. For instance, if a staff member made an interpretation comparing the patients to animals in the zoo, the patients were mostly unable to see how this related to their own particular feelings and tended to resent the analogy. This was not due to deliberate perversity or because their personal problems blinded them to insightful remarks, but rather because the staff never made it clear how the analogy was supposed to be applied.

Like anyone else giving an explanation, a therapist often finds it useful to present an analogy to express a point in other terms. The difference between this and the usage in the day hospital was that verbal exchange employing analogy came to be a game in itself. Not only did this kind of language help the therapist resist attack, it also seemed to be enjoyable for its own sake. The overall aim of helping the patient understand himself better was lost as the staff enjoyed communicating with each other in a kind of double talk, a code. When a rule of behaviour created to obtain a particular result becomes an end in itself, then we can talk of ritualization: it was not a case of the staff searching their imaginations for some alternative way of expressing the interpretation, but rather that they used the ritual of expanding their explanation and conveying meanings in a language exclusive to the initiated.

Listening to a number of staff talk together often added to the patients' confusion. It was not unlike hearing adults playing the role of children sharing a phantasy. Such world-sharing can perhaps be helpful as well as enjoyable if all participants are conversant with the language used, but to those for whom the overt meaning remains obscure such talk conveys an aloof, facetious attitude. On hearing a totally foreign language one can simply ignore the unfamiliar sounds; but the patients knew that such utterances were supposed to aid their understanding; they understood the individual words but lacked the key to their meaning. This opacity only added to the feeling of being excluded from certain vivacious interactions; such a feeling tends to exaggerate the supposed importance of the conversations from which the individual is excluded. If the words in a foreign language are incomprehensible the listener relies more heavily on tone, facial expression and other nonverbal communication signals. The day hospital conversations were often conducted in bantering tones and with amused smiles, rather like adults 'fondly' explaining their children's follies. As Freud argues, the humorist takes

118

Strategies of control

*. . . the attitude of an adult towards a child, recognizing
and smiling at the triviality of the interests and sufferings
which seem to the child so big. Thus the humorist acquires
his superiority by assuming the role of the grown-up . . .
while he reduces the other people to the position of children*
(Freud, 1950, pp. 215–21)

A provocative, bantering tone is felt to be an invitation to take
up a position: either to join the joker or to show anger. At the
day hospital the response was a polarization into opposing
groups. Since the individual could not respond to the invitation
to laugh at his ridiculous stance without a clarification (which
was rarely forthcoming) of its wording, this led not only to the
humiliation of not understanding but to the further exclusion of
having failed to see the joke. Shared humour implies equality
of status and highlights group consensus; neutrality is impossible – the audience has to choose to join in the laughter or not,
and joining in implies acceptance of the humorist's definition of
the situation. While humour is often a permissible form of
aggression, it also eases tension and conflict between members
with different status and so contributes to the maintenance of
the social structure. When patients rejected the staff's interpretation of their actions as pathologically determined and tried to
shake off their 'sick' identification by maintaining they had *social*
problems, the staff's jocose responses to this effectively smoth-
ered opposition by presupposing a common definition of the
situation.

The patients could not easily counterbalance this staff humour
with similar attempts of their own, because jesting behaviour
was tolerated only from status superiors. Coser's (1960) analysis
of humour in a mental hospital shows how the status structure
was supported by 'downward' humour, with the targets tending
to be the junior staff. For example, only the chairman of a
meeting could initiate humour safely, as the making of jokes
implied a withdrawal of focal attention and a permissiveness
that might completely disrupt the structure of the meeting. At
the day hospital, similarly, it was only the qualified analysts
and psychotherapists who initiated humour, as this deliberate
reduction of social distance was the perquisite of status

superiors. If patients made jokes, this was taken as a sign of aggression and further evidence of their condition.

The humour initiated by the staff upheld their definition of the situation (it confirmed that the patients were sick and that all their actions had to be regarded as supporting evidence), but the patients' humour broke away from this definition and, by asserting individual perspectives, ignored common or dominant group values. It was through staff humour, however, that socialization of both staff and patients took place, through the joke highlighting dominant group values related to psychoanalytic interpretations of the patients' unconscious motivations. If the patients were told they were like animals in a zoo, for example, then responding laughter implied acceptance of this definition.[5] Amusement at a joke always implies acceptance as well as fostering an in-group feeling; a poker-faced reaction spells refusal to accept this group identity – an experience likely to be particularly painful to a patient who desires the safety of being part of a group. Taking a joke seriously implies a breakdown of this consensus. In the following example we see how a therapist attempted – not altogether successfully – to reinstate the jocose status of his remarks.

Shortly after the complaint, on a rare occasion when the collusive joke game was openly mentioned, therapist B expressly dissociated himself from the jocose derision technique referred to in the letter of complaint.

Therapist C: Yes, it offends and insults the patients.
Patient 1: If this is a technique, you ought to be ashamed of yourselves. No wonder we feel we can't trust the staff.
Medical director: The derision is to make you recognize those parts of the self you want to discard. Laughter is a defence against the self. If we cried then we'd all drown, and no ark has been built to save us.

[He exchanges a smile with another staff member, then giggles.]

Patient 2 [to the medical director]: You're talking about yourself. Why don't you shut up?

Strategies of control

Patient 1: It's a shame that Adrian spoilt what he'd said by making a joke at the end.
Patient 3: What do you mean about the 'bits you want to discard'? It sounds interesting. Could you explain it a bit more because –
Medical director [interrupting him]: What would happen if the ark sank in our tears?
Therapist C: I don't think you should interrupt 3 when he's taking what you said seriously.
Medical director: I'm showing him what he is doing.

This was a reference to the fact that this particular patient had been one of the main instigators of the complaint which, according to the medical director, interrupted the therapeutic work.

Therapist D: This is like an experiment with animals in the zoo, with the spectators interpreting the behaviour of the animals.

In this example the medical director was trying to revert to humour when his joke had been taken seriously, whereas the patient had been trying to translate the joke into a more meaningful statement.

The flavour of any jocose interactions is unfortunately almost impossible to convey second-hand. If few of the exchanges reported seem genuinely funny to the reader, it is because within the situation humour depends on the actors recognizing the values that are being made fun of and is therefore confined to a momentary context from which the reader is inevitably excluded. Humour is effective because a serious reply – an attack or display of hurt feelings or anger, for example – always seems maladroit and out of place in an unserious exchange.

A knowledge of the way in which these interactions were conducted, however, is important for understanding the threat they posed to the patients' self-identity. Failing to participate and in general to understand when one is expected to can make one feel intellectually or emotionally stupid. Attacks on self-identity in the day hospital were often compounded by the patient's questions being met with silence and avoidance of eye contact, leaving him with the unreal feeling of wondering whether he only imagined he had spoken. Since he was also deprived of ordinary, common-sense roles, he often ended u' denying himself any form of expression in situations (such as the large group) where it is common to feel one's identity and self-boundaries threatened.

It remains unclear why the staff did not make it easier for the patients to understand their interpretations. It was rare for them to translate analogies back into ordinary language or to interpret directly rather than through analogy. Perhaps they could then be challenged – to be incomprehensible is to defy refutation. As one staff member put it, following the exchange in the example above:

> I could be as clever as you [laughter], but you're being too clever, always going one step ahead – jumping the gun.
> You don't put enough emphasis on the dynamics that are actually going on in the group.

In other words, he was asking for the connection between the analogies and the current interaction to be clarified. But the staff as a whole resisted that idea. Possibly they regarded providing clues or links as 'interventions in the therapeutic process'. Or perhaps they feared that the patients, having learnt the rules of the game, might begin ridiculing them in the same way, or play well themselves. As it was the patients seemed to have been permanently handicapped participants – neither untouched outsiders nor competent insiders, but victims. Generally speaking, their lack of comprehension was regarded as evidence of the pathological condition to which the analogy was meant to refer, and the staff did not seem to realize that the patients simply did not possess the required tools for understanding.

At times the verbal exchanges between staff were, of course, deliberately obscure. But the mocking tone in which they were delivered always implied that it was the patients' 'sick' unconscious that prevented them from understanding. It is also possible that this defensive, bantering position was adopted by some staff members as a way of coping with an often painful and threatening situation.[6] Because they themselves felt reduced by the ambiguity of their roles and the uncertainties inherent in the experiment, they may have needed to reduce others in their turn. (Coser argues that humour eases the tensions of role conflict.)

The following statement by a member of the staff about his role in the day hospital, made one month before the official inquiry, may provide an insight into how the experimental setting was experienced by the actors. It may also contribute to an understanding of the games that were played.

Therapist: I'm disillusioned with the day hospital . . . B [another therapist] is useful as a counter to Adrian because he's always confronting, challenging and interpreting him . . . I feel that Adrian's idea of freedom is simply to allow him to come and go as he pleases. B says that Ezriel seems totally obsessed with his three-part interpretation . . . I wonder if Adrian's cracking up too. I feel the least he can do is support his own staff. There's an insidious power thing going on. I can't see it, but I can feel the change in atmosphere when he comes in . . . I think his interpretation of everything as symptoms is insidious and castrating. I can understand that the patients reject all our interpretations, because if everything is seen to be an inner problem, then how can one distinguish between inner and outer reality? I know myself now how the patients feel, because Adrian's been interpreting everything *I* say just like he does with them . . . This idea of the correct interpretation is very seductive, but I can also understand how the staff refuse to answer, or look vacant sometimes, because I used to do it myself when I was copying Adrian so I'd learn how to do an analyst's job, and I felt powerful then and untouchable . . . It keeps you from contact with patients that might make you anxious . . . It's quite true, though: Adrian, does have seductive charm. If you go along with him you feel you're on the inside, not excluded. You're laughing *with* rather than being laughed *at*. That mocking attitude is so belittling.

While the division between the two sides – staff and patients – was more apparent earlier on in my research, as the crisis deepened new alliances were constantly forming, dissolving and re-forming. Sometimes staff allied themselves with the patients, refusing participation in the collusive staff games and earnestly requesting that the situation be examined on a conscious level to protect the hospital. At other times patients, especially old-timers, would join the collusive game of the staff and play therapist to the other patients. One member of staff actually referred outright to the mockery as a technique:

The theory behind the day hospital is good, but the technique of laughing at people, and saying everything is just part of a person's pathology, is most damaging.

Goffman notes that where there is an additional, non-addressed participant in a discussion between at least two or three, a collusive net and a distinction between colluders and ex-colluded is created:

Then it can be seen that an unaddressed recipient, especially a chronic one, may stand back somewhat from ordinary participation and view the speaker and his addressee as a single whole, to be watched as might be a tennis match or a colloquy on stage.

(Goffman, 1975, p. 565)

The esoteric syndrome

Related to the collusive game was the esoteric syndrome, a process whereby a therapist might borrow an analogy used by another in an interpretation in order to argue a point with a colleague. Since the medical director tended to avoid contact outside the large group, and since common-sense discussions where the talk was not wholly on the unconscious level were not possible with him, this syndrome appeared regularly among therapists adept at using the language of the unconscious. For example, when the medical director remarked how hungry the

Strategies of control

patients were for 'cabbages' – that is, psychoanalytical interpretations – another therapist said that they had 'indigestion from too many cabbages'. Here is another example, from a large-group session when a patient had just lost his lighter:

Patient: I just drop in to say hello and I lose my lighter. [He searches another patient.] Someone's nicked it. Really, you guys.
Therapist A: Everybody loses something here they'd valued.

The staff here were actually making covert fun of the confusion they felt existed in the day hospital.

Sometimes esoteric language would be used to express staff conflict. In the next extract, from another large-group session, a therapist interprets a patient's statement and another therapist retaliates on the same level. Eventually a third translates the discussion back into less analogous language.

Patient: I don't want to work. The problem would be solved if we could be paid to come here [to the hospital].
Therapist A: Yes, the goodies are okay. The trouble is that Big Daddy [the state] gives them to you free, and you don't think you're good enough for that, so you hurt yourselves.

He is suggesting that the patients are doing one of two things: undervaluing themselves or feeling guilty.

Therapist B: Ah, but the staff like to guzzle the goodies too, and they eat so much they feel sick.

He may be saying that he feels the staff are taking too much out of the situation – being greedy with the freedom it allows, for instance.

Therapist C: Yes, the same applies to staff. They don't allow their superegos to function but chuck their consciences out of the window. If they don't work enough, it's because their consciences are so painful.

125

He has picked up the barely concealed criticism of therapist A and endorses it.

Within this syndrome the speaker can, of course, make use of analogies without necessarily talking in terms of the unconscious. However, as generally used, analogy became part of the control process, and in the example above it was quite deliberately employed to criticize another staff member. Also, the remarks were probably made in this form rather than directly because the analogy partly masked the criticism and disagreement among staff which may have been thought unsettling for the patients.

The new staff syndrome

One of the most interesting processes at work in the day hospital was the way in which new staff members gradually lost their individual approaches in interaction and treatment as they became involved in the experiment. Initially new staff often felt pleased to work in this open situation, which compared so favourably with their experiences in more traditional hospitals. They frequently considered the day hospital as a useful and safe testing ground for their ideas and development. Gradually, however, they would become aware that stepping out of line would expose them to attack from the patients and lack of support (or even indirect attack) from the staff. This made them feel insecure, and rethinking their early impressions only exacerbated this insecurity because they now saw that their assumptions about the hospital's freedom had been wrong.

While they were re-orientating themselves, they would retreat and watch how the other staff worked. They noted the protection obtained from the silent, stereotypical psychoanalytic stance and, aware of their own relative lack of qualifications and experience, took their lead from the more established staff. In a situation without overt rules or guidelines, the new staff member seemed to have a bewilderingly unlimited choice of action and, while trying to find his feet, would latch on to more implicit rules of behaviour such as the 'collusive game' or the 'bring it all to the group' process. There would be no theoretical

Strategies of control

reasoning behind this; such a move would be adopted almost entirely to protect the individual rather than to facilitate therapy and help patients.

In the absence of more thorough therapeutic training, unqualified staff in general and novice staff in particular tended to imitate the 'grand masters' (Ezriel and his disciple, the medical director) when they were unsure of themselves in the large group. If they were sanctioned for deviating from the approach, they were also rewarded for adhering to it. People rarely like to be excluded, and the feeling of sharing in the giggly amusement of the therapists after a mocking interpretation may well have been more attractive than the risk of putting forward an independent view. Because of the difficulty of distinguishing between different levels of meaning, an unconfident staff member would in any case not be sure he was on the right track and other staff members, who also feared being ridiculed and excluded, were unlikely to offer support or elucidation. This confirms the appeal of the 'in-group', who re-affirm their superiority and prevent deviance by ridiculing outsiders.

The following extract from a discussion I had with a new staff member gives a good idea of the latter's thoughts as he considered what his function might be. I had asked him: 'How do you feel about working here? Has the experience in the day hospital turned out pretty much as you expected when you first came, or not?'

New therapist: On the three-day visits, before I was taken on as a member of staff, I was impressed by the way people here expressed themselves in the large group. I remember one patient saying, 'Oh, he'll never get the job', and I was really worried. I now feel that there should be more interaction and self-expression. I think we can leave the three psychoanalysts to their stereotyped role and interpretations, and we others can do our own thing. After all, we aren't therapists and can try our different ways. But there's this hidden pressure to conform. It's often happened that, when I'd thought of something to say in the large group and someone else on the staff got in first, they were giving a totally different interpretation than I'd been about to make, and I decided that they were more experienced, knew more about the place, and knew better what was going on. It really does require a lot of courage to stick your neck out and give more individual therapy, because you run the risk of the staff disliking you for being different. Everyone says it's Adrian laying down the law, but I've never heard him say what people must or mustn't do. Perhaps his is a kind of unspoken power. I think the patients realize that the stereotype psychoanalytic silent role is a defence. They even say so. Psychoanalysis is such an individual thing, you can't find two analysts alike. It depends so much on intuition. If the ideology is that all other interaction and interpretation interferes with the three-part relationship, then how do they expect a new person, who knows nothing about the theory or practice of Ezriel, to pick it up? People criticize B for laughing. I suggested to all the staff that we must meet to discuss our particular approaches and look at the differences, but they all stared at me as if I were mad, and someone said, 'We don't have leadership here'.

The above discussion took place not long after this staff member had joined the hospital. He was still feeling confused and angry at what he saw and experienced, and he was quite conscious of the hidden power structure. In time he subdued these feelings somewhat and became more 'conventional' in his approach – that is, he too eventually used the silent stance to avoid diffi-culties and stopped making suggestions about different approaches. He was, in other words, gradually being socialized into a day hospital therapist's role.

Perhaps he had to adopt the interpretative stance of the blank-screen syndrome to create for himself a sufficiently comfortable atmosphere in which to work, when so much seemed to consist of unflattering comment and so little of support and any action appeared to elicit an unpleasant reaction. In such a situation impassivity is quite a good strategy. Two other new members of staff who came to the day hospital with their own ideas initially expressed a 'warm human caring' for patients, but similarly modified their attitude as the months passed, partly because they were criticized for their non-interpretative approach. This change was commented on by a therapist who lamented the loss of the earlier enthusiasm and human warmth:

Therapist: How you've changed! When you first came you responded to the patients in a human way; now you're making interpretations which aren't half so useful. When you tell me we therapists can't have an honest discussion of our own and must always discuss everything in front of the patients, you're acting just like little Adrians to protect yourselves. In real families parents talk things out and fuck together on their own, without the children.

It is not clear how long an individual can keep up strong opposition to the institution in which he is working. Either open conflict leads to a parting of the ways between the individual and the organization,[7] or the conflicting feelings lessen and the individual adapts. In the day hospital, such adaptation included participating in staff strategies.

How can these staff strategies be explained? Deprived of their formal roles and the skills appropriate to them, the staff almost certainly felt insecure and in an ambiguous position because they were answerable to two sets of managers who placed contradictory demands on them. They had to control the patients' behaviour without the help of any formal rules or roles, and at the same time differentiate themselves from the patients since they were also liable to psychoanalytic interpretations if they decided to question the values and norms of the day hospital. By emphasizing their membership of the staff in-group, they created a measure of distance between themselves and the patients; and by not responding to patients, they controlled intrusive questioning or participation.

As we have seen, because overt behavioural control was not permitted, staff tended to fall back on an informal code which emphasized in-group feeling through shared jokes and language. This made them feel less isolated from their colleagues, and their lack of contact with their own professional hierarchies seemed to matter less.

Asylum to Anarchy

The correct interpretation game

The day hospital's permissiveness and the hidden control behind these staff games were, then, a major source of confusion for new staff members. Beneath the professed democracy lay a hierarchy of authority based on expertise, knowledge and skill, as well as a formalized qualification in psychoanalysis. Although it was a basic tenet of the ideology that all its members were equal, it was quite evident that some were more equal than others in their licence to interpret the unconscious. In fact so pronounced was this difference, and so far-reaching the effects of interpretation in terms of controlling deviant behaviour, that it amounted to a very real differential power to define reality. This differential power was further enhanced by the rule that only the *correct* interpretation was an entirely valid statement. In turn, the correctness of an interpretation was implicitly decided by those most qualified to sit in judgement on matters psychoanalytical – who were, of course, the staff members who had had the most thorough training and experience.

The greatest possible emphasis was placed on the correct interpretation being given of any feelings expressed in the large group. It was believed that failure to make this correct interpretation would result in the patients 'acting out'. So in discussing the reason why the patients should have complained, a staff member suggested: 'Something must have gone wrong with interpretations for us not to be able to contain the trouble downstairs.' She argued that the complaint resulted from the staff's failure to make the correct interpretation after a patient had thrown a lighted firework into the large-group session, or to understand the importance of the act and its meaning for the patients. As she saw it, the patients must have been afraid and wanted the staff to take action and then the staff had not realized just how much the firework incident had upset them.

This view was echoed by another therapist, who felt 'very concerned' that somehow the staff had missed an opportunity for interpretation a long time ago, when the main activist patient had been making 'revolutionary noises'. These noises were discounted by the staff, arguing 'it's because we failed to under-

130

stand what that was all about that we're getting this acting out now through letters of complaint, etc.'

The emphasis on the correct interpretation meant that only one of other possible interpretations would unearth the real meaning of a particular feeling, so that by definition all other comments or actions constituted 'non-interpretative interventions'. So it was felt that a correct interpretation had been made when it was suggested that the leader of the patients' activist group (see next chapter on patient groupings), which was then opposing the staff, was trying to compete with the medical director, who had interpreted: 'He wants to have a penis as big as Big Daddy's.' This interpretation was then seen to be confirmed as correct when the patient remembered how, as a small boy, he had felt envious of the size of his father's penis when he saw him half undressed one night.

Rycroft has defined as 'correct' those interpretations which

> . . . both (a) explain adequately the material being interpreted, and (b) are formulated in such a way and communicated at such a time that they have actuality for (make sense to) the patient.
>
> (1968, p. 76)

In the day hospital, however, the search for the correct interpretation came to be used as a competitive game that functioned to confirm the hierarchy of psychoanalytic knowledge and interpretative capacity. The concept of the correct interpretation was referred to so constantly among the staff, and such a premium was placed on its attainment, that its ordinary meaning was distorted. It became a prize coveted for its own sake rather than part of the process of helping patients understand themselves. In fact, it was given such emphasis that when some statement was given the accolade of 'the correct interpretation', all other statements were automatically inferior or invalid.

Whether to designate an interpretation as the correct one or not is a matter for contention, but when it really is accurate this may be confirmed by the patient's response – for example,

131

if he remembers a connected event as a result of hearing the interpretation. It could be argued that whether or not such corroborative 'confirmation' has taken place or not is again a matter of interpretation by the therapists since, by definition, a patient cannot know his unconscious. When, however, the interpretation really is correct – both in content and the time and manner in which it is delivered – the patient may experience a feeling of recognition, often accompanied by a sense of relief. Moreover, since psychoanalytic interpretation is concerned with illuminating and exposing aspects of the hitherto unknown unconscious, the patient would then know that it is correct, since it has made him consciously aware of what he did not understand before. In fact, the above interpretation of penis envy was a classic example of apparently overt confirmation of accuracy – so that at least two members of the staff wanted to write it up for publication.

Although patients can verify, therefore, whether or not an interpretation is the correct one, the day hospital reduction of all interactions to psychopathological manifestations confused the issue. As psychotherapy was not separated from discussions of material administrative and political matters, the question of the correct interpretation became implicated in competing definitions of reality – between those who defined reality solely in psychopathological terms and those who defined it solely in material/political terms. Of course the two sides exist concomitantly in all situations, and it is the overall context that provides the meaning of a statement or interaction. By contrast, the day hospital maintained that psychoanalytic interpretation would sum up all the various meanings contained in the situation as a whole, and the concept of 'the correct interpretation' developed into an idealization of what was possible. Like doctors anywhere, the staff did not wish to admit uncertainty in case the patients would think they did not know their own business.

The ethos of the correct interpretation provided the ideology with a strong motivating force. Like searchers for perfection in the eyes of God, participants strove for the unattainable, always failed and were therefore prompted to renew their efforts. It was also a way of asserting the potency of the leader. Since the participants did not realize that there is no such thing as an

Strategies of control

all-encompassing, absolute interpretation, they depended on outside judgements (mostly negative) of the correctness or otherwise of those interpretations they themselves were putting forward. On the other hand, the staff assumed that the medical director's interpretations were always correct, except when he and staff discussed having 'missed' an interpretation. In other words, all behaviour and feeling could be interpreted in terms of the unconscious and so brought into consciousness and made 'knowable' – a process which endowed its leader with apparent omniscience and omnipotence.

The process of 'correct interpretations' that flow from a given ideology and thereby generate a hierarchy of competence and credibility may be discovered in religious sects, in political groupings, and elsewhere. For example, just as the hospital rejected traditional psychiatric treatment methods and ideology, religious sects challenge the old order and frequently, if not always, gather round a charismatic personality as the focal point for restructuring the social order. Just like the medical director, whose professed desire for patient participation in a democratic system contradicted his rigid control of deviant views by psycho-analytic interpretation, charismatic figures in sects often enunciate contradictory principles. In neither case do these contradictions impair the ideology; they simply deepen the mystery that lies in accepting the charismatic leader's will (Wilson, 1970, p. 191) – in the case of the day hospital the medical director's definition of all contexts as reducible to the psychological dimension. The following examples show parallels between the two types of organization.

Firstly, the Oneida Community, a nineteenth-century utopian sect that believed in the community of property, sex and children, assumed that man can be perfect. Sickness was a sin that could be exorcized by self-criticism and mutual criticism. Once the individual had enunciated his sins to the group, others present listed his failings and then the leader made the final summary exhortation. It appears that this process released personal tension. Members, having been purged of their short-comings, then re-dedicated themselves to the community, finding satisfaction in the sect's acceptance of them despite their acknowledged deficiencies.

133

The parallel of this process of self- and mutual criticism with group therapy is obvious: the individual patient tells the therapy group of his problems, the therapists point out the weaknesses in his unconscious that have led to these difficulties and, having dared to expose himself in this way, the patient is reassured by the group's acceptance of him despite his failings. Just as the members of Oneida assumed that man could be perfect, the assumption behind the medical director's approach implied that perfection was attainable if the 'sickness' could be dealt with. The chief difference between the two is that the Oneidans assumed that people create their weaknesses and even illnesses consciously, while at the day hospital it was the unconscious that was held responsible.

Secondly, the theory of Scientology, a therapeutic system controlled through a church[8] founded and led by M.R. Hubbard, maintains that mental problems are the result of pre-natal impressions, 'engrams', received by the embryo in the womb. Hubbard trained 'auditors' to direct (like therapists) the patient's thoughts back to his or her earliest impressions in order to eradicate this engram from the unconscious mind and so liberate him or her from behaviour rooted in the compulsive fear produced by it. If all such engrams were eradicated, the individual became a 'clear': a member of an elite group in the organization who had undergone extensive training and therapy.

The assumption here is that the effects of earlier suffering can be removed mechanically, much as the day hospital maintained that a problem could be eliminated if the correct interpretation was given. Again the assumption behind both theories is a state of perfection, attainable after long years of therapy.

Legitimations of control

There were three justifications for this control emanating from the psychoanalytic reduction of social, economic, physical and material problems by the above strategies. First, the employment of psychoanalytic interpretations was regarded as 'scientific' – that is, the principles used were part of the body of knowledge in which staff members had qualified (notwithstanding that qualifications in terms of previous training were

Strategies of control

being denied). The staff were saying, in essence, that the social, material and other issues raised in the large group were matters neither of personal preference nor of social or practical fact, but required for their explanation the kind of scientific understanding which the patients lacked and the staff were trained in. If the patients said they would prefer to have encounter therapy in the afternoons rather than no therapy at all until the next morning, the staff's psychoanalytic interpretation of this would point out (however obliquely) that this discussion had grown out of a number of psychological and interactional dynamics which the application of science could uncover: only psychoanalysis could provide an understanding of the 'real' meaning of what the patients said they wanted. This constant reduction to inner meanings implied a mechanical view of humanity with all opinions, tastes and preferences regarded as nothing but expressions of uncontrollable hidden drives.

The second legitimation of control through psychoanalytic interpretation lay in the hospital members' acceptance of psychoanalysis as a more 'humane', liberal and less authoritarian treatment than traditional psychiatry's mainly physical methods. Most of the patients had personally experienced the latter, and regarded psychoanalysis as a liberating type of therapy based neither on physical intervention by drugs or ECT nor on the authoritarian enforcement of rules.

Thirdly, the emphasis on psychological explanations of all issues accorded well with the patients' acceptance that the unconscious can lead one to feel, say and do certain things which consciously seem to have a quite different significance. The day hospital, however, took the psychoanalytical approach to an extreme and, by assigning validity only to psychological explanations, denied the differences in personal make-up that constitute the so-called political dimension of human thought and activity.

Ideological totalism

Although in many ways the day hospital system of control through psychoanalytic interpretation resembled a totalitarian democratic regime – in its all-embracing nature and the much-reiterated claim that the unit was democratic, while the control mechanisms remained concealed – perhaps thought reform is a more useful concept to apply here, as the chief objective of its approach was to persuade staff and patients to adopt a different view of themselves and so pre-empt the legitimacy of their queries and criticisms of, and deviance from, the experimental perspective. Robert Lifton's book *Thought Reform* (1961) shows how in the Chinese labour camps the prisoners were brainwashed into regarding themselves as wrongdoers, and so became deprived of any legitimate basis for rejecting their guards' theory or behaviour. The parallels between brainwashing and the therapeutic process practised in the day hospital are quite marked, even though the staff could not control the external world of the patients as they could the inner.

Lifton defines ideological totalism as the coming together of an immoderate ideology with equally immoderate individual characteristics. He argues that any individual can get caught up in ideological totalism and that any ideology ('any set of emotionally charged convictions about man and his relationship to the natural or supernatural world') can be carried by its adherents to a totalist extreme, but that it is more likely to occur where the ideology is sweeping or messianic. He notes that any scientific, religious or political organization can come to resemble nothing so much as an exclusive cult – and become more or less brainwashing in so far as it exhibits the latter's criteria. Every one of the criteria Lifton enumerates as totalist depends on an equally absolute philosophical assumption and mobilizes certain individual assumptions.

I shall take a closer look at those of his criteria that are relevant to the day hospital experiments, bearing in mind that as the day hospital was non-residential it could not be described as a total institution and that only psychological pressure, not physical threat, could be brought to bear. In consequence its influence was restricted, though quite profound.

Through 'milieu control' the organization has power over the individual's communication with the outside as well as with himself. Although at the day hospital the therapists had no control over the patients' communication and interaction

Strategies of control

outside clinic hours (nine to five, five days a week), there was an attitude of omniscience in their conviction that reality was their own exclusive prerogative, as expressed by their insistence that only their psychological interpretation of reality was the 'true' reality and overrode all others. If the effect of this attitude was tempered by patients being exposed to other, external information, the continual reduction of even statements of personal self-expression restricted their capacity for internal reflection that would have created the phenomenological space for them to view reality in perspective before judging it.

By means of what Lifton calls mystical manipulation, the individual is manoeuvred into trusting the organization that possesses a mystique and higher purpose, and whose agents are 'the chosen'. So Henry Ezriel was regarded as a guru and the medical director by charismatic succession his spiritual son; many of the staff attended weekly seminars with Ezriel and became disciples of both. The patients, whose status prevented their knowing the content of their unconscious, had to trust in the staff's interpretations of their statements and interactions.

The messianic organization's demand for purity posits a world divided between the 'pure' and the 'impure', good and pure being those ideas and feelings that fit in with its ideological totalism, and everything else being 'bad'. In the day hospital ideas and feelings were moulded to fit in with the hospital's reductive interpretations, and any challenge to this perspective was regarded as symptomatic of disease. The paragon of purity in this context was the 'good patient' who trusted and accepted these definitions. One such patient took on the role of therapist and, like the experienced prisoner in the Chinese labour camp, tended to merge with the tide to avoid painful disagreement. Such an individual becomes skilful at analysing or criticizing others, helps them make their confessions, or explains how their psyches are distorting reality and communication for them. This judge–penitent bases himself on the assumption that the more he accuses himself, the more he has the right to accuse others.

In both day hospital and concentration camp, confession as such goes beyond its legitimate legal, religious or therapeutic function and becomes a cult. The prisoner has to confess to things he has not done – to the point where confession becomes a means of exploitation rather than a solace. Even if the day hospital patients probably did not confess things they had neither felt nor done, in the prevailing all-embracing therapy any innocent statement could *post facto* be turned into a confession by the interpretation placed on it. Where a patient did confess to anti-social feelings and/or illegal acts, the often abstruse interpretations of his unconscious motivation would frequently leave him feeling unsupported by the group and not much the wiser – as if it had been the confession *per se* that was all that mattered.

This was clearly felt by two patients (a married couple) when the husband admitted to the group that he frequently exposed himself in public. Just like the totalist confession in the Chinese camps, such an avowal became an act of inner surrender and a vehicle for personal purity. The unveiling of guilty secrets is often followed by a 'dissolution of self into the great flow of the Movement' (Lifton, 1961). However, because the interpretations in this case were not directly related to the husband's confession, the patients concerned simply felt angry and cheated at the lack of help – particularly in view of what it had cost the husband to make this inner surrender.

Where the dogma has a scientific basis and is held out as the ultimate moral vision, any questioning of the basic assumption (for instance, whether the psychological reality is really the sole relevant question) is prohibited. Not only is the individual prevented from using his own judgement but the scientific quest for knowledge is also hampered and, with no distinction between the sacred and the profane, all thought and action are related to the 'sacred science'.

In Chinese thought reform it was 'dispensing of existence' differentiating between 'people and non-people' – that gave the peasant and working classes the right to exist and excluded the rest, the 'reactionaries and imperialist lackeys'. Similarly, the only people taken seriously at the day hospital were loyal members and those sympathetic to the experiment. Anyone else, including the majority of the staff of the rest of the institute, who were critical, were 'non-people' who could be discounted.

Not all Lifton's criteria of ideological totalism apply to the

138

day hospital,[9] but the fact that the patient must see himself in pathological terms as a means to salvation shows that there were elements of thought reform in its ideology. The individual patient was guided by an instructor or therapist, made to analyse the causes of his deficiencies and work through his resistances until he thought and felt in conformity with the doctrinal truth to which everything was reduced.

In the process of either thought reform[10] or psychoanalysis as practised in the day hospital, the individual's identity is assaulted. To some extent there is a threat to identity in most therapeutic contexts, but this was exacerbated by the lack of any formal rules, leaving the patient no clear points of reference by which to guide his behaviour. When therapy – as it inevitably does – jolts a person's ideas of what others expect of him, it makes patients look for support from each other; the new social relationships may then constitute a counterbalance for the old ones which were stripped away in the course of therapeutic treatment. The support obtained from other patients is that of people 'in the same boat' who can identify with the individual patient's fears (many in the difficult process of therapy) and who, because of their similar fears, are ready to band together with him in self-defence. The therapeutic role of the staff, on the other hand, is to make patients confront their hidden conflicts squarely, not to retreat behind the masks that hide such conflicts; their aim is to change, not to maintain, the individual's *status quo*. So while a therapist is concerned with *why* an alcoholic drinks, patients may be happy to join him in his drinking. Looking at the example of the alcoholic from a psycho-analytic perspective will show more concretely what is meant by the process of weakening ego-defences and its effects on the person's self-image.

Through analytic interpretation, an alcoholic patient may begin to see how his drinking is physically as well as emotionally self-destructive. Even a partial understanding of his drive to drink may prevent him from automatically using it as an escape the next time he feels anxious. If no other protective measures have been built up, however, abstaining will leave him with the undiluted anxiety and feeling of loneliness that the drinking had masked. As an added burden to his psychological discomfort, he may feel that his social image is endangered. Having been regarded as a good drinking companion whom people can rely on to be easy going, entertaining, a wit and so on, he worries about what they will think of him now when they see him (so he imagines) as a pitiable and cowering figure. Will they not feel disappointed in him, and even actually cheated because he is no longer available to play his former social role? Such loss of a known self-image is one of the added difficulties to which a person is exposed when undergoing therapy, and patients often develop modes of adaptation for protecting their particular self-image – for example, in the day hospital some patients said they simply needed the day hospital for companionship, for its facilities as a social club.

Whereas in Chinese thought reform a person's general conduct was attributed to his imperialistic or bourgeois greed and desire for exploitation, so reducing the individual's short-comings to those of an opposing ideology, in the day hospital it was his unconscious that was seen to be at fault. In both instances a threat is posed to the personal autonomy, self-expression and independent judgement of individuals caught up in the system; both contexts place the person concerned in a regressive stance and deprive him of his adult self. Each attempt to assert his own will or identity is considered a show of resistance and calls for new assaults. But whereas in thought reform these assaults – which included violent brutality – generally led to an inner surrender of personal autonomy, in the day hospital many patients could and did resist the psychological pressure and actually dared to re-define the reality proffered by the analyst. Those who did adapt were rewarded. Both patients and prisoners found that the process of adaptation allowed them to feel in harmony with their environment again: all problems could now be solved and the surrender of self to an all-powerful force provided a sense of group identity and intimacy – for the patients this lasted until they complained.

Chinese thought reform based much of its persuasion on the real fear of actual physical annihilation (prisoners were threatened with execution); the day hospital counterpart to this was the fear of emotional annihilation, the possibility of becoming lost in madness. This added to the pressure on inmates to

Strategies of control

'accept help' – the patients by confessing their weaknesses to the therapists, the camp prisoners by admitting their crimes, both encouraging others to do the same.

Having made an initial confession the prisoners began to accept the image put on them by the reformers, actively sought out the evil in themselves in order to reject it, and by gradually accepting authority's version of themselves developed a new identity as a 'receptive criminal'. Abandoning their own beliefs and values, they turned to the morality of the higher group, whose harshest judgements fitted in with the most tyrannical aspects of their own personality. In the process of re-education, the prisoner had to extend his self-condemnation to every aspect of his being until his final confession summed up and discarded his past identity.

This psychological pattern was not followed to this extreme by patients at the day hospital, even if many of the elements of ideological totalism were reflected in its ideology. The different ways in which patients resisted the psychological pressures to which they were subjected was paralleled in a number of patient groupings, which I shall discuss in the next chapter.

Concluding remarks

In this chapter I have shown how staff communication strategies such as collusion and the use of an esoteric language became mechanisms of control – especially when, in crisis, the staff felt a greater need to defend themselves. What had been patterns of interaction which were merely congruent with a psychoanalytic perspective were now employed more instrumentally to assert control when the hegemony of the analytic world-view was threatened. I have likened these control processes to the psychological pressures and manipulation of brainwashing as described by Lifton in the Chinese labour camps. Although the day hospital's psychological and social control was not a direct parallel of 'ideological totalism', a thoroughly undemocratic and tyrannical system did emerge, despite the ideological claims to the contrary. The hidden nature of the power structure made it particularly strong, for it was masked by the members' assumption that the authoritarianism associated with hierarch-

141

ical control had been dissolved once rules had been abandoned and roles blurred. Being hidden it was less easy to attack.

I hope that the extent and nature of the manipulation with which the patients were faced has become clearer in this chapter. This was not a typical Goffmanesque situation, where the rules and mechanisms of control are relatively clear-cut. Here we have a much more subtle and at the same time much more invasive exercise of power.

Goffman's patients were literally stripped of their clothes, but at the day hospital the mortification processes were far more internal. At the traditional institution the possibility of self-presentation through clothes may have been denied, but at the day hospital every statement or action that expressed the self was annihilated by critical interpretation based on the so-called pathology of the individual. This was particularly pernicious because the actual means of healing, the interpretation, was made the vehicle of control. The patients' receptiveness to the healing role of the staff meant that interpretations as control mechanisms went very deep. In this sense it is true to say that the political forms of manipulation have moved on since Goffman's analysis. The subtlety of control that has its parallels in thought reform was simply not available to him. In the new context the nature of the relationship between manipulator and manipulated was established by virtue of the fact that the individual is dependent on taking a 'poison potion'. No doubt the patients accepted the control for some time because the day hospital in the first place represented an attitude that was against the authorities from whom they had suffered for so long.

In the next chapter I show how the patients did manage to defend themselves against the impact of the imputation of pathology that reduced and belittled their contributions, and how their different reactions were related to their view of themselves and of therapy.

6

The struggle for a definition of reality

What were the effects on the patients of the day hospital's experimental treatment methods? How did they cope with the control strategies that had arisen to deal with the *anomos* threatening the hospital as a result of the abolition of rules? How did they react to the therapeutic environment that challenged their conceptions of themselves? In this chapter I shall outline a typology of patients to show how they defined and responded to the situation in which they found themselves, and the subsequent impact of this on their informal organization. The focus will not be confined to patients' group formations alone, but will also include the types of reaction and modes of adaptation that cut across these groupings. The kind of 'games' played between and among staff and patients will then be examined, in a number of linked sessions.

To begin with, although the staff and patient roles had been consciously blurred and there was no strong class-like cleavage between the two groups such as Goffman describes in *Asylums* (1968, p. 196), there remained a clear differentiation between them in terms of the use of psychoanalytic language. The staff did not wear uniforms, they shared food with the patients and attended, as they did, the large group in the mornings, but mobility between the two groups was none the less restricted. Even if the more obvious 'abasements, degradations, humiliations and profanations of self' (Goffman, 1968) could not be found in the day hospital, the imputation of pathology in the staff's psychoanalytic interpretation did leave the patients feeling 'inferior, weak, blameworthy and guilty', while the staff retained its 'superior and righteous position',[1] as emphasized by the collusive staff games.

Even if the patients were not deprived of their own clothes, names and personal belongings, nor mortified and degraded by constantly having to obey staff orders, their personal identity was under attack, and in that sense they did experience a re-socialization process. While patient participation was indeed encouraged, it is an ironical fact that the more therapeutic and less custodial the institution, the more the staff tend to impress on the patient that he is ill and that the trouble lies within himself: he must change his conception of himself and start relating to people differently.

However, even when people are constrained to consider themselves as sick and cannot therefore get what they want or show their anger and alienation, they will still continue to try to obtain these ends by whatever means are available, including unauthorized ones. Even though social control in the day hospital did not lie in the more obvious formal constraints of a total institution, the totalizing tendencies of its ideology required those secondary adjustments that make up the underlife of an institution – which is, in Goffman's words, 'to a social establishment what an underworld is to a city' (1975).

Even in the absence of any elaborate formal control system, there will still be expectations which the participants may choose not to meet:

Where enthusiasm is expected, there will be apathy; where loyalty, there will be disaffection; where attendance, absenteeism; where robustness, some kind of illness; where deeds are to be done, varieties of inactivity.

(Goffman, 1975, p. 305)

Although there were no rules of attendance the patients were expected, for example, to turn up to the large-group session – and sometimes, especially after the complaint (a case of the patients quite consciously posing a counter-system), very few patients attended. And whereas the streamlined approach valued only large-group therapy, the patients produced their own encounter-group therapist. During this period especially,

144

The struggle for a definition of reality

the patients countered the psychoanalytic version of themselves as sick by a view that was socially determined.

Goffman argues that the tragedy of mental illness lies precisely in the fact that every expression of alienation and dissatisfaction is read as symptomatic. This was particularly true at the day hospital, where organizational and physical realities and all other aspects of life were interpreted in this way despite the fact that the ideology rejected the rigours, deprivations and attacks on self-identity found in the traditional psychiatric hospital and the usual ways in which people try

> *to hold off the embrace of organizations – insolence, silence,* sotto voce *remarks, uncooperativeness . . . and so forth; these signs of disaffiliation are now read as signs of their makers' proper affiliation.*
>
> (Goffman, 1975, p. 306)

The other side of the coin is the way in which patients new to the day hospital, after experiencing staff expectations of mad behaviour in residential hospitals, would put on a show of being crazy. There is no doubt that some patients did suffer considerable culture shock as a result of the initial breakdown of defences inherent in the therapeutic process. During periods of increased vulnerability, acting mad at least ties the person down to a particular role.

In attempting to adapt to a new environment, the individual will search for a new 'vocabulary of motive' and with no formal rules for patients' behaviour, new patients often made a quite exaggerated pretence of madness. One patient for example, held the floor for a large part of a group session and became frustrated by the therapists not answering his direct questions. Calling himself Dali, he then proceeded to give a very graphic account of his life. He described how he had 'sucked a man on Hampstead Heath – soft like a baby's teat – an initiation ceremony'. He said he was getting ready for his mother's return from abroad and that he was going to make up for the baptism she had given him 'when she pushed faeces in my mouth when I was a child'. Playing with the hat on his head, he declared: 'I don't know why I wear it. Maybe it makes me sure my head is

145

still on.' It was almost as if this patient had a set idea of the preoccupations of very disturbed patients and was imitating such a state.

While it is difficult to be absolutely certain, it is probable that his mad behaviour was aped rather than genuine. This patient had been a tramp for many years and in his wanderings he had come across the day hospital, where he found he could get free meals and coffee. He was delighted that there were none of the formal rules banning him from membership which generally applied in other institutions, but he may have felt it incumbent upon him to make himself appear mad at first to prevent others from accusing him of 'dossing'. After a few weeks he became a very active member of the large group. He cleaned himself up, cut his long matted hair and beard, acquired new clothes, and showed himself to be very well acquainted with modern poetry and a writer of poems himself. He may not have been 'cured' but this radical change does suggest he was adopting a mad role when he arrived.

In general, when a new patient made his first appearances in the large group, 'old' patients often attempted to exclude the newcomer. For example, in the middle of a large-group session a new patient joined in the discussion, excusing himself for talking off the point:

New patient: I wonder if this is irrelevant, but would anyone here subscribe to the view that a sacrifice is used to maintain the tribe?
Therapist A: Like 2 or Adrian or someone being used as a scapegoat to keep the rest together?
Patient 1: This is not a suitable forum for discussing that. You understand you'll have to bring in the context.
Therapist A: It's quite valid. He's giving *his* perspective.
Therapist B: Old patients are telling the new patient how to behave as a patient.
Patient 1: He shouldn't interrupt, that's all.
Therapist B: Oh yes, there's a definite hierarchy of patients, too.

In addition to the threat to identity posed by therapy the new

146

The struggle for a definition of reality

patient must therefore, as the above example shows, face up to the aggression of established patients, and may well try to mollify them by acting mad to legitimate his presence in the therapeutic arena.

Sharp (1975) has argued that this type of adaptation leads to even less rehabilitation than that of the isolates and was at the other end of the continuum. The individuals concerned in Sharp's therapeutic community, a 'hip' subgroup, were very skilled in therapy jargon and involved in informal groups. They developed a dichotomizing perspective, lauding an alternative society that rejected the values of established society together with the idea of getting a mental patient fit to work again as a proper aim for his rehabilitation. They implied that most 'normal' people are stolid and that those who break down under the dulling influence of most jobs were always the highly sensitive ones. This argument can lead to a form of neo-institutionalization as the individual comes to rely on the organization for maintaining his self-identity. An individual employing such a mode tends to 'perform' in the group, being very articulate and able to *ad lib* without hesitation.

At the day hospital, some of the main activists in fact used this strategy. They formed a hard core of patients who had been attending the clinic for years, were well accustomed to the forum of the large group and made use of it to expound their ideas. However, it was a strategy which did not seem to be employed with the same urgency as in Sharp's community. Sharp says it seemed to ward off the stigma attached to being labelled mentally ill. The day hospital situation was in any case rather different. Both staff and patients largely subscribed to the anti-psychiatry ideology which argues that madness is but sanity in an insane world, even though for the staff this created a contradiction between acknowledging the patients' need for treatment and not being able to establish an image of normality in any way different from the conventional view based on ability to cope with responsibilities and earn a living.

There was also in Sharp's community a group called the conformists or elite subgroup who adopted the stance of the staff, used staff terminology and employed a strategy of 'therapeutic hegemony'. Sharp defines the latter as the way in which

147

they deflected talk away from themselves in the name of caring for others. These so-called elite members prided themselves on their intelligence, perceptiveness and analytic skills. The day hospital parallel to these conformists was the activist group before the complaint. They too valued therapy greatly and played the therapist role frequently, apparently finding it a stimulating mental exercise. Therapeutic hegemony was more often used by the staff, but at times the patients did attempt to retaliate by arguing that staff interpretations were based on the therapists' own insecurity.

As soon as the new patient made his adjustment to the therapeutic setting and process, the all-pervasive character of therapy forced him to build a private world for himself by finding 'free places' (Goffman 1968) where the organization cannot intrude and where support for selfhood is gained through resistance and solidarity with other patients. When the day hospital patients had complained and organized counter-groups running alongside the large group to discuss the next political move, their morale seemed to lift as a result of setting up this resistance movement. Similarly, throughout the period of my research, certain areas of the hospital were taken over as the exclusive preserve of certain individuals. The rooms previously reserved for small-group therapy became general free places shared by many patients; the library, taken over by a group of patients for drinking, became group territory and was sometimes referred to as the drinking room. More personal free places were adopted by individual patients: one, for example, always spent the day in a particular corner of the art room, leaving it only for lunch, which he took alone at one specific table.

In this way, then, there was quite an array of secondary adjustments making up the day hospital underlife. Although at first glance the situation appeared highly fragmented, among the patients as a whole distinctly different modes of adaptation to the organization could be discerned. The response was either completely individual or one where several patients sympathetic to each other responded similarly and could be designated as a subgroup.

The struggle for a definition of reality

The subgroups

The isolates

The isolates were patients who, if they attended the large group, remained silent throughout or missed the therapy sessions altogether while participating in 'extra-curricular' activities such as yoga, drama or art. They were often very withdrawn and rarely communicated with other people. They therefore represented a quasi-group.

In Sharp's therapeutic community this 'situational withdrawal' was regarded as less affronting than dissidence but, since it gained the individual no support from other patients, it was rather an unsuccessful mode of adaptation. Any attempt at participation in the form of aggressive rejection of others would be so awkward that it did nothing to help the individual fit in. According to Sharp, situational withdrawal resulted in a negative spiral of ever-decreasing help, usually ending with a crisis and the individual's transfer to another institution.

At the day hospital too such withdrawal met with no active patient support, but neither did it elicit verbal attacks from patients or staff. Members employing this mode were largely ignored – a stance which did imply at least a measure of acceptance (much as furniture or Musak might be relied on to be permanently there), especially at the time of continuous conflict. Indeed, during the crisis this mode of adaptation was rather successful, as maintaining a low profile seemed a way of avoiding being drawn into the conflict.

The social-club group

One subgroup of patients used the day hospital almost purely as a kind of social club. Although most patients made use of the social side of the institute, there were some who regarded it in and of itself as a possible solution to their problems, and gave more importance to it than to psychotherapy. For those who defined their sense of loneliness as springing from social isolation, the hospital provided a setting for sociability. One patient quite openly acknowledged that that was why she came:

'We all have personal problems like loneliness. That's why I come here, to be with people.' When these patients attended the large group they often did not participate in the therapy; they remained either silently passive or rejecting.

Goffman (1975) holds that where patients follow a rather 'contented' life, using the organization's facilities to the full and making merely token contributions to the therapy group, colonization occurs. Sharp, who applied Goffman's modes of adaptation in his examination of a therapeutic community, argues that this adaptation cannot last long, as those employing it are soon accused of lacking motivation. At the day hospital patients who seemed to value it for these facilities in themselves annoyed the staff, who regarded this as an abuse. What were meant to be frills or conveniences additional to the main goal of analysis were being used instead as the chief reason for attending. In fact, when the conflict over whether or not the day hospital should provide meals ended with the staff deciding to stop this facility, this was the catalyst which triggered the patients' complaint.

The drinking group

Among the patients with the social-club attitude were four who proclaimed themselves in mock rivalry with the therapists and who were also generally known as the drinking group. These four had been attending the clinic for longer than most patients. They spent much of their time drinking together, both inside and outside, and they would sporadically go to the large group with their bottles, brazenly flouting the large-group emphasis on self-understanding rather than escaping from problems by any available means.

The staff, however, would argue that when psychoanalysis breaks down the defences the patient has built up to protect him from anxiety-provoking internal conflicts, a confrontation with necessarily painful feelings is brought about which the patient will use a variety of tactics to avoid. These may range from complex psychological mechanisms to a plain refusal to listen to the psychoanalyst's interpretation, or the use of alcohol to dull the pain and 'cheer him up'. Since this was understood,

150

The struggle for a definition of reality

drinking on the day hospital premises (unless it seriously
disrupted daily life) was mostly accepted, and therapeutically
legitimated as a communication from patients to staff – an
expression of misery, a 'cry for help', and so on. Opinion about
tolerating it within the large group was, however, divided.
Some argued that it was pointless trying to do therapy with a
person who was drunk, did not know what he was saying, and
would not remember the discussion later; others thought that
if a patient needed to drink in order to be able to say certain
things about himself, then this must be accepted. They felt it
was better for a patient to 'bring his problem to the group' in
this way than to get drunk and into trouble in the unsympathetic
world outside.

Shortly before the inquiry, positions among staff and patients
were hardening as a result of formal pressure, since by then
everyone realized that the day hospital's viability would be
under scrutiny. These divisions are revealed quite clearly in the
extract below from a large group session, which relates to 'social-
club' and 'gangster' patients.

Therapist A: It smacks of omnipotence if you think you can
treat alcoholic patients who in the normal way aren't
accessible to therapy.
Therapist B: That one there [indicating a patient] is a petty
thief who could become a big-time criminal . . . and there
are another two I could put in the same category.
Patient 1: We're the three musketeers! Why pick on us? We're
plain honest, not like some people – not like those who come
in for meals, collect their fares and piss off. Or that one there,
who neither smokes nor drinks, who can cope and doesn't
need this place. If you want to discharge people, let's put it
to the vote. You can discharge me if you want to. You seem
to think all I do is drink all the time. I go to the flicks and the
library and attempt suicide about once a fortnight, so I do lots
of other things besides drinking.
Therapist C: Of course, there are some who are afraid of
leaving the nipple or the bottle.

The therapist is relating the drinking problem to a child's reluc-

151

tance to being weaned, whereas the patient has been concerned with his legitimate status as a patient.

[Patient 1 laughs.]
Therapist C: I'm not sure that B should single out 1 to accuse him of not being here for therapy. Maybe 1 represents the rest of the patients' disillusionment.
Patient 2: So you say some people should be discharged for not coming in for therapy. But if you look at this place properly, you'll see there isn't much therapy going on to come in for.
Therapist C: I agree there isn't much therapy going on, or can be in the present circumstances. And though people may just come for meals and fares, we must bear in mind, as he said, [indicating a patient] that it takes a new patient some time to settle down, to feel brave and at home enough to join in large groups, so he's bound to stay on the fringe for a bit.

The last point certainly seemed to be true, although initially the discussion had concerned patients of long standing who, irrespective of their interest in therapy, were engaged in various rackets that had become so obvious they could hardly be ignored.

The gangsters

Linked to the drinking group was a small number of patients who had adopted what seemed to me a gangster-like role and seemed to be paying mere lip-service to the concept of therapy. Their rare attendances at the large group were regarded by some staff as arising more from a feeling that their presence was required once in a while to legitimize their membership of the day hospital than from any serious desire for help. Despite the absence of rules they felt there might be a limit to what kind of behaviour was ultimately tolerated, and they were quite aware that some staff members questioned the validity of trying to treat such reluctant patients at all. By putting in the occasional appearance at therapy groups, these gangster patients managed to work the system to their own financial advantage

152

instead, apparently, of being motivated by the formal goal of self-understanding through therapy.

This group, relying on the hard drinkers' need of money for the next bottle, would organize members of the drinking group to shoplift for them. For the sake of a little cash, the latter were willing to ignore the risk of being caught. On one occasion one of the drinkers got into trouble with the police for trying to obtain a refund on a stolen railway ticket. It was generally thought at the day hospital that one of the gangsters had stolen the ticket and passed the 'hot stuff' on to a lackey in return for a share in the proceeds. The more vulnerable drinkers were thus involved in a number of rackets organized by the gangster group, including procuring buyers for drugs and fake social security cards. Their organization was never very efficient, and sometimes the pawns in the game were prosecuted, but the connection between them and their ringleaders was never formally brought to light, though it eventually became common knowledge. This may have been because the drinkers were afraid of the ringleaders and reluctant to forfeit their social and financial support, or it may have been a case of honour among thieves.

This sub-organization had managed to operate for some time before the staff became fully aware of it, because the rackets were carried out in informal patient settings away from staff scrutiny. In theory, of course, information about the gangsters' activities should have been fed back into the large group but the staff were kept in the dark for as long as possible, perhaps because the 'victims' preferred this more concrete attention they were receiving to the vague help of therapy. Besides, the obvious disagreements in the staff group offered little sense of security and made such reporting risky. When these activities eventually came to light, staff reactions were predictably split. Some preferred not to believe it, or concluded that if it were true the most significant element was the indirect 'cry for help' from the instigators of the illegal activities. Others were outraged at the exploitation of the needier patients, telling the ringleaders to stop 'playing around with petty crime' and become 'legitimate entrepreneurs' instead. They wanted them

153

to be discharged, but as they could not get everybody to agree the matter was left unresolved.

The different staff reactions to the gangster element are shown in the next extract from a staffroom discussion, in whic¹ there was disagreement over whether a patient who had been discharged by a minority of staff should really be regarded as discharged or not. The circumstances had been as follows.

Six months after the complaint had been submitted there were some burglaries in the day hospital. As a result of these – and following recommendations from the Area Health Authority to implement formal regulations such as keeping a register of patients and clinical notes – some staff began to reconsider the lack of rules, and how their response to illegitimate actions would look to outsiders (the inquiry was only a few weeks away).

Therapist A: I don't want to go to the PSC about patients' illegal actions because it's a medical matter that's going on there. If I single out [the patients concerned] . . . I have a close relationship with them, and to have a go at them for stealing . . . ?

Therapist B: I *know* patient 1 steals. The patients have told us. Should we put up with that? He was supposed to be discharged and here he is again. Unless we have a consensus of patients and staff about who's supposed to be here, it's no good. Now staff are getting hit [while intervening in a fight among patients]. That's never happened before. Patients used to protect staff because of this consensus.

Therapist C: If our theory of a three-part relationship between the therapist, the NHS and the patient is correct, then if we dismiss stealing from one of the parties as a joke, we're messing it up.

Therapist D: But do you think punishment is treatment?

Therapist C: Yes. If a patient stole an ashtray from your house, what would you do?

Therapist D: That's different. What's been stolen here?

Therapist C: Typewriters.

Therapist D: You automatically think it's the patients.

Therapist C: Well, and a telephone was stolen from

The struggle for a definition of reality

downstairs. We need a different attitude to the damage to our third party.

Therapist D: I welcome people telling us our mistakes, because we're bound to make some.

Once only did the staff agree in their criticism of one of the members of the gangster group (in my presence, anyway). However, they failed to discharge him because he disappeared at the moment when, as a group, they were prepared to take action. He returned only when the storm had blown over and the staff had fallen back into their customary divided allegiances, so that by default he was allowed to remain.

Some three months later, when the staff were divided again and still feeling strongly about an incident where one of the gangsters had thrown a lighted firework into the large-group session, therapist A left the room when she saw patient 1.

Therapist B: I wonder how everyone else is feeling about patient 1's appearance in the large group.

Therapist C: Well, I must say I thought he'd been discharged.

Therapist D: Not as far as I recollect.

Therapist C: I thought we'd decided as a group to discharge him.

Patient 1: If three patients got together they could discharge therapist C. I've just been with a group of patients, and they say they want me to return.

Therapist E: That's because they're afraid of you. You belong outside, because you're really an entrepreneur. What are you doing, getting fat on the NHS? You only come here to wheel and deal and get X to go to [the big local department store] to shoplift for you. Why are you here?

Patient 2: That's slander! You can't say things like that.

Therapist E: Well, if you think it isn't true you must be deaf and blind.

Patient 1: I'm here because two psychiatrists think I need treatment.

Four months later, however, opinion had hardened somewhat after further dubious activities had been discovered. In this

155

instance the staff suspected a patients' group of having recently
burgled the day hospital, and felt more certain about the latter's
motivation for attending: 'It's ridiculous to attempt to give
interpretations to people who just want to make money out of
the situation.' This group became known in the hospital as the
'capitalists'.

The activists

At the opposite end of the spectrum from the gangster model
was a group of patients I shall call the activists. They were
deeply involved in the therapy, were always the most active in
the large group, and in general seemed to take the whole
therapeutic experience very seriously. For example, one patient
said in answer to another's purely social explanation for coming
to the hospital: 'I come here to solve my problems. I've got to
talk about my personal problems to try and understand why I
feel certain things.'

These patients tended to appear more outgoing than others.
They were intelligent and extremely articulate. They seemed
more highly motivated towards understanding themselves and
their social situation through a desire to realize their potential.
Until they came to believe that the situation in the day hospital
was hopeless, they were the ones whose purpose appeared most
fully to accord with the therapeutic aim. Initially, they were
the most open to psychoanalytic interpretation and tried hard
to remove blocks to their understanding. They seemed more
sure of themselves and less threatened by therapy. Unlike the
isolates they had no need to protect themselves behind a wall
of silence; they did not seem to see the day hospital primarily
as providing a social life, nor a base for illicit personal gain. In
fact, they were often antagonistic towards what they regarded
as its misuse.

However, having been so active in their support of the hospital's primary goal, they were equally active in their rebuttal of
the approach once they had come to define it as counterproduc-
tive to their own aims and interest. Better able than others to
express themselves in therapy, they also had greater facility in
airing their grievance. When, having taken psychotherapy so

The struggle for a definition of reality .

seriously, they came as a group to regard the situation as one of manipulation, their annoyance with the staff was the more intense. They felt that the unilateral staff decision to withdraw meal facilities reflected a concealed control mechanism that had been operating under the surface all along. From then on, rather than trying to understand the psychoanalytic interpretations of their unconscious they rejected the idea of unconscious motivation altogether, realizing how they had let themselves be used as 'guinea pigs in some bizarre experiment'. They felt that accepting further psychoanalytic interpretation would lay them open to the ideology's totalizing tendencies. In order to fend off the more extreme attacks (as expressed in their being defined as driven *solely* by pathological motivations), they had to reject psychoanalysis *in toto* and put forward alternative views of what really did motivate them: that they were victims of social circumstances, that they were lonely, and so on.

It was this group that organized the complaint. After their frustration at the confusion at the day hospital had made them write the letter of complaint to the Area Health Authority, the Minister for Health and Social Services and the Professional Staff Committee, they organized other groups to discuss tactics to ensure that the authorities would take the complaint seriously. They canvassed other patients, regularly boycotted the therapy sessions and, if they did attend the large group, refused to participate in therapy and attempted to force the staff into discussing their criticisms on their own terms – in terms of a 'real' situation rather than individual psychopathological symptoms. When they thought therapy was being used to inhibit or belittle their attitude, they rejected it outright. For example, in these sessions such patients declared that psychoanalytic interpretations of the inner meaning of their criticisms of the day hospital were merely red herrings. This is illustrated in this extract from a large-group session:

Patient 3: Interpretations are no good. When an inspector comes here he can *see* a dirty carpet when he's shown one. You don't need interpretations to know a carpet is dirty.
Patient 4: Hear, hear! Psychotherapy is just manipulation.

157

Patient 5: Why should anyone want to come here and express their feelings and problems?
Patient 1: I do. But that doesn't seem to be happening.
Therapist A: Why don't we enjoy it, or do more work here?
Therapist B: Masochists can only work when it's difficult and miserable. The patients are rejecting interpretations because they think apathy may prevent intercourse between staff.
Therapist C: I don't agree. I think the patients are saying they have indigestion from having been fed too many interpretations.

During this session one of the activists left, returning shortly afterwards to tell another patient that someone wanted to see him, and then a third that he was wanted on the telephone. The telephone had not rung; it was rather that this patient wanted the others to attend the alternative patient group for discussing strategies for further action on the complaint, instead of participating in the large-group therapy session.

It is clear that the activists' endeavours in the counter-organization were every bit as busy as their earlier support had been. They had taken the day hospital and its aims seriously, but when they saw it becoming chaotic, dominating and unhelpful to them they applied the same kind of earnestness to its destruction. In fact, the activists resembled Sharp's dissidents, but only after the complaint. This dissident group would angrily and verbally reject the staff and their values, and if a resident was being confronted by a staff member the others would rally round and attempt to defend him.

Sharp argues that their dissidence did not provide these patients with a clear self-image and identity, because they did not form a real subculture group with its own rationale and the ability to neutralize the conventional and stigmatizing attitudes towards mental patients. Dissidence alone did not provide a distinct definition of the situation such as would have enabled the residential patient to combat 'the assault on self-identity of the therapeutic-community experience'. The transformation of some of Sharp's dissidents into conformists vis-à-vis the therapeutic-community goals implied a 'transformed subjective

158

The struggle for a definition of reality

reality'. Like religious converts they now had a new definition of reality, a new plausibility structure for understanding life.

At the day hospital, the transformation was in reverse. The activists who had been converted to psychoanalytic goals went back to a new/old definition of reality which was opposed to the analytic world-view. Having strongly adhered to psychoanalysis, they then apparently wholeheartedly rejected it, concluding that analysis was a mask concealing manipulation and control. Unlike Sharp's dissidents, they did gain a certain sense of identity from this because they did form a separate subculture in their attack on the hospital methods. Having something clear to fight for, they developed a distinctive self-image. There was one patient in this group, however, who retracted part of his denunciation of the medical director and thereafter would often parrot the prevailing ideology[2] – and this way of taking the day hospital approach too literally annoyed the staff as much as the patients.

A patient subculture?

These subgroups of the patient collectivity were, it must be remembered, more accidental than deliberate groupings. Until they had collectively re-defined the treatment they were receiving as manipulation, the very activity of interpretation was an individualizing process. However, as time passed affiliations were made initially on the basis of either shared tastes or friendship. Thus those who felt lonely but shy would drift towards the library and the relative conviviality of those who drank cider there. They were not, in this sense, consciously organized groupings. Once the situation became more polarized, however, the rejection of the therapy was accompanied by a re-definition of the meaning the day hospital held for them. Hence from that point on the activists, for example, saw the day hospital in political terms, whereas the isolates saw it as a haven.

In Sharp's terms, the key to a true subculture is the existence of a plausibility structure, a new definition of reality, and perhaps it was this that gave the activists' group such resilience in the face of months of turmoil and crisis. Whether they were

159

championing psychotherapy or rebelling against it, the activists had a peculiar buoyancy that allowed them to thrive on either situation.[3] Having a strong sense of what it was they valued and what they were aiming for (whether the furtherance of therapy or its destruction) helped them to see their common interests, orientate their actions to a particular goal, and organize as a group. Apart from the strategic value of such clarity about goals and values, the very fact of having a value system and collective goals seemed to sustain them. Although the gangsters were not much involved in either therapy or rebellion, they evinced a similar resilience because they too provided an alternative definition of the situation (in their case as a base for illegal activities).

The activists, therefore, did set up an alternative definition of the situation in both word and deed. The social-club group, with its subgroups of drinkers and gangsters, defined the hospital as a place for meeting people, drinking and making money, and explained their attendance as stemming from social difficulties. It was only the isolates who lacked an alternative rationale and a true subculture. Although this left them without support for combating the attack on their identity inherent in the therapeutic-community experience, their survival may have been due to the fact that the day hospital, unlike Sharp's community, did not press them to confront the reasons for their withdrawal from both informal patient associations and therapy sessions. They were left alone and allowed to go on existing in an empty, isolated world where – despite the lack of contact and development – they felt a degree of acceptance because they were not actually rejected.

Each subgroup of patients, therefore, used a different way of coping with the threat to self posed by therapy, but within each rough grouping there were variations in the mode of adaptation to the process. Among the group I have called isolates, for example, there were also 'retreatists' and 'ritualists'.

The retreatists withdrew completely from the general therapeutic area, inhabited little-used rooms, hardly communicated with others, and developed their individual styles of living within the hospital – for example sleeping in the library, painting quietly and in an uninvolved way with the others in

The struggle for a definition of reality

the art room, eating alone and separate from other patients. It looked as if such a patient's purpose was not to gain self-understanding through therapy but to follow his own quiet interests in the shelter (asylum) of the day hospital.

The ritualists conformed to the general expectation of attending the large-group therapy sessions in the morning and did not miss a day, but they never spoke and so never contravened the implicit rule against introducing ideas extraneous to psychoanalysis. Nevertheless they were hardly pursuing the prime therapeutic goal as defined by the medical director, and the hospital simply represented to them a shelter or a haven.

Additionally a member from a group would sometimes react in a way different from his peers. Thus, within the overall group of the social club which largely ignored the hospital's therapeutic function, some members would occasionally try hard to pursue psychotherapy, perhaps because they were feeling particularly worried at that point.

Interestingly, it was a member of the isolates (who from time to time became involved with the drinkers) who founded the Mental Patients' Union (MPU), a self-help group for protecting the interests of patients in or from psychiatric hospitals. This association, with its own magazine, was founded in the early 1970s and held meetings to provide information and support for patients. It faded out in the second half of the decade, but many of its members joined a similar group called People not Psychiatry – also opposed to electroconvulsive therapy and drugs. (It still publishes a magazine.[4])

The patient who founded the MPU had been in and out of psychiatric hospitals for about thirty-five years – most of his adult life – and had devoted much time to studying anti-psychiatry literature, especially the works of R.D. Laing and Thomas Szasz. He saw the reasons for his own predicament as 'problems in living' (Szasz's term) and completely rejected psychoanalytic interpretations. Only rarely did he attend the large group in the morning, although he was a well-known and much-liked figure who had been attending the day hospital since its inception.[5]

At the peak of the crisis, after the patients had filed their complaint and in reaction to the staff's decision to terminate

161

the provision of meals and fares, the patients closed their ranks and the response was more uniform. In a situation where the patients were in direct opposition to staff, the polarization of attitudes imposed greater conformity than previously; in other words, there was stronger allegiance to each given group. While the majority of patients were united in general condemnation of the staff, many of the isolates withdrew from the hospital completely and failed to reappear for a long time. There were a few cases of overdosing among the isolates, as among the more active patients, but the majority reacted with hostility towards the staff rather than violence towards themselves.

Whether the patient subculture is regarded as a potentially important instrument of therapy (as the therapeutic community sees it) or as subversive to the formal treatment aims (as Goffman argues), the relationship is both problematical and vital to therapeutic-community methods. Bloor (1981), for example, examines activities regarded as beneficial and others supposedly detrimental to treatment and shows how the same activities can be seen in a different light at different times. For example, the patient culture provides a social learning experience for fellow-patients, but this can also serve as an opportunity to learn counter-cultural behaviour which will be rewarded by the patient group. On the other hand in some therapeutic communities this contradiction, confusing as it is for patients, is regarded as helpful, because life *is* contradictory and the therapeutic community can thereby prepare its patients for dealing with the outside world.

Interaction in the day hospital

The patients' secondary adjustments and the staff's strategies were both syndromes which influenced behaviour, although they had not been developed for that specific purpose. They were the patterns emerging from the anarchic situation that ensued when all rules and clear authority structure had been abandoned. When no formal rules can be brought to bear on a situation, participants rely more heavily on the structures that have developed spontaneously in interaction. By examining a

The struggle for a definition of reality

number of consecutive sessions, the process of informal
patterned behaviour will become clearer.
   I shall take a particular Thursday, 11 March 1976. The date
was three months after the complaint, and the Area Health
Authority had recently announced its agreement that an inquiry
should be held.

Before the large-group session a new patient was talking to a
therapist:

New patient: We've [the patients] had two meetings and
people seem quite interested, so I'm going to get someone
from [a private clinic] to do an encounter group.

Being new, this patient was unsure of the rules and spoke to a
staff member outside the formal therapy session in order to a
certain staff reaction. He may also have been hoping to get
informal advice. He had not yet learnt that patients never
approached staff directly; neither was he aware of the more
overt prescription against small groups of any kind that might
interfere with the workings of the all-important large group. The
therapist he wished to introduce to the day hospital belonged to
a private centre practising Gestalt therapy.

Therapist: Perhaps you should bring it up in the large group.
New patient: I don't really want to. I'm kind of afraid in front
of all those people, if you know what I mean?

Keeping to the implicit rule of not giving a direct response to
appeals for advice, the therapist refers the patient back to the
large group. He does not wish to be thought to approve of
something he knows will be seen as an intervention and might
be interpreted as an 'acting out of the patient's unresolved
feelings'. He is also teaching the patient that individual unilateral action is not encouraged, since the group always takes
priority over the individual.
   During the large-group session later that morning there was
a phone call from the encounter therapist. The new patient
answered it and returned to the large group, where he explained

163

what he had arranged. He asked if this was acceptable, and mentioned the patients' demand for it.

Medical director: Anyone can come and use the place any way he chooses.

This was in keeping with the rule-less nature of the day hospital, which appeared very liberal and democratic. After the large-group meeting, however, the following exchange occurred:

New therapist: I can't understand Adrian. His answer to the patients wanting the encounter group seems odd as he has always said that small groups split the transference of the large group. Freedom is the main problem here, as far as I can see. Leaving it wide open as it is just seems to lead to confusion.

The new staff member had hit on a basic conflict in the approach. On the one hand there was support for the idea of 'democracy', which here meant that people could govern themselves and do what they liked; while on the other, without making any overt rules, the medical director always vetoed any extraneous group activities by inferring that they interfered with the therapy.

The next day, in the large-group session:

Therapist B: I think the patients are wondering if the staff are all going to go off and have sex together over the weekend.

It was a Friday, and it was assumed that in the transference relationship patients are overly interested in the activities of their staff/parents, especially at the weekend when they are excluded from contact with them. The assumption was that this temporary separation stirred up feelings of sexual jealousy, as in the classic Oedipus or Electra complexes.

Patient 2: [activist]: All the staff seem to be interested in is sex. They're obsessed with it.

The struggle for a definition of reality

Patient 3 [activist]: Well, I'm certainly not going to play silly 'cuckoo' games with them.

As mentioned already, at this time just before the first inquiry many of the patients had reached the point where they simply rejected all interpretations, fearing that what they said would be invalidated by the staff who had recourse to the language of psychotherapy. The activists kept up the most solidly negative attitude. A frequent way of ridiculing the staff's interpretations was comparing them to the therapists in the book – later filmed – *One Flew Over the Cuckoo's Nest*.[6]

Therapist A: Of course not, not just before the weekend when the staff might play their own games together.
Patient 2 [activist]: Putting all these things about sex on to us is pretty degrading, and I wish you'd all stop it.
Patient 9 [social club]: I'm sick of all this. This place is no good. I'm going to put a big fat bomb under it.[7]
Therapist C: The patients' worrying about the weekend seems to be getting worse as the inquiry gets closer. Maybe on Monday they'll find the inquiry in full swing and no staff in the clinic.

She is here making explicit what she imagines to be the under-lying phantasy of the patients' 'separation anxiety'.

Meanwhile the encounter-group therapist had arrived upstairs and was shown into the staff room.

Encounter therapist: The administrator says it's okay if I do a group in the day hospital if the staff and patients are willing. As the patients seem keen, could I discuss it with the staff?

He is of course aware that the medical director is responsible for the patients and, since he has prescribing authority, would have the right to deny him access.

Therapist D [looking away]: Anything to do with the day hospital should be discussed in the day hospital.

For the reduction to psychopathology to be able to operate, all psychoanalytic interpretations had to be made in the setting of the day hospital. Outside this context the psychoanalytic language becomes meaningless or unacceptable. This particular staff member was within two months of rejecting the hospital's approach, but while he was still undecided he clung to the protective rules that had helped him so far.

Encounter therapist: Okay, would you be willing to do so now?
Therapist D [rustling in his briefcase]: I'm busy, I'm afraid.

Staff members B and C say they will discuss it with him downstairs. They all three leave together. Fearing he might not have support for his action, therapist D has avoided taking responsibility. However, he joined the other staff within a few moments.

The subsequent discussion in the large group is mainly between staff and patients. The encounter therapist (W) is not asked any questions. The patients, having talked with him, know what to expect and the staff seem interested only in the rights and wrongs of letting him practise in an NHS institution when he is not an NHS employee:

Therapist H: I can't accept W as a staff member because he hasn't been invited to join our team.
Patient 3 [activist]: That's not the point. Do you mean you don't want him and just want to stop him coming?

[Therapist H averts his eyes. A long silence ensues – an example of the non-response syndrome.]

Patient 2 [activist]: Who's this place for? We're free to do what we want, aren't we?

[Therapist H remains silent and looks at the floor, employing the blank-screen role.]

Therapist G: If the patients have paid him, we could be

The struggle for a definition of reality

contravening the NHS ruling that doesn't allow NHS
buildings to be used for private purposes.
Therapist I: Although if he's a patient he can do as he likes.

They were divided between their own rules and those of the
NHS. If they were to define the encounter therapist as a patient,
then – according to the prevailing day hospital approach – he
would be free to do anything he wished, legitimized by the
medical director's professional autonomy over all matters falling
within his clinical area, as defined by him. Since this prerogative
applied only to the medical director's patients, the staff felt they
must not blatantly flout NHS principles. Also, since they took
their treatment directives from the medical director, they knew
they were expected to go along with his approach and not dilute
the transference by allowing splinter groups. No such formal
expectations extended to the patients, but they knew as well as
the staff that small-group activities were disapproved of. There
can be no doubt that they were fully aware of the significance
of their desire for an encounter group, and it was during this
particular period that they showed their most pronounced opposition to the day hospital approach through deliberate patient-
group organization.

Patient 3 [activist]: We've had two patient meetings about it
already. I really feel it's unnecessary to go on discussing this
over and over again.
New patient: Yes. If the patients want W, then it's okay. Let's
go to the library now, all of us who want him, and we'll wait
for him there.

Patients 1 and 3 get up to leave, but nobody seems about to
leave with them. Having organized themselves for the
complaint, some of the patients still felt militant and did not
mind organizing active opposition to the experimental approach.
But not all of them felt so confident. The new patient, who had
not yet learnt the rules, was probably unaware of how far he
was challenging the approach.

Encounter therapist: I'm sorry, I'm not happy with that. I want it formalized. I have the administrator's and the patients' permission, but I still need the agreement of the staff here. In any case, the administrative agreement was formally conditional on that of the staff, and I think some of the patients here feel they need the approval of the staff though they talk and act as if they don't. In any case, I want it to be formally correct. Can I please have an answer from the staff?

This was followed by silence, with nobody looking at him. Again the staff were avoiding a direct answer by adopting the stereotyped, non-responsive role. The encounter therapist knew that to protect himself he must go along with NHS rules which say that the consultant alone has the right to dictate treatment. He was insisting on being formally correct, even though he knew the hospital had jettisoned formal rules, but was met with the silent, lack-of-eye-contact syndrome. In terms of both verbal and nonverbal response, his question appeared not to have been asked. Indirectly, he was being told not to put direct questions.

Patient 4 [social club]: The consultant [absent] is the only person able to make decisions about who can be admitted.
Encounter therapist [looking at therapist D]: Is it okay? [Silence, and D looks away still.] I'm sorry – I only want to know if it's okay. [Silence.]
Therapist D [finally]: Am I the medical director's deputy? [Peals of laughter from the patient.]
Therapist G [smiling at therapist E]: We can't have more than one Big Daddy.

In collusive interaction, these two staff members (G and E) were indirectly telling D that they thought he was trying to compete with the medical director, and were getting some amusement out of their shared joke while at the same time diverting attention from the immediate issue of the encounter therapist. Uncharacteristically, D could not maintain the silent defence of the blank-screen role when challenged twice, perhaps because the questioner was an outsider unversed in the rules of the game. But he did avoid showing his personal

168

The struggle for a definition of reality

attitude by referring to the medical director, opting for calling on NHS rules of seniority in decision-making although he knew that the hospital ignored these rules, but still feeling unsure how far the democratic rights of the members really went.

Patient 5 [old experienced patient, reciting in a mechanical singsong way, as if he had learnt it off by heart]: Everything in the day hospital is a clinical matter and it therefore is the responsibility of the consultant in charge. But he has delegated authority to each member of staff and all patients equally, therefore we are all responsible as individuals and must take on this responsibility and decide.

He was parroting the consultant's declared position, as he always did whenever a patient expressed any doubt. Patient 5 often assumed a staff role. An activist and one of the longest-standing patients, he had learnt over the years to imitate the staff by making interpretations. This often made him very unpopular with the other patients in group sessions, who would charge him with having gone over to the 'other side'.

Therapist D: Isn't that the trouble? If we're all equally responsible, who'll put a stop to anything that happens here – such as therapists going off together in pairs, or patients' phantasies about what staff do together during lunchtime? Will other staff, the consultant, the encounter therapist, or an investigating team stop these things?

Focusing on the unconscious level, D was here saying that the patients were afraid of the lack of rules because it meant they could not stop staff from getting together. He may have been suggesting that the internal need for control had pushed the patients into asking for an inquiry.

Patient 2 [activist]: I'm not sure what is right.
Patient 6 [activist]: Look, while we're sitting here discussing this we're missing our small group. I'm upset that it's being messed up like this. I'll only accept the encounter group idea

169

if it's after small-group time. [At this point some small groups still existed.]

There was a general murmur of patients agreeing with this. They were aware that small groups were disapproved of, but there was still sufficient patient support to make them viable. However, a further splitting-off from the large group, especially when it lacked widespread support (and had no definite staff support) seemed rather more risky and worth exchanging for the known benefits derived from the small-group therapy.

Patient 7 [activist]: I don't agree with anything that splits off from the large group and the day hospital way of working, so I'm against the idea.

He was playing the role of therapist and mouthing the medical director's ideology. General angry murmurs from the patients answer him.

Patient 3 [activist]: How can you say that when you don't know what an encounter group is anyway?
Encounter therapist: To settle this – who *is* in charge?
Therapist E: That's the thousand-and-one dollar question. We'll be having an official inquiry shortly into precisely that.
Encounter therapist: As everything seems so confused, I think it would be better if the patients wrote to me at [his organization], and then we can perhaps arrange something separate in another place.
Patient 8 [isolate]: What a waste of rooms. There are lots of them here, standing empty. It's okay with me if the majority of patients want the encounter group.

[The encounter therapist leaves, and the group disperses rather quickly.]

The visiting therapist had been treated in a way that accorded with the attitude that interference of outsiders could only spoil the current large-group therapy. Instead of discussing the matter openly with him outside the day hospital, where the stereotyped non-responsive therapist role would have been out of place and regarded as ill-mannered, the staff had insisted on directing him to the large group, where such behaviour was accepted as a normal part of the therapeutic process. In this way it was the staff who chose the context and therefore defined the meaning of the exchange. Individual responsibility was avoided, and the decision left to the patients and their visitor. The staff's very silence and lack of commitment acted as a form of pressure on the other participants. The matter became one where the patients wanted to break the implicit rule that the large group was the only legitimate therapeutic vehicle, and the staff could not overtly prevent them. No one was interested in the practical content of the problem – exactly what kind of group the visitor was proposing, how it would relate to their own therapy, and how people felt about trying a new kind of therapy. The question became one of the relative power of the two groups involved.

The patients' attitude in the matter was partly meant to show a dissatisfaction with the therapy they were receiving in the day hospital. It demonstrated that they were able to get some other therapy, one which they had chosen, a therapy that would not only be fixed in time and space but arranged by themselves. The staff, on the other hand, were concerned with whether the patients were 'acting out' and trying to avoid relating to staff. Despite the talking action was paralysed in the end, and I wondered how far the two groups were being constrained by fear of acting without the approval of the medical director, whose position in the matter remained ambiguous and who was not present at the discussion.

At the large-group session on the following Tuesday the matter was referred to again. The day before, the large group had been well attended by patients but there were few staff members. At the Tuesday session the ratio was reversed, and only ten patients came to the hospital in the course of the whole day.

Patient 5 [activist]: The reason there are no patients here is because of last Friday. They're showing their disgust at the way the staff behaved over W [the encounter therapist]. Let's

171

begin again, with just Adrian and the patients. Let's get rid
of the staff because they interfere with Adrian's idea of
delegating responsibility equally to all members. The staff
didn't exactly stop the encounter group, but they produced
such a lot of confusion that W just gave up.

Staff always put things in the way when patients try to do
things for themselves, to help and understand themselves.
I'm not going to be told by others what I want. If we had had
just W and the patients, there wouldn't have been any of this
confusion.

New therapist Z: But some patients left the room when the
group was still talking with W.

Patient 5 [activist]: They were just showing their disgust at
the discussion and acting on what they wanted. If Adrian will
sort out his staff, then we can begin again.

Patient 9 [social club]: I'm fed up with my wife. [He is
referring to his actual private life outside the hospital.] I don't
see why I shouldn't have custody of the children.

Patient 5 [activist]: Same here. Let's end the marriage
between the staff and keep just Adrian.

Having become adept at manipulating interpretations, patient
5 here entered the esoteric syndrome by using psychoanalytic
language based on the previous speaker's remark to communicate something on a different level.

Therapist E: Whose penis is patient 5 trying to make use of –
Adrian's or W's?

Patient 5 [activist]: My own. Why shouldn't I be allowed my
own desire for growth? I want an ideal penis and erection.

Here the activist is acting like one of Sharp's conformists and
'colonizing'.

Therapist E [to patient 5]: You want to keep Mummy all to
yourselves and Adrian, then he can't have intercourse with
the other staff.

Therapist G: For when he does that he forgets all about
everyone else.

The struggle for a definition of reality

Therapist Z [exchanging an amused grin with G]: He certainly wouldn't be thinking about the patients, anyway.
Therapist G [returning the glance and smiling at the patients generally]: Much better to keep him with you, then you can see what he's doing and make sure he doesn't do anything that would make you feel ignored.

The inference, once again, was that infants/patients in the transference state accompanying therapy wish to control the actions of the staff/parents in order to prevent the phantasized intercourse that leaves them feeling jealous, ignored and lonely. Being a party to the esoteric syndrome, patient 5 was actually rather unlikely to feel excluded; but other patients, newer to therapy, were less likely to understand these tacit references and assumptions, and their exclusion was liable to have been compounded by the nonverbal communication of significant glances and smiles.

Patient 5 [activist]: I'm disgusted with the behaviour of the staff today.
Patient 9 [social club]: Therapy is inhuman. If I say 'Hello' they don't even answer. Talk about identity! I think the staff go all blank because they are unsure of their own identity.

This·was one of the few direct references to the staff's silent non-response tactic.

[Walking up and down]: And I'm sick of my wife. I'll tell her I can't take her attitude.
Therapist E: Patient 9 is very angry.
Patient 9 [social club]: I could do her, I could. I don't see why she should have the children. Why can't I have them?
Therapist E: What about the chil . . . ?
Patient 9 [interrupting]: Why can't I have them? I'm just as good as her. What's wrong with me? I'm sick of it all – sick of it all. Why can't . . . ?
Therapist E [breaking in]: What about the child that's inside you?
Patient 9 [interrupting again]: I don't see why. Why don't you

173

shut up? I warned you the other day that I'd put a bomb under . . .

Therapist E: Patient 9 wants us to know how angry he feels, but also that he needs looking after. And actually, even though he feels very angry, he isn't as angry as all that since he didn't really bomb the place.

[Patient 9, finding himself out-talked by the therapist, walks out of the session.]

Patient 5 [activist, also walking out of the room]: Well, I've said all I want to.

Two patients enter, look around the room, and laugh. One says: 'Just look at that! Ten staff, with only two patients left.' They go out again, and within a few minutes the room empties.

Conclusion: the phenomenology of power

Although the sessions described above were not altogether typical of large-group sessions, they are useful in that they illustrate some of the group processes and strategies described earlier. When the day hospital members had to try to solve a particular problem – in this case whether to accept the encounter therapist – large-group sessions were rather more focused than at other times. Usually the discussion topic would be much more dissipated. Any issue would be reduced to its meaning in unconscious terms and rarely taken up again in later sessions.

To some extent the same process was at work in these sessions too, but here the issue revolved around a person who was not a member of the day hospital, who wanted a response to his request to practise in the hospital, and who was not reducible to anyone's unconscious. Even if the patients' request for his services could be explained psychoanalytically, the fact remained that, confronting the staff directly, he needed a commitment one way or another. As the encounter therapist was an outsider and not therefore part of, or involved in, the hospital ideology and practice he was not willing to drop the matter and did not see why the staff kept avoiding a clear answer about who was in charge. In the end he backed away from the confusion, preferring to deal with the patients separately and outside the organization.

By tracing through these sessions and indicating the group membership and strategies of the speakers, I hope to have shown that there is more meaning in everyday conversations than the words themselves express. By taking as problematical what others take for granted, I have attempted to unearth the implicit rules that provide the routine grounds of everyday activity.

It may be asked whether I am justified in presenting either the staff or the patient groupings in the day hospital as typical. I do believe this is legitimate because, as Schutz (1962) notes, 'Everyman' orientates himself in terms of typical facts, events and experiences. A detached observer trying to discern the meaning behind a transaction between actors will always relate it to other, similar transactions in a typically similar situation, and then construct the participants' motives from the limited and fragmentary section of their action he has observed. The resultant interpretation will not, of course, be the same as an actor's own, because the observer's interest and objective are different from his, hence also the meaning constructed from watching the event.

Rather than limit myself simply to describing the numerous possible subjective meanings of other actors' motives, I have attempted to interpret by means of common-sense typical constructs. This perspective gives greater meaning to everyday verbal exchanges than can be expressed in words, because all conversations presuppose that the participants share a mutually meaningful context. In order to get at implicit rules, at the 'routine grounds' of everyday activity, it is necessary to treat as problematic what is generally taken for granted.

In this chapter, as in Chapter 5, the focus has shifted from the roles of day hospital members in terms of formal and informal obligations and expectations to an outline of their attempts at shaping and reshaping their world. The method of 'feeling inside the actor's experience' (Mouzelis, 1967) replaces a more conventional approach that assumes a rather passive stimulus/response image of human behaviour. In general terms, the perspective emphasized here implies a concern with meaning and process rather than with a completed act or finished cultural product. As Punch argues:

What people appear to be doing may not be the most significant thing to them at that moment. Behind the public façade lies a private reality, and to reach that other reality one has to peel away the layers, the masks or the public fronts that protect people from scrutiny.

(1974, p. 38)

I have tried to go beyond the formal and informal rules of accountability to give an idea of how the game in the day hospital was actually played, how actors responded to the situation, and the kind of groupings they made according to their individual mode of adaptation. The more conventional approach sees institutions and their goals, rules and norms as out there and given and as controlling the individual, who is portrayed as a puppet. From that point of view a patient in the day hospital was, for example, constrained to act 'sick' and had no choice of how to react to the situation.

It is precisely this rule-bound basis of everyday life that I have treated as problematic, for social reality is socially constructed, socially sustained, and socially changed by actors who themselves act *on* the social world. This perspective allows the actor a greater degree of autonomy. For example, despite overt and covert controls (which have their parallels in thought reform), patients have a certain degree of manoeuvrability. Given certain social and psychological constraints, they can still choose whether to 'act mad' or which subgroup to identify with. Psychological and social forces set limits on behaviour but they do not determine it, and some phenomenological space, however small, is left for actors to make decisions. As Goffman (1959) has observed, definitions of reality are 'the accomplishment of actors engaged in a cooperative task'. A rule or goal does not just happen but is part of a process of men working and acting together. I am not suggesting that organizational crisis and/or change are simply aspects of a communication problem. If there is conflict, it arises out of competing interests and definitions of the situation.

The struggle for a definition of reality

Despite the totalizing tendencies of the ideology, the day hospital patients did have a limited choice of *whether* to accept the staff's reductionist view that encompassed all things, material and spiritual, or to accept what was useful about these interpretations when they were relevant, *or* to reject explanations in terms of the unconscious altogether. I have tried to show how different patients reacted differently to the psychoanalytic pressures and the assault on their identities experienced in the hospital.

I have also examined how, although structural features such as hierarchy and its derivations of rules, roles and norms do impinge on individual perception, actors also contribute to the maintenance and creation of the social world – which they may oppose, attempt to change, or accept according to their own interests. Exactly how constraining these social structures are is dependent on the actors' interpretations of the situation.

Goffman (1968) sees the attempt by the patient to protect his self-hood as 'not an incidental mechanism of defence, but rather an essential constituent of the self'. The actor can shape his world even in a total institution:

We always find the individual employing methods to keep some distance, some elbow room, between himself and that with which others assume he should be identified.
(Goffman, 1961, p. 279)

Although he later takes a more socially deterministic view, in *Asylums* Goffman emphasizes that in all social situations there remains the possibility of the phenomenological space where an individual can exercise choice. He is a stance-taking entity who is not simply driven by external forces. In the day hospital, although the patients were under pressure to assume the role of the 'sick patient', there were some who managed to resist this despite interpretations that this was yet further evidence of precisely their sickness. It was not simply a matter of their passively turning from one role to another, from sick patient to rebel, it was rather that they actively and spontaneously created an alternative 'political' group to combat the attack on their identity and to create an environment for self-expression.

177

In the same way the inmates of Goffman's asylums are seen to be actively creating secondary adjustments and finding 'free places' to meet their own needs, whatever the aims of the organization; but later, in his essay on 'Role distance' he has lost this insight and man is enslaved by a multiplicity of roles:

Various identificatory demands are not created by the individual but are drawn from society which allots them to him. He frees himself from one group, not to be free, but because there is another hold on him.

(1961, p. 280)

In this view the individual can no longer resist roles: he can only turn from one set of roles to another; there is no area where social forces do not constrain him. Now there is no doubt that in a total environment or ideology limits are set to the individual's freedom to manoeuvre, but within those limits he can exercise some degree of choice and ignore the dictates of the external social world.

To emphasize this room for creative self-expression, I have described the behaviour of some rough groupings of patients in the day hospital. The behaviour exhibited in each category arose out of their particular definition of the situation – for example the day hospital as a social milieu – and I have compared these groupings with the resident subgroups and strategies described by Sharp (1975).

By following a series of sessions, I hope to have demonstrated how the syndromes described in Chapter 5 not only represent mechanisms of control but were part of an organic process. They were not just specific techniques adopted for the purpose of social control, they were valued for themselves as part of daily spontaneous – if patterned – interaction. Their prime motivation was the strong need for protection against the vulnerability experienced in the group session. Given the usual fear in therapy groups of, for example, violence and verbal personal attacks – and, as I have shown, the degradation of having one's every statement reduced to a psychopathological symptom – this need for defensive behaviour applied to patients and staff alike.

178

The struggle for a definition of reality

I hope to have indicated how spontaneously created patterns of interaction can eventually be experienced by the actors (the creators) as outside them and influencing their behaviour in the same way that formal rules bind or structure action. The staff did not set out to control the patients through their in-group communication games, but under pressure in the crisis these processes stopped being games in and of themselves and became instead control mechanisms. Likewise the perspectives of group interaction amongst the patients, having been modes of adaptation to therapy, became during the crisis ends in themselves, and a new anti-psychoanalytic perspective developed to counteract the control they experienced through reductive psychological explanations.

PART
3

THE PROCESS OF
CRISIS

7

The crisis

This chapter will describe what has been called the crisis in the day hospital, focusing mainly on the year 1976. It will give a chronological outline of the events already referred to in earlier chapters (see Appendix for a brief chronology). Rather than interpreting these events, however, I shall provide a purely factual account and leave it to the final chapter to relate the events recounted to some of the ideas mentioned earlier.

Gradual and undirected as the change in therapy was, as a result of the introduction of the experiment by 1975 a quite marked position had been reached where all administrative and concrete factors were defined as of clinical interest alone. For instance, staff no longer signed medical certificates although the patients' need of social security payments was very real.

When I queried this decision in the staffroom, some members replied that they felt that if they signed such certificates this would constitute an ignominious label for the patients by putting them into a static category that emphasized illness rather than a move towards health. One staff member put the problem this way: 'The doctors who have to sign forms for patients who want sick pay feel that this may undermine the patient further by encouraging his negative and sick side rather than the healthy part of him. It's better to let the administration or general practitioners do it.'

By the end of 1975 the 'total therapy' of the day hospital had not only come to encompass all aspects of the patients' lives, but was also beginning to include elements of the NHS structure. It was the implication of this challenge to the NHS, following endless arguments about the meaning of administrative issues, that culminated in a letter from the staff to the patients: 'by

183

majority decision' the staff had decided that there should be no more meals or fare restitution from a date set one week later. This happened on a Friday, a day which the staff later agreed was an unfortunate moment to communicate such a statement because patients experience 'separation anxiety' especially strongly at the weekend. In psychoanalytic terms they are presumed to feel anxiety at being left alone, mixed with angry envy for the idealized staff who, it is sometimes phantasized, will go off (like the child's parents) to have sexual intercourse and forget all about them. This anger is said to be so painful that the patients refuse to countenance it and project it onto the staff/patients instead who, they fear, may retaliate and punish the patients/children. It was suggested at the hospital that this separation anxiety was part of the reason for the patients' strong reaction to their letter. At the same time the staff were aware that 'no day could be a good day for learning of such a decision'.

The patients' complaint

The reaction of one of the patients to this staff move was: 'Taking meals away from people who have nothing is an act of violence. The staff are all screws.[1] After the bread-and-water diet comes the physical violence.' Within a few days (on 11 January 1976) the patients, led by the activists, had responded with a strongly worded and articulate letter of complaint about conditions and treatment in the day hospital. It was signed 'The Day Patients' and sent to the Area Administrator, with a copy to the Minister for Health and Social Services and another copy to the chairman of the Professional Staff Committee (PSC) of the institute. This letter contained a list of items which the patients regarded as facilities they had been led to expect when they were first admitted. These included availability of staff from 9 a.m. to 5 p.m., small- and large-group therapy, medical certificates, occupational therapy, cleaning staff, lunch, fares, table tennis and tea. They criticized the withdrawal of these facilities, in particular the unavailability of staff and the small amount and choice of therapy being offered. With respect to cleaning (there had been no cleaner for six months by this time), the patients noted that though they could clean for themselves, a 'subtle

184

means of control' had been used to prevent them. The medical director was quoted as saying that if a patient could clean up after them all, he needed no medical certificate.

The patients' letter also expressed doubt whether any treatment was taking place at all. In any case, many felt that 'they could not present themselves in the therapeutic arena' because of the collusive, jocose mode in which psychoanalytic interpretations were delivered (see Chapter 5) and said that their problems 'were so often met with derision and jokes'. They alleged that as a result of this situation many had 'left, withdrawn or overdosed'. They refused to be ridiculed or used as 'guinea pigs in some bizarre experiment'. They also argued that meals and fares were an administrative matter and not something with which clinical staff should concern themselves. They wanted improved conditions in terms of therapy and environment and emphasized that as the NHS financed the day hospital it should be aware of the falseness of the claim that the hospital was open for therapeutic treatment. This was not the case. They were asking, in other words, for the reinstatement of their rights, that rules be followed, that the day be structured, that staff do their jobs and that the day hospital be run as required by the NHS.

In fact the patients were invoking the very NHS rules that the day hospital had spurned. Not only did they want the formal structures reinstated, they were also asking more senior NHS staff to apply them so as to control the staff.

Now that senior administrators had been informed through the patients' complaint of these possible breaches of NHS regulations, it would mean neglecting their own responsibilities if they were to ignore the matter. So far, the power structure had remained hidden and control had been a conjunction of informal assumptions and expectations, but now the patients' action had put the whole problem on a formal level where the medical director could no longer cold-shoulder criticism and fail to answer requests and statements. Similarly the staff had to face more directly their conflicting attitudes to the experiment. In fact, by formalizing their complaints the patients had raised the problem of the managerial control of professionally autonomous doctors and their staff. The latter were caught in the classical dilemma of dual accountability to their consultants and to the managers of their own discipline. The Area Health Authority (as the medical director's employer) had no managerial control over him other than the ultimate sanction of dismissal, bu senior nursing and occupational therapy staff could place legitimate pressure on their subordinates, even though this would conflict with the medical director's managerial prescriptions. (See Chapter 4 for a discussion of dual accountability.)

The patients' firm and strong response to the staff's unilateral decision may seem a surprisingly coordinated action in view of the more usual lack of cohesion in patient groups. It certainly surprised the day hospital staff. However, although psychoanalytic interpretation is designed to produce an individual response, we have seen in Chapter 6 how the patients had already spontaneously created informal groupings, and it was these (led by the activists) that provided the base for their concerted action. Having been somewhat vague in form and membership, the activists as a body now had a definite aim: to enhance group cohesion and encourage the support of others especially social-club and gangster-group members.

During the period when psychotherapeutic activity had seemed rather unclear in its objectives the feeling of being controlled had been no more than a suspicion, although while they were concealed the rules of behaviour were all the more powerful. However, once the staff had acted in an openly authoritarian manner, by unilaterally deciding to discontinue meals without even a pretence of consulting the patients, the latter as a whole could at last identify staff behaviour as authoritarian and controlling. The ideological tenet that they were free to participate in decision-making and could criticize the views of others now stood revealed as a myth.

It must be pointed out that the medical director himself had been ignorant of the decision over meals since, working on a part-time basis, he was not present when his staff arrived at it; subsequently he neither condoned nor condemned it. In fact it is unlikely that he would have become involved in writing to the patients on such a matter; he relied on more hidden controls. Still, once the patients' complaint had been submitted and the issue became public and formal, he did defend his staff's action and carefully justified himself in written statements.

Professional judgement and clinical freedom

In response to an official letter asking for an explanation, the medical director as consultant in charge of the day hospital explained his position to the district administrator (16 January 1976). He saw the day hospital's 'primary task' as that of psychotherapy and considered that all activities taking place inside its boundaries should be seen as part of this process. For him, this was a matter for clinicians alone in that it represented a derivative of pathology. He thought that the matter *could* be discussed by outsiders, but never fully understood by those not experiencing the whole day-to-day situation. However, he was prepared to discuss the complaint if the patients would identify themselves, if they persisted in their complaint, and if this would further the aims of therapy.

The medical director's explanation therefore rested heavily on the consultant's right to clinical autonomy. In the British NHS it has been a tradition that in such critical matters as health care each person is entitled to his own named doctor, who is not managed by anyone – that is, the patient can negotiate directly with the person who makes important decisions on his behalf. In order to maintain this right, the doctor's autonomy over his clinical decisions is limited only by law and certain professional standards. Within these limits the consultant must treat his patient as he himself thinks best. The medical director rested his case on the contention that the treatment and assessment of his patients (including their making formal complaints) was a clinical matter subject to judgement based on the wealth of his professional experience. By calling on his professional autonomy he denied any legitimacy to the queries of either administrators or patients, none of whom was endowed with such knowledge or experience.

Having rejected the NHS bureaucratic rules in the running of his community, the medical director now relied on the NHS regulation that gave him the right to clinical autonomy. He was stating what *he* considered to be his clinical arena and threw

187

out a particularly large net that covered 'all activities happening inside the boundaries of the day hospital'.

This was possible because medical autonomy not only excludes external managerial control but also permits the practitioner himself to define that very area of autonomy.

His letter stated that in his clinical opinion the activities at the day hospital were all derived from pathology and made no reference to the points in the patients' complaint likely to alarm the administration most: that the staff were not available all day; that cleaning services and meals as well as occupational therapy were not provided and, in particular, that their problems were 'met with derision and jokes'. On the contrary, his letter seemed almost designed to provoke still more apprehension. He seemed to be saying: you can discuss these matters if you insist but (a) you do not have the professional right to interfere, as it is a matter for clinicians alone (that is, medical practitioners have professional autonomy); and (b) these things can be understood only in their full context, of which you are not part (that is, he was indirectly asserting the primacy of the large group and calling on an experiential ideology whereby he excluded from comprehension all and everyone who did not daily participate in the day hospital). He was making it extremely clear that the position of senior administrators and outsiders was very weak. Still, as he was running a democratic enterprise, he would discuss the matter if his patients insisted, 'and if this would further the aims of therapy'. This was another way of saying that in accordance with his version of democracy he was prepared to raise the issue in the large group where everything was defined in psychopathological terms – and that he would not just acquiesce or 'collude' with the patients, even if they insisted, but would make a 'clinical' decision about how helpful such a discussion would be therapeutically.

It is not clear quite what he meant by this. Given the medical director's general approach, it would seem that if the patients persisted with their complaint, such 'therapeutic usefulness' might be reckoned in how far their individual criticisms could be explained in psychopathological terms. In the large group, this was in fact the interpretation he made. He said it was rather like the situation of children seeing adults coping with life and,

The crisis

feeling frustrated at the long and tedious process of growing up, finding it far more exciting to pretend to be adult and bypass those immediately present. Although the people in the day hospital were able to help them learn, the patients turned to a more senior/remote and impersonal authority. The staff on the whole accepted this reduction to internal reasons. It was suggested, for example, that the patients' action had been a way to 'avoid a confrontation'. One member of staff told the patients they had obviously thought it 'better to find a third party to act as mediator, for then you won't have to consider internal motives'. Another line was to see the letter of complaint as a challenge to the potency of the consultant's interpretations. But despite all efforts by the staff to discover who exactly had written the complaint, the patients refused to give out information.

At the district administrator's request, the chairman of the PSC included the patients' complaint on the agenda of its next meeting. Three days later the medical director argued in a letter that since psychotherapy was the primary task, and to 'avoid colluding with anonymous blackmail', the discussion should be held with the patients concerned present, preferably on the day hospital premises. Unless these conditions were met he would be unable to discuss the letter, although he was quite willing to discuss any 'individual issues' about the day hospital. In effect he was refusing to discuss the matter head on but concealed this by accepting a discussion of details, while insisting that the main issue was a clinical matter which fell entirely into his all-embracing conception of psychotherapy.

By tacitly re-defining the problem in terms of the primary task of psychotherapy, the medical director defined the situation as one in which other personnel could not intrude: in clinical questions (as defined by himself) he, as medical director, had an undeniable right to professional autonomy and could justifiably shake off outside intervention. In addition – and in keeping with his ideology that all matters relating to the day hospital must be considered in the large group – his attempt to re-locate the discussion in the day hospital environment meant giving it a context where his definition of the situation would be more readily accepted and, being on home ground, he would be at a psychological advantage. He may also have suspected that

189

within their treatment setting the patients might find it more difficult to maintain a political stance (a position adopted on the basis of values and choice) and would more readily succumb to a psychoanalytic explanation of their complaint.

However, the PSC chairman was not prepared to comply with the medical director's wishes. His reply (on 19 January 1976) – without stating that he refused to enter the medical director's territory, and without formally acknowledging the latter's right to professional autonomy – pointed out the inappropriateness of the PSC discussing the day hospital's psychotherapy, even though this was the subject of the patients' complaint. If this matter was not to be discussed, then it was also inappropriate for the patients to attend. In conclusion he asked once more that the medical director should come to the meeting, because it concerned 'the relationship of the Professional Staff Committee as a whole with the day hospital'. He 'welcomed' the medical director's offer to discuss individual issues, and felt that the possibility of a later discussion of the day hospital's psychotherapy in the patients' presence could be raised at the meeting on 21 January.

The Professional Staff Committee

In the meantime the patients had written asking to attend this PSC meeting (letter of 16 January 1976), as they had been told that decisions affecting them were to be made there. The letter was bitter in tone, mentioning a 'day hospital policy to progressively deprive the day patients' and how it had become 'normal practice' for the medical director and his staff to make decisions affecting the day patients without any prior consultation or agreement with them. In other words, they were adding to their complaint the charge of authoritarianism at the day hospital with lack of democratic participation and asking whether the PSC was in fact any better. There was also a defiant note: 'The practice [of leaving patients out of decision-making], we say, has got to be stopped.' In conclusion they warned: 'If our request is met with no response, as has been the normal practice, or you cannot agree to our representatives attending this meeting, we shall have to consider some alternative form of action.'

The PSC chairman's reply three days later tried to be concili-
atory while still refusing the patients' request to be present at
the PSC meeting. He explained that because the PSC would
have to reply to the district administrator's request for
comments on the issue, the meeting would have to be properly
constituted – that is, without visitors – but said he would put
the request to the PSC and be pleased to sponsor it, 'as the
Professional Staff Committee's main task is to look after the
welfare of the patients'. He also assured them that they need
not worry that major decisions about the day hospital would be
made without them, and expressed surprise that they had not
been party to previous decisions, as 'we have always been
informed that the day hospital is run as a therapeutic community
in which the patients participate in every aspect of decisions
concerning the treatment of patients and the running of the day
hospital'. In this way the PSC chairman appeared to be trying
to give support to the patients and, without openly taking sides,
was indirectly querying the medical director's assertion that
there was genuine patient participation.

On 21 January nineteen patients (almost all regular attenders)
signed the reply to the PSC chairman. In it they accepted that
they would not be able to attend that day's PSC meeting, but
asked that another be arranged with 'our full representation as
soon as is conveniently possible', since in view of the seriousness
of the matter a PSC answer 'could only be made after a meeting
between the Professional Staff Committee and the patients in
the day hospital'.

In return, the PSC immediately arranged a meeting with
the day hospital patients or their representatives for the next
scheduled PSC meeting on 28 January.

The relationship between the day hospital and the institute

Five days later, at their first meeting after receiving the signed
letter of complaint, the PSC members confessed themselves
very worried about the bad reputation they thought the day
hospital had earned for itself, as evidenced by the lack of referrals from, for example, general practitioners.[2] They were most

emphatic that any such negative view by outside referral agents should not extend to the rest of the institute, and felt they had to dissociate themselves from the day hospital. They were not, however, sure what rights they had to interfere with its running. In the end they decided that the PSC had the same basic functions as the medical committe which it had replaced and which had been required by the NHS to make sure that 'certain minimal standards of care are maintained' and 'to protect patients from disturbed members of staff'.

They kept coming back to comparing the present situation with that of a department of another hospital under a similar experiment, which had since been closed. A formal inquiry had concluded that 'the inexperienced staff' could not cope with the situation in a relatively unstructured crisis-intervention centre. They felt that if the complaint was, as some claimed, an 'acting out' by the patients, then this had come about because inexperienced staff had wrongly interpreted the ongoing conflicts inside the patient group, and that this had resulted in the unresolved feeling being converted into complaints. They agreed that it was fortunate that the possibility of violence had been averted and were astonished at the patients' saying they had not been allowed a voice in decision-making.

The members of the institute's other departments, therefore, did what they could to defend their own interests against possible repercussions. Lacking a constitution, the PSC had in fact no formal rights over its members; it existed only in an informal, advisory capacity. In its discussion, reported above, the PSC edged around the issue of clinical freedom, since deciding how far it could intervene in the consultant's clinical arena was particularly difficult when the latter defined the compass of his prerogatives so widely. The matter now became one of delineating in concrete terms exactly what limits should be ascribed to clinical freedom. By so doing the PSC was taking on a quasi-managerial role *vis-à-vis* the day hospital, perhaps as a consequence of the way in which the medical director had attempted to replace the administrative area of authority with his own professionally autonomous authority.

The PSC decision to refuse the patients entry on this occasion seemed to contradict the democratic ideal held by the institute in general. But however vague its members might be in this issue, they seemed to act with a sense of purpose in their discussions with colleagues. It was this type of professional discussion that was lacking in the day hospital since, with staff meetings abandoned, it had become increasingly difficult for the staff to have such a level of discourse with their medical director. In a sense this meant a degree of freedom as well as privacy, since anything of importance said to the medical director in the staff common room would be fed back to the large group – and the staff member pulled back into line by an interpretation of his unconscious motives.

It is interesting that at this stage the PSC's professional psychotherapists were making their own psychoanalytic interpretations of the situation: 'unresolved feelings' had been 'converted into complaints', for instance. But at the same time they were taking the actual content of the complaint very seriously. When they manifested their astonishment at the way in which patients had been excluded from decision-making, they did not yet know that on the whole no decisions were made by the day hospital in any case; it was purely the consultant's policy and treatment programme which dictated how things would go. Whenever such 'decision-making' evoked discontent and disagreement among members, these signs of independence were promptly quelled by psychoanalytic interpretations. When members of the large group wanted to discuss the inquiry, for example, the medical director said: 'The patients are always wanting to bring in outsiders as third parties. This is a shame, as it prevents people from really expressing themselves and their phantasies of one-to-one therapy.' Another therapist contributed to the same theme with: 'If staff and patients started interacting, the inquiry mightn't like that at all.' To this the medical director replied, smilingly: 'It might even get rather messy.' He seemed to be suggesting in this esoteric way that the demand for an inquiry represented a defence against 'authentic' feelings and communication with therapists. The theory was that being in touch with these feelings, as shown in the interaction with therapists, is resented by that side of the individual which seeks to defend the self from exposure and likely hurt.

The role conflict of the staff

As mentioned already, the day hospital staff felt torn, in problems of accountability, between their allegiance to the medical
director and their interest in his work and their professional
consciences about the work for which they were originally
trained. The staff's ambivalence is demonstrated by the fact
that despite their dislike of this kind of conflict, they gave their
support to the medical director's statement that the PSC and
anyone else participating in an inquiry would have to realize
that the day hospital situation was understandable only in terms
of an 'ongoing day-to-day' process. They argued that only
confusion could ensue from explaining one small part of the
whole in isolation. They were again reinforcing the ideology
that helped to protect the day hospital from external control by
insisting that only personal participation could legitimate any
criticism of its methods. This implied that once such a critic
became part of the large group, he would be exposed to the
psychoanalytically reductive definition of the situation and any
criticism could thereby be ignored and denied intrinsic validity.
At the same time such a critic would no doubt be thoroughly
mystified by the staff's esoteric and collusive games (see Chapter
5) and, not suspecting the staff of attempting to control the
participants, might merely imagine himself not *au fait* with this
particular large-group culture.

The argument that outsiders could not understand what went
on in the day hospital was constantly reaffirmed during the
crisis. Although it implied an exclusiveness that worked as an
excellent defence against intrusion, it is probably true that the
staff believed their own personal daily knowledge of the situation could not be acquired by some transient outside investi-
gator. An exact explanation of just what comprised this superiority of knowledge was not forthcoming, but it seemed to be
something more than the usual familiarity with his surroundings
that anyone will obtain about the organization of which he is a
member. The implied exclusiveness appeared to indicate that
those involved had a particular way of seeing the situation that
could not be achieved without the necessary experience.

But there was also a certain reluctance on the part of the day hospital members to let outsiders see what they could see. In this respect it could be said that such characteristics of the hospital as its exclusiveness, theoretical perspective, control over knowledge and attitudes did form a close parallel to a religious sect with a seductive and charismatic leader as its motivating force (see Chapter 5 on ideological totalism). Thus deviation from seeing all things in terms of psychic reality was controlled by denying any value to deviant statements and actions through a totalist, psychoanalytic interpretative mechanism. In such a closed, self-confirming system, dissent implied sickness.

United in their support of the leader as they may have been in the public forum of the day hospital therapy sessions, some staff did dare to express dissent in the privacy of the staffroom with others who also did not mind questioning the 'party line'. They were not openly 'deviating' so much as saying what they thought. Moreover, as time passed after the complaint and it became clear that there would indeed be an inquiry, staff members realized they would have to rethink the situation. It is also true that their individual futures were at stake in no uncertain fashion.

In the following example, some three months after the complaint, a number of staff members reconsider admission groups, which had been abandoned two years previously as 'bureaucratic' and unhelpful.

Therapist A: We do need an admission group for those referred here. We should take the names and addresses of patients for when doctors ring up and ask if a particular person's been a patient here. It's okay not to bother with those who come with other patients, or with self-referrals who don't mind wandering around and fitting in. But I do think we should just explain to new patients what the situation is, how vague it is, how it doesn't suit everybody. Why don't we have one day a month when we see a group of potential new patients and include some patients in the group to explain things to them? But not like it was before, with staff and patients deciding whether to take them or not.
Therapist B: Yes, that would provide a little 'holding' for our

195

new patients, especially those who find its vagueness so frightening.

Therapist A: Yes. As it is, the situation is so frightening that only the real toughies who can just walk into any situation can stand it, and the result is a kind of selection which is partly due to the organization and partly self-selection. You end up with an elite group of tough nuts.

One form of active opposition to the experiment had been the maintenance of small-group therapy. Earlier in the year, before the complaint when all the staff were less sure of their position regarding the medical director's experiment, most of them were still conducting small groups, but gradually the pressure mounted to disband them. Being more intimate (with no more than eight to ten people attending) these groups were initially seen as an important part of the therapy, but as the experiment became more rigid they came under increasing criticism. At first they were accepted as long as important issues arising in a small group were reported back to the large group, but in time small-group therapy came to be regarded as an 'impermissible intervention'. In attempts to control this stepping out of line, the group leaders (each group had two co-therapists) were mocked for their 'secret' work – being asked, for example, 'What goes on behind those closed doors?' As a result the staff became unsure whether to conduct small-group therapy at all, as a discussion in the staffroom shows:

Therapist A: B and I have started an afternoon group. Adrian may think it's splitting, but the patients feel they talk there and not in the large group.

'Splitting' here means splitting the patients' transference to the large group. Alternatively the concept may have a number of meanings, from reflective self-awareness to a schizoid defence mechanism.

Therapist B: I don't care what Adrian thinks.
Therapist A: He says we can do what we want but, very subtly, he's controlling us.

The crisis

Therapist B: We'll just have to go ahead.
Therapist A: I think [a named patient] is right when he says Adrian's on a power trip.

As time passed, criticism of the small groups became more open. It was said in large-group sessions that people who continued to run small groups were 'working against the large-group therapy', since the large group became less effective if patients could avoid expressing themselves there by discussing in small groups instead. Some patients may also have come to mistrust their small-group therapists. Although they seemed to find it easier to be frank in the smaller group – and even though they partly accepted the rule that all information must be fed back to the large group – as they became more critical of the experiment they may have felt that the therapists were betraying their confidence by informing the large group.

Eventually all but one small group stopped functioning. The others just faded out. Being expressly against hierarchical authority the critics of small groups would not admit they were making a rule and actually banning small-group therapy. Neither did the therapists who dropped the small groups admit that they had been wrong in running them or that the day hospital was definitely better off without them; they seemed more concerned with justifying themselves than explaining in terms of a reasoned decision why their small group had stopped. It is quite likely that they wanted to neutralize the conflict they were feeling between finding this particular work professionally satisfying and therapeutically important and the disapproval meted out to them for deviating. So they said that there had not been sufficient demand for the small groups, and now there was not enough time.

The abandonment of the small groups made the question of the experiment's value even more urgent, because now it had become even more rigidly focused and less diverse. While the therapists were running small groups they were doing what they regarded as important and difficult work; they had to be reliable about the groups, were seen to be so by both other staff and patients, and the groups largely justified their employment in the hospital to themselves and others. On the other hand many of the staff felt constrained in the large group by the narrow limits of the new therapy and the control they were subjected to if they moved outside those limits. There were many large-group sessions with only four staff members present, or when the whole group spent a large part (if not all) the session in silence. At such times the therapists may well have wished their input had been greater.

(Interestingly, the one therapist who continued with her small group until long after the others had given up was the only one among the 'ambivalent' staff who finally decided to identify with the medical director's group. Whatever she might say in support of the experiment, however, the fact that she persisted with running her group against all opposition did imply some disagreement. Alternatively, the fact that she could continue small-group therapy may have seemed to her evidence of the 'freedom' of the approach, proof of democracy in action.)

One of the main dividing lines between staff was the full-time/part-time distinction. All the qualified psychiatrists and psychotherapists attended on a sessional basis, while the rest of the staff, nurses and occupational therapists (except one) worked full-time in the institute's adult department, devoting only a few hours to the day hospital. Generally, it was the part-time staff who were pioneers of the Ezriel approach, and it was often argued by the others that it was the full-time staff who had to cope with the day-to-day living situation; that this was perhaps a more important task, and that an interpretative stance was quite impossible to maintain through the whole of the eight-hour day. So for example in one large-group session (on 5 February 1976) a nurse said:

The doctors are here for only part of the day to make interpretations. Since you're not here all the time, you don't realize how important it is to 'hold' patients sometimes. It's us who put in the hard work, cope with emergencies and hold the patients, so you can have some patients to make interpretations to. And then you have the cheek to say only interpretations are possible.

The daily presence of staff untrained in psychotherapy was

therefore the backbone of the day hospital. For over half the working day they were free from the control of the analysts and therapists at the top end of the hierarchy of expertise and qualification. However, as noted already, many of these staff members were ambivalent about the experiment, though they rarely opposed it consistently. Yet notwithstanding their equivocal stance these staff members did create a certain ambience when left to themselves to work in small groups: one that was strikingly different from the morning group ritual. The atmosphere was more relaxed and patients felt able at times to say more directly how they were feeling. The large-group sessions were more like being on stage; the afternoons gave a behind-the-scenes feeling.

The medical director's response

The main element of disagreement between the PSC members from the day hospital and those from other departments of the institute remained the question of what aspects should be defined as administrative and what as clinical. Although this decision was crucial for determining the areas in which the PSC could involve itself, the issue remained unresolved. The day hospital's medical director maintained his original decision that everything that happened within the confines of his premises was clinical and so lay outside PSC jurisdiction; the PSC members for their part felt that, though they were free to voice disagreement about methods, they could not dictate what therapeutic techniques another department must employ. The PSC debates about the day hospital's 'primary task' and psychotherapy were very heated – perhaps because, no matter what particular school an analyst belongs to, his method will be very much his own in that it is related to his personal psychoanalysis and, as he tends to rely heavily on his own resources of intuition and imagination, any criticism may be felt as a personal attack.

After long discussions, the PSC finally decided to dissociate itself from the day hospital and agreed to invite the patients to its next meeting. On 21 January 1976 the chairman wrote to the district administrator informing him of these decisions. His letter reported that the PSC had rejected that part of the patients' complaint which referred to 'a gross abuse of a hospital', since this was a matter which 'does not concern any of the departments other than the day hospital'. The PSC had apparently been afraid that the criticisms might be read as referring to the institute as a whole, and although the patients' wording made it quite clear that this was not the case the PSC wanted to be sure the district administrator understood this correctly. The chairman advised the latter that the patients were to be invited to the next PSC meeting on 28 January, 'to establish whether there is a *prima facie* case for an urgent inspection and subsequent inquiry as they have been requesting.'

Despite its lack of constitution and formal authority, the PSC was being allowed considerable power. The district administrator stood in a managerial relationship to the day hospital (excluding the consultants, who as doctors had professional autonomy), but before he started inquiry proceedings he wanted to be sure it was really necessary. He himself had no psychotherapeutic training and was geographically separate from the day hospital, so he had to rely on the specialist and more intimate knowledge of the PSC members.

The day after the PSC meeting of 28 January the day hospital medical director/consultant wrote a letter to the district administrator. He explained the complaint in terms of the patients' understandable rejection of the help offered in psychotherapy at the day hospital and as a retaliation against their life experience of continual rejection through incarceration in mental hospitals and prisons. He argued that the day hospital was trying to help people who had been subject to gross material and emotional deprivation. None the less, they were properly representative of patients asking for therapeutic help under the NHS who would otherwise be 'screened out' of the system for being 'too sick' or 'not intelligent enough'. He explained that the treatment aim was to understand the individual patient by resorting to an examination of his functioning within the hospital – 'the hospital is the drawing board on which patients are invited to portray themselves' – and that this necessitated a simultaneous understanding of both the patients and the hospital. He suggested that any outside interference in this complex task was due to 'envy of an open working situation' that allowed great 'freedom of expression'. He felt that the approach adopted was unlikely to please either the patients (because it explored their anxieties rather than placating and repressing them) or the NHS (because of the kind of behaviour involved in testing out new discoveries of self), but he felt it would please those who wanted to see a flourishing NHS give the treatment that was necessary.

He said that the complaint was a matter of the patients drawing in outsiders as part of their 'testing out' their understanding of themselves. He asserted, however, that the work in the hospital must be restricted to what was happening inside the patients within the hospital's boundaries. He thought it understandable that external bureaucratic agencies would respond through the means available to them – that is, with rules – but he expected those who knew the unit well to respond with its 'best interest at heart'. He pointed to the health authority's inconsistency in failing to inform him about a letter from the public health inspector about the state of the day hospital, while reacting with no delay at all to an anonymous letter of complaint from the patients: 'I know that direct and honest communication is being avoided and the conservation of bureaucratic power resorted to instead.' This, he felt, was reminiscent of the lack of communication in the earlier fight against closure.

Finally, he said he welcomed an inquiry, 'an open forum to assess our work here', which would guard against unhelpful interference, and suggested a panel to include an NHS administrator, a patient representative, an 'unprejudiced' psychoanalyst, and a colleague experienced in this type of work. He insisted that the complaints should be assessed with certain essential factors in mind, such as whether or not patients returned for more treatment, whether other treatment had brought greater benefit, and in what different ways the administration could participate. He did, however, maintain his original position that anything concerning the patients would be brought up for discussion in the treatment context – that is, the large group. Although he did 'welcome' the inquiry, he proposed as an alternative that the hospital should continue as it was while a scientific report was prepared. He was being rather disingenuous here, as he almost certainly would have preferred to be assessed by fellow-psychotherapists (preferably of his own choosing), but presumably did not want to seem afraid of an inquiry.

In short, the medical director's letter simultaneously criticized the way the administration had resorted to 'bureaucratic power' and the fact that it had not followed the same bureaucratic rules in the matter of informing him of the health inspector's report. It also appears that he had realized he would not be able to stop an inquiry, and so made known his wishes concerning it and almost set its terms of reference.

In this way the medical director neither entirely rejected the bureaucratic NHS hierarchy nor accepted its view of the situation. He manipulated both frameworks, that of the NHS and his own, to defend his position.[3] However, he did maintain a consistent approach when he used psychoanalytic interpretation (of envy, etc.) to explain the criticism of his work by patients and 'outsiders', and when he reiterated that he would bring the inquiry back into the treatment context. This can be read as either internal theoretical consistency or as blind dogmatism in imposing his own theoretical perspective on every situation, even where the people involved could not possibly understand or sympathize with his argument. Adopting an entrenched position, he was saying that whatever might happen external factors would not alter *his* way of working, since external factors were precisely what his experiment had rejected as irrelevant.

The patients attend the PSC meeting

The next PSC meeting on 28 January was attended by seventeen patients. The committee members continued to worry about the definition of clinical and administrative issues respectively, on which would hinge how far the medical director could encroach on other areas of work such as the administration's. They declared that as they were ultimately responsible for the building as a whole, they were entitled to the opinion that the correct level of treatment was not being maintained at the day hospital and that this indicated the need for an inquiry. Since

The crisis

it was proving too difficult to define the boundaries between clinical and administrative matters – and hence the field over which they saw themselves as having the authority to comment – the PSC now concerned itself with the limits of clinical freedom, that is, the 'correct level of treatment'. In this respect it was their right and actual duty to protect the patients.

The patients for their part said that the complaint had arisen from just such a confusion between clinical and administrative matters, and asked that the PSC clarify these respective areas of responsibility since the day hospital could not even agree over, for example, the question of cleaning, and this made the patients feel anxious. Against the medical director's claim that he could only 'advise' the administration, the patients argued that this was 'an oblique way of telling the administration what to do'. They reiterated that they had had no part in decision-making and said they felt that any suggestions they put forward 'were frivolized by the staff'. One patient had agreed with the idea of the patients cleaning up after themselves but this had been made nonsense of by the lack of admission groups and so on, so that any 'dossers' could come in and make a mess of the place.

On request by the committee, all but one of the patients voted in support of their letter of complaint and its request for an inquiry. The one patient who withdrew did so on the grounds that although he had agreed with the letter as a vote of no confidence, it contained untruthful statements such as the claim that the staff worked only forty-five minutes a day: they did work somewhat longer than that. (This was the patient who had spent many years at the day hosptial and tended to adopt a quasi-therapeutic role himself. Because he largely identified with the staff, he may have found it difficult to join in a formal criticism of them.)

The patients then left the meeting, followed by the medical director (to demonstrate he believed only in democratic discussion). The committee decided to press for an inquiry by an independent body, as it did not want any further 'splitting' of the institute. Members felt an inquiry was necessary in view of their concern about the chaotic situation in the day hospital. They were worried by the patients' feeling that they were excluded from decision-making, although this could well be expected given the absence of organization in admission and discharge procedures. This disorganization led to outsiders using the building and left the patients unclear about their own status as patients. When the latter also disagreed with the medical director's definition of 'clinical' and queried his idea that 'all matters pertaining to the running of the day hospital had to do with the treatment of patients', they were actually rejecting his reduction of all material and organizational matters to pathological symptoms. It is ironical that, had the medical director stayed until the end of this PSC meeting instead of making a point about democracy, the decision to endorse the patients' complaint by calling for an inquiry might have been averted – at this stage, at least.

The PSC could act without any formal vote being taken and in the absence of a prime participant because it had no constitution regulating how decisions were to be made. By the same token it had no official authority to make decisions at all, but as the Area Health Authority took its opinion seriously, the committee felt free to give it. However, since the PSC knew that the formal grounds it stood on were shaky, it felt obliged to put forward an explanation of its decision to press for an inquiry. After the meeting, therefore, and with the agreement of the rest of the PSC members present, the chairman sent the district administrator the unconfirmed minutes of the meeting by way of giving him a report of the discussion.

Rulelessness and the problem of dossers and hygiene

The medical director also wrote to the district administrator (who managed the administration in the institute) because, although he was 'sure much of this discussion will be minuted and conclusions forwarded to you, I am equally sure that certain factors will be omitted which have an important bearing on the whole situation.'

By this he meant the patients' accusation that because of the lack of rules on admission (and discharge), dossers were dirtying the hospital. In addition to this criticism of the experiment and

204

The crisis

its deliberate lack of structure, another and related contentious issue was that of cleaning – equally seen as a clinical matter in the terms of the experiment. When the usual cleaner had left, the medical director advised the administrator not to employ anyone else because this was an issue to be dealt with solely on the unconscious level. As a result the hospital became very dirty and the subject was continually being brought up at large-group meetings. Eventually someone must have complained to the district administrator as an inspection was made by the chief environmental health officer and a report sent to the district administrator. In his original letter about the patients' complaint the district administrator had asked the PSC for comments on this matter of hygiene; this is why it was on the agenda of the PSC meeting at which the patients were present. The medical director was highly incensed that he himself did not receive a copy of this report until a month later.

In his letter of 30 January he mentioned how one patient apparently felt that 'dossers' were responsible for the dirt, but said that he himself had advised the district administrator against hiring a new cleaner, so that he alone was answerable. He pointed out that as they had been unable to agree how to define dossers, this indirectly proved his theory that the issue of cleaning was one of clinical relevance only: 'Ultimately some patients, the less sick, began to realize that they were not talking about others, but about themselves, about rejected parts of their own personality.' The implication that the more a patient insisted on the material need for a cleaner the sicker he was is a clear instance of how psychoanalysis was used to control dissent in the day hospital.

The medical director felt that the clinical basis of the dossers and cleaning problem was not proved: 'This mechanism of defence is called Projection and is well known to Psychoanalysts. Any Psychoanalyst worth his salt could have forecast that this would be the case' (his capitals). This allowed him to go on to argue: 'I, however, predict that all other complaints and allegations will turn out to have the same basis once the disguises are understood.' Once again he was reducing statements about material facts to psychological defence mechanisms.

Since the district administrator was not trained in psychoanalysis, it would seem unlikely that he would concur with the medical director's contentions. Nevertheless, the latter continued in the same vein and implied that the argument about unconscious motives also explained the complaint. The day hospital's treatment 'aims to put people in touch with what they do to themselves and others, to rediscover discarded parts of themselves. When the people who make the mess ultimately realize what they are doing they will no longer need to function in this way and will, in fact, be able to clear up any remaining' (remaining mess, that is). Translated, this means that once the psychopathological meaning of the complaints and criticisms was recognized by the 'sick' patients, the complaint would be seen to be void of substance.

He concluded that his colleagues were being either 'naive' or 'malicious' about his approach and that he would not 'brook interference' from either colleagues or administration. Although he himself had defined the complaint as based solely on his patients' pathological condition, he implied that by taking the complaint seriously his colleagues and the administration were being malicious in rejecting his definition.

The division between the medical director and most of his staff on one side and the rest of the PSC on the other – a division which had already made itself felt at the first PSC meeting following the complaint – had now become a gaping schism, with the disagreement formally and publicly documented in letters.

The minutes of the PSC meeting a week later again recorded a discussion on the day hospital's views. Since the PSC could not accept the medical director's view that administrative (for example, cleaning) and clinical (that is, related to the unconscious) matters could not be separated because all rested on unconscious motivation, and since the PSC was unable to settle the question satisfactorily itself the committee argued that both matters should be investigated by the inquiry. The PSC justified its request for an inquiry by referring to its specific role of 'upholding professional standards'. Having come to this conclusion, it was then agreed that 'these discussions should now be abated unless further questions of principle or problems arose'.

The crisis

In the day hospital the patients' letter of complaint remained a burning issue. Despite the fact that privately the staff expressed a good deal of anxiety about it, they hardly ever mentioned it publicly in the large group in any terms other than the unconscious motivation of the people involved. Only rarely did they discuss strategies for coping with the situation in practical ways, or review where they might have gone wrong. In one large-group session four weeks after the complaint (on 3 February 1976) there was an exchange which was exceptional in this respect.

Therapist A: I disagree with having an inquiry. It interrupts work.
Therapist B: We have no choice.
Therapist A: We have to find out why all this has happened. Why the patients wrote the letter. Where we failed.
Medical director: Well, you call it a success in that the patients were able to get together and write letters.
Therapist A: Yes, in one sense. But it also represents a past failure to recognize the patients' concern.
Therapist C: It's really a row between consultants, the medical director and the rest, and the patients are being used and affected by this.
Medical director: Ah, but it's the patients who started it. They must accept responsibility for their actions and see the consequences of their actions.
Therapist A: The fact that they 'started it' doesn't justify their being further hurt.
Medical director: I've tentatively chosen consultants A and B for the inquiry panel. Some administrative medic has asked me who I'd suggest.
Therapist A: It's worrying that you're fighting it alone. I have nothing to hide. Let's get the inquiry over quick, and then we can work again.

Polarization

The gradual polarization between most of the staff and the patients may be seen from the exchanges in the large-group

207

session of 26 February, a month after the complaint. The staff group was still busily interpreting but the latterly more cohesive patient group, led by the activists, had already begun to react to all such contributions as negative. Instead of merely rejecting reductive interpretations aimed at controlling their deviance, the patients now did not permit any unconscious-orientated definitions at all. At the beginning of the session there were eight staff and two patients, but by the end there were about twenty present in all.

Patient 1: I wonder if the staff ever thought of being veterinary surgeons. They treat us like animals anyway.

[Silence.]

There is a high rate of suicide among psychiatrists. Three commit suicide every day of the year. If Adrian did, I tell you, I'd laugh so much I'd have to change my trousers. I wonder what would happen if his neck was wrung – I expect he'd walk round afterwards like chickens do.

[He gets up from his chair between two therapists, to sit next to the only other patient present at this point.]

I feel safer here.
Medical director: Really, these patients must let the staff get on and teach the new staff member what her role is.

He seemed to be implying that this rebellious talk was a way of countering the anxiety engendered by the presence of a new therapist.

Patient 1: I want to report that two patients are in possession of a letter that shows that one of the staff has applied for a job in another hospital and there is a reference from Adrian. I think it's bloody cheeky of this therapist to think of leaving now. I also think those two patients shouldn't interfere in staff business. What's more, I resent their suggestion that I stole

208

The crisis

their baby's feeding bottle. What would I want with a bottle anyway?

A baby's parents had earlier accused this patient of having stolen the child's bottle.

Patient 2: But I thought they'd apologized to you?
Patient 1: I don't care – I didn't accept their apology.
Medical director: Which baby needs his bottle [implying that the patient himself has need of nurture and comfort]?
Patient 1: Shut up, you! I'm not interested.
Patient 3: Don't you see what psychotherapy is all about? They just try to make you feel angry and impotent, and then you'll get 'insight'.

He was putting forward an anti-psychiatry criticism of therapy.

Patient 1: I'm not impotent, I have two babies to prove that.
Patient 3: I'm talking about emotional impotence . . .
Patient 1: I suggest the patients move to another room to avoid insults. It would be much more productive.
Medical director: People can use their tongues here but they do make slips. Staff too can use them, but in a more subtle way. What's important is how long and how wide they are.

He may have been referring (again) to the penis envy he supposed patients felt for the staff, implying envy of the staff's capacities.

Patient 1: Come on, let's all move somewhere else and discuss what's wrong with this place.

There was a notice on the board, written by a group of patients, informing others that a meeting was to be held at 1.15 p.m. It was during this period that the patients had set up 'patients' groups' to compete with the large group and to undermine it in terms of attendance, and it was at these groups that they organized future tactics.

209

Medical director: [Two named patients] can seriously confront [that is, the staff's authority], but [patient 1's] attempt is only funny.

He was saying that the patients' rebellion, especially that coming from patients prominently involved with the complaint, was rooted in unconscious rivalry rather than a justified stance.

Patient 1: I've been thinking of how to bug the place. I wonder if V [a foreign staff member] has had much experience with bugging?

He was trying to impress the group with his expertise in electronics, as well as needling a member of staff whose country of origin is regarded as prone to such secret-police methods of control. [As therapist D enters the room:] Look, (D)'s back! I thought you'd been sacked.

Therapist D: I've looked over the building, and there's an eating group in the canteen, and a drinking group in the library.

He was informing the large group about what he regarded as rival (social-club) groups in the hospital.

Patient 1: You'd make a good spy.
Medical director: The poor patients. They can't eat in the large group but must feed and entertain the staff to keep them happy.

Here he is implying that the patients do not feel they are getting a 'good feed' – help – in the large group but rather that, to keep the staff interested, they must entertain them. This implied that they were avoiding or defending themselves against analytic understanding.

Patient 1: The staff don't know how to entertain. They're here only because they can't get jobs elsewhere. I saw a job

advertised for a dustman. That's a good job for Adrian. A shit
collector.
Patient 2: I think they call them refuge collectors these days.

[Laughter at the unintended implication that the medical
director was providing a refuge.]

Medical director: You see? Babies can't articulate properly.
[Laughter.]
Patient 1 [to 2]: Why are you here?
Patient 2: Because I feel better here than I do anywhere else.
And I'm using my letter to the district administrator as a
forum for my ideas as an individual and to explore myself.

He was corresponding with the district administrator to make
his position clear concerning the complaint; although he had
signed it, he disagreed with some of its charges.

Patient 1: Why not get a sexy penfriend instead?

[Within a few minutes the group disbands.]

The extract shows how the patients, mainly activists, had recognized the staff interpretations as forms of control, and were
beginning to see their own problems in terms of social rather
than psychological causes. Although they had swung from a firm
belief in purely psychoanalytical understanding to this equally
firm interpretation of overt reality, their position still remained
strong because they still had an overall framework from which
to view events. As they began to see things more clearly the
influence of the activists on the rest of the patients became
ever more pronounced. The reason that the patient subculture
developed so markedly in this crisis period of uncertainty was
that its plausibility structure (Punch, 1974) was more accessible
and realistic than what the patients were being offered through
psychoanalysis.

Four weeks later, the patients' attitudes had become more
mixed. Some were less uncompromising in their rejection of

the therapy, and inclined to be less sure about the outcome of the complaint.

Patient 1: If Adrian can't decide what is 'clinical' and what is not, then he's had it. With the inquiry we have the choice of continuing as we are, or going back to being controlled.
Patient 2 [a relatively recent member]: None of you realize how lucky you are. This is better than outside; here you can do or say anything you want, except get violent, and yet you're all complaining. You needn't be frightened of what you say here – it's a wonderful opportunity.
Patient 1: Better make use of it while it's here, because this freedom of taking your own responsibility is going to be destroyed.
Patient 2: You can't destroy what's good, what's the point of . . .
Medical director: It's a shame people can't stand this 'good'. They need to bring in outsiders to stop it for fear of what might happen if we could really work together.

It will be clear by now that the patients, despite their anxieties about the outcome of the inquiry, at times became militantly anti-analytic and that the medical director maintained his interpretative stance throughout.

The power of the PSC

The question of how much authority the PSC had over people and events in the day hospital was taken up again in its meeting of 12 May 1976, when a case of violence had been brought to its attention. Two male patients had begun to fight and hurt a visiting woman ex-patient as well as a nurse and a therapist who tried to intervene. Fearing a possible recurrence, the PSC called an emergency meeting to see what could be done to safeguard patients and staff alike.

The PSC was unsure whether or not the day hospital staff had dealt with the incident in the proper way, and wondered if the violence might not have been prevented. To understand what had happened exactly members needed a full report of

The crisis

events, and the chairman even argued that this was important because they might have to 'answer a Queen's Counsel's questions'. The PSC chairman insisted that the day hospital registrar provide him with a clinical diagnosis of the violent patient in order to let him see how much danger was involved. Presumably this request was made on the basis that if the patient were diagnosed to be in a condition where he could not, for example, distinguish between his own phantasy life and reality, it could be argued that he should be committed to a residential hospital to protect others as well as himself against his future possible violence. Here the PSC chairman was acting in terms of his managerial authority over a junior doctor (the registrar). But whether this was appropriate in this context, or relevant to the registrar's work in the day hospital, is another question. The latter offered information about the situation, but felt that a diagnosis would be unhelpful.

The issue reflects the problems of professional autonomy and the delicate balance between the different sub-systems in the organization. By adopting a managerial role towards the technical staff in the day hospital the chairman was prejudicing his role as chairman of the PSC or 'institutional sub-system' (Parsons, 1956): by defining his role in this way he was making it easy for the managerial hierarchy at District and Area Health Authority level to hold the PSC, as lower-level managers, responsible for not keeping more control over their subordinates. Had he concentrated on the PSC's public-relations role, the committee would not have felt so implicated in the deviance of the day hospital, and would not have needed to dissociate itself so strongly. As it was, the PSC chairman laid himself open to the medical director's criticism that his position was 'unwarranted'. Having technical knowledge as a therapist the medical director could legitimately argue that his specialist skills gave him more authority in the managerial hierarchy of a hospital than a technician such as, say, a front-line worker in a car factory. He could claim the right to negotiate with the administration their relative areas of authority, and was justified in rebuffing the PSC chairman's interference in managerial matters.

In fact, of course, the medical director rejected all inter-

213

vention in his work, legitimate or not. In this case he was correct
in rejecting the PSC, but for the wrong reasons. Whereas the
administration had a legitimate managerial role, the PSC did
not, and by taking a managerial stance the PSC put itself in a
negotiating situation with the therapist in the day hospital.
Indeed, when the PSC chairman subjected day hospital staff to
accountability for the incident of violence, most other PSC
members felt he had gone too far. And when he kept on saying:
'as a consultant psychiatrist, I demand that you as my registrar
give me a clinical diagnosis', he was stopped from causing more
than considerable embarrassment only by other PSC members
pointing out that the registrar was being put 'in an impossible
position' and that the situation was intolerable for everybody.

As a policy-making body, the PSC was open to any qualified
member of the institute. Its chairman could act on its behalf by
conveying to the District Health Authority decisions made at
PSC meetings, but as his chairmanship was not by election
or appointment, but merely a carry-over from his previous
chairmanship of the medical committee,[4] it was not clear how
far his authority actually extended. In any case, lacking a constitution the PSC could impose no sanctions if some 'unanimous'
decision was not implemented by its members.

The conflict in which participants find themselves when an
authority structure remains undefined is seen from the following
verbatim report of a discussion between two members of the
PSC before the meeting at which the violent incident was to
be raised.

PSC member X: Do come to the meeting, because we have
got to work out the rights and powers of the professional staff
committee, and we need everyone involved to come. I believe
in democracy – I must fight for it. If we give it up, we'll go
back to the medical committee of the rule by two consultants
alone, and that was not democratic at all.
PSC member Y: I don't think the PSC works in a democratic
way. Democracy is one thing, but when it gets out of control
and people's careers are involved, it's different. I can talk
there, but not freely.
PSC member X: I see your point – so what do you do then?

214

The crisis

If we go and say we can't speak freely, then we're inviting
their attack. And *we* can get sacked, whereas consultants can't
be.
PSC member Y: If there's no hierarchy, then what you say is
evaluated. If this is a pecking order, I can speak but not
safely. I can really only listen. If people are not prepared to
listen to *me* because I'm not a consultant, I get frustrated
and my patients suffer, and I'm not prepared to let that
happen. The PSC is a controlling body and unnecessary. *I*
don't want power – as long as I can do my work I can share
with anyone, staff or patient.
PSC member X: I *must* go. If the minutes of the last meeting
refer to me in some untrue way I'll have to defend myself.

Apart from the confusion over function and the role conflict
this entailed, the friction between the PSC chairman and the
registrar arose out of two very different approaches to mental
illness. On the one hand there was the radical idea prominent
in the day hospital, (as well as in society at large at the time)
that negative labels are harmful and that the violent incident
could be assessed correctly only through full understanding of
the context; on the other hand the more conventional psychiatric attitude was that a diagnostic category would immediately
indicate what kind of person a patient is and, therefore, his
likely future actions. This is a good illustration of the current
debate in psychiatry between conventional treatment methods
and the alternative view that saw the former as concerned more
with control than care (see discussion of Goffman's theory in
Chapter 1). At the same time the issue at stake was what might
happen if the day hospital staff were found to have been acting
irresponsibly. The PSC would then be able to dissociate and
clear itself by reporting the matter to higher authorities. This
in fact was what did happen, and as a result the staff were
divided into two camps: day hospital versus the rest of the
institute. There were a few exceptions: those who insisted that
it was important to examine the authority structure of the PSC,
both the power of its individual members and especially that of
the chairman who, acting on behalf of the PSC, had reported

day hospital negligence in connection with the violence without consulting the other PSC members.

It was generally agreed, however, that in this particular instance the chairman could not have acted other than he did in making a written report to the Area Health Authority (AHA). The question of the power of individuals or groups was suspended by falling back once more on the general statement that the PSC's functions were similar to those of the earlier medical committee, but that clinical matters ultimately came under the jurisdiction of the AHA. It was the AHA that would decide just how reasonably the violent incident had been handled. The question for debate was whether the PSC had the power to insist that a consultant attend a meeting of such urgency. The medical director had sent his apologies for being absent, on the grounds that the PSC had agreed not to interfere with the day hospital until after the inquiry into the patients' complaint. Although the conflict between the day hospital and the other departments of the institute was never resolved, everyone agreed that the area administrator should be asked to hasten the inquiry so that issues of treatment could be clarified, and patients' and staff's anxiety about the hospital's future relieved.

As a result of the PSC chairman informing the Cogwheel committee of the Division of Psychiatry about the violent incident, the Cogwheel committee chairman made a visit to the day hospital. Having discussed the hospital's relationship to the PSC with the medical director, the latter wrote to the Cogwheel committee (18 May 1976) following up some of his ideas. Although the Cogwheel committee did not have managerial control over the medical director, it could – if it wished – exert internal pressure on him as a colleague, and if its members were to suspect negligence at the day hospital they could inform the AHA and the British Medical Association accordingly.

The letter expressed well the medical director's view of the situation concerning the violence and the complaint, and how such conflict between the patients, staff, the PSC and the Area Health Authority had arisen. As in his day hospital work, the medical director presented a purely psychoanalytically reductive explanation, arguing that if all the parties involved

216

The crisis

had been aware of their unconscious motivation, there would have been no conflict and no complaint. He saw it largely as a matter of 'sibling rivalry', of brothers and sisters (the different compartments in the institute) competing for the love of the parents (the AHA). In particular, he saw the day hospital treated by the rest of the institute as the 'unruly younger child' creating a persistent state of conflict, which continued because

the psychopathology of the individual staff in respect of their own unresolved sibling rivalry keeps it going. Patients naturally enact the problem on behalf of staff . . . leading to complaints to external agencies and acting out of sibling rivalry between themselves, for example arguments and fights.

This picture of the situation allowed the medical director to emerge from the dispute without a blemish and as the only one who understood the content of the psychopathology of all concerned. In this position he could ignore the content of the complaint (whether or not the patients had any justification for it), as well as the actual organizational relationship among departments and with the AHA.

According to a letter from the area medical officer to the PSC chairman (dated 24 May 1976) the Cogwheel committee chairman felt that in respect of the violent incident he saw no need for instant intervention in the day hospital, but that 'procedural guidelines for the centre as a whole and also for such matters as case records, drug charts and minimum standards of administration and cleanliness, should be drawn up and implemented as soon as possible'. In other words, he did not accept the medical director's psychoanalytic explanation of the day hospital's problems in terms of sibling rivalry. By recommending the creation of 'procedural guidelines' he was overruling the medical director's perspective that all matters, including the material and organizational, are in the end reducible to psychopathological terms and so a matter of clinical judgement. His apparently simple sentence about 'minimum standards of administration' was actually a wholesale contradiction not only of the medical director's perspective but of his entire experiment.

217

The medical director's written response to the area medical officer's communication with the Cogwheel committee chairman on 7 June (which had been circulated in the centre) was an attempt to explain the crisis. The letter can be read in tw(parts. The first gave a fairly cool-headed explanation of the day hospital's approach to therapy, and how this must exclude bureaucratic control procedures. Surprisingly, the reasons given for this included the admission that he had attempted 'to define and enlarge the area of clinical responsibility at the expense of those dealt with by the external administration' which 'has lead [sic] to testing out of the boundary between "clinical" and "administrative" responsibility' – that is, he had been fully aware all along that by re-defining administrative issues as clinical he was expanding his area of authority. He also argued that selection procedures would run counter to the letter and spirit of the NHS, a service intended to provide treatment for all patients who present themselves. In the matter of 'acting out', he advocated 'interpretative intervention' where possible.

In the second part of his letter, the medical director's analysis reverted to an explanation in psychoanalytic terms. He said that in order for the patients to understand the omnipotent unconscious phantasies which underlie their disorders, 'the relevant therapists must be seen to be responsible for what is offered to patients.' Further on he remarked on a public-holiday closure of the hospital ordered by district-level administration:

If others outside the immediate treatment situation exercise real power which interferes with that offered by the clinician, then the exploration of unconscious phantasy will cease or be seriously impaired.

In this way he laid the blame for the crisis at the door of administrators at district level who had been arranging for the day hospital's specific organizational features.

Phantasy and reality in psychoanalysis

In individual psychoanalysis, the knowledge a patient has of the analyst's life is kept to a minimum so that he may see more clearly how his phantasies and feelings about the analyst are more a function of his own psyche than matters of external fact. Where external reality coincides with phantasy – for example, if an analyst takes a session off because of a bad cold, at the very time when the patient has felt destructively angry towards him – then it is more difficult for the patient to distinguish between his phantasy and real life. He may ask himself whether the analyst has fallen ill because he (the patient) had wished him ill. The attempt to make such differentiations between fact and fiction is of course one of the main analytic tasks.

In respect of the day hospital the medical director was arguing that if the 'omnipotent phantasies' of making organizational changes were reflected in *actual* changes executed by outsiders (instead of therapists), then this would constitute a confirmation of the phantasy and be unhelpful. In fact the argument hinges on the perspective from which the patient's wishes are seen. The day hospital patients had been making conscious criticisms of the hospital on the basis of feelings springing, they felt, from choice and preference, and it was these the medical director re-defined as 'unconscious phantasies' and so as psychopathological. Instead of answering this problem in the language of organizational affairs, as used in the first part of his letter, he reduced it to the unconscious level over which he, as analyst, had greater say.

In any case, from the point of view of psychoanalytic practice it is impossible – even in individual work where the intrusion of external matters is kept to a minimum – to control completely the external world so as to prevent reality from reflecting inner phantasies. The medical director imagined he had more control over the analytic situation than is possible in real life. It also seems as if he resented other people exercising their legitimate authority (that is, doing their jobs), as it interfered with his idea that he had total control over the situation.

The remainder of the letter of 7 June referred to 'envious attacks' and

collusive help from those who might be expected to know better, leading to support for their unresolved perverse

219

*infantile wishes, from those who, although they are not
designated as patients, struggle with the same problem.*

He had therefore contacted the Medical Defence Union 'to
counter malicious attacks based on personal animosity, not to
protect the working methods which *per se* will speak for
themselves'.

The strength the medical director derived from reducing
discussions of material reality to psychopathological motivation
is made explicit in his letters. Seeing the situation based on
unconscious elements allowed him to ignore everyday tangible
facts. The area medical officer, however, a member of the
medical profession, could reject explanations in terms of sibling
rivalry and propose bureaucratic procedures for dealing with
practical realities. But mere common sense could not deter the
medical director: he blamed the administrators for the
complaint because of their interference in interpretative work.
It was the issue of the extent of a consultant's clinical freedom
that lay at the root of the inquiry and which, having remained
unsolved, had to be re-examined eighteen months later by a
second inquiry.

The first inquiry

The decision to proceed with an inquiry was in accord with
the code of practice for dealing with hospital complaints as
recommended by the Davies Committee in 1973. The
committee had suggested that where patients were not satisfied
with attempts on the ward to deal with the problem, they
should be advised to write to the district administration.

As a result of a patient contacting the newspapers, a number
of press articles about the complaint began to appear. In a
pointed article published shortly before the inquiry *The
Guardian* mentioned that the Davies Committee had laid down
that it was the staff's responsibility to report patients' complaints
alleging they had been 'deprived of treatment, care, food,
comfort or other benefit to which [they] were entitled.' These
were precisely the things of which the patients at the day
hospital had been complaining for months before they made

The crisis

their official complaint. The article further mentioned how the Davies Committee had left unresolved the problem of complaints against the clinical judgement of doctors. *The Guardian*, as well as a local newspaper, also showed some interest in the 'story' side of the affair and a few articles appeared, chiefly outlining the basis of the complaint and the decision to hold an inquiry.

On 24 May 1976 the patients were informed by the AHA who had been chosen for the inquiry panel that shortly after 1 June they would be invited to submit their evidence.

An incident of violence became of crucial importance in the development of the crisis by raising the questions of safety which any employee in a psychiatric hospital has to confront and, as it affected the whole institute, legitimated more external interference than would otherwise have been feasible.

As a result of this stimulus, the members of the PSC drew up their own suggestions. They recommended among other things:

(i) an intake procedure, including collecting information on the patients' history, diagnosis, treatment plan, and the name of the latter's doctor;
(ii) a register of patients;
(iii) a discharge procedure;
(iv) a staff 'system' to ensure some staff coverage of patients at all times;
(v) an on-call roster for doctors;
(vi) some form of case notes;
(vii) a report back to a general practitioner about the patient's condition.

These recommendations were put to the chairman of the Cog-wheel committee of the Division of Psychiatry, and accepted by the area medical officer as measures ensuring the safety of patients and staff until the results of the inquiry should be known.

During the period of the inquiry – from 1 June and for about three months until the report came out – the staff group in the day hospital became increasingly worried about their position. Realizing that their futures might be at stake, individuals began to clarify their stance *vis-à-vis* the experiment. Apart from a few who had remained loyal to the medical director's approach throughout, there was more and more unqualified criticism of his theory and methods. Even so, staff members as a group could not reach sufficient agreement for unified action. So while some agreed that interpretations could not help all patients, they felt they could not accept the recommendations for the reintroduction of ordinary bureaucratic procedures of admission, discharge, clinical notes and so on. Their resentment of such regulatory structures being imposed from outside is shown by a staffroom discussion on 16 June 1976.

Therapist A: Let's say we'll consider your recommendations if you'll consider ours. We could say we want to chuck out the art department and only have help from porters or social workers if and when it's really necessary.
Therapist B: We're being asked to work in a different way. Now it's vague about how people join in the large group so that a person can choose to get involved slowly. They want regimentation.
Therapist C: The boundary is not clear now. We have to have meals and fares, so if we have a clear boundary we can choose from there.
Therapist A: I don't think Adrian cares about us.
Therapist B: He doesn't.
Therapist A: He only cares about the external fight.
Therapist B: We can either fight on his behalf, or say we can't work that way with external interference . . . or simply not work.
Therapist C: How *do* we want to work?
Therapist B: We all have different ideas.
Therapist A: Let's write individually to the inquiry and let them sort it out – that's their job.
Therapist C: Why not talk about it together first?
Therapist D: We *should* get together and decide as a group.
Therapist A: We'll never agree.

Later this group of staff did try to draw up a list of the recommendations they disagreed with – and ended up by

222

The crisis

rejecting almost all the proposed bureaucratic procedures. Though they had previously been divided, the suggestions from outside made them close ranks.

When it became clear that records would have to be kept once more, some of the staff started to get the books out. In making up the records they realized that only two new patients had come to participate in the hospital during the past six months (before June 1976). They confronted the medical director with this fact; he, perhaps annoyed at their following the AHA recommendations, told them they were being 'silly'. This made one staff member quite angry: 'Oh yes, only doctors are right. There should be *two* large groups – a "silly" one where you talk about everything, and an "intellectual" one where there are only interpretations.' Another supported her: 'We're fed up with Adrian coming to the large group for five minutes and then leaving'; but one of the medical director's supporters accused the other two of merely scapegoating Adrian and the violent patient. Although the proposal to have two types of group was only a bitter joke, the day hospital did later split up into two groups, one providing more conventional psychotherapy and one following the medical director and making interpretations.

The closer the inquiry came, the more critical the staff attitudes grew towards the medical director's methods. On 9 July 1976, in a large group at which the medical director continually interrupted a patient who was trying to explain his feelings, one staff member became very angry. The ensuing exchange shows that there was now some identity of attitude between some of the staff members and the patients.

Therapist A: Adrian's very clever, but he can't stand it if someone else is too, because he thinks only one all-powerful interpretation is possible . . . Why do you ignore so important a statement from a patient as that he feels there isn't enough space for him to grow?
Medical director [teasing and smiling]: A is very clever too. He's very good at interpreting.
[Therapist A sits poker-faced and silent.]
Therapist B: I think this is all about control, especially the

223

way the patients are trying to control the movement and words of staff.

Patient 1: It's the other way round.

Therapist A: Adrian was controlling just a minute ago what patient 2 said by deliberately interrupting him.

Meanwhile the patients as a group remained quite clear about their position. In the main they stuck to their complaint, rejected the psychoanalytic interpretations, and continued to hold their own patient groups, sometimes issuing bulletins. One patient even approached the media and, as mentioned above, a number of newspaper reports of the pending inquiry resulted.

During the inquiry period, members of the panel visited the day hospital to talk to the patients and see the situation for themselves. On 17 June one of the external assessors, a professor of psychiatry from a large hospital, made one such visit. He talked to about twelve patients and asked about their feelings about art therapy and the groups. During his visit he met only one member of staff, because he had arrived at 9.30 a.m. when only patients were present. The patients were rather amused and pleased by this, as it showed the inquiry member that their criticism about staff attendance had been justified.

Although the division between those who supported and those who fought the experiment was sharply felt at this time, occasionally there would be a kind of truce when both sides would lay down their arms and try to resume therapeutic work. However, once staff members began giving evidence at the inquiry, those waiting for their turn became very anxious. Some of the nurses felt particularly upset as they had always been in a conflict about the contradictory demands of psychotherapy and the nursing profession, and would now have to justify their position, knowing full well that the approaches of the day hospital and the nursing hierarchy were irreconcilable. If they worked efficiently according to one perspective, they failed in the other.

The registrar felt a similar conflict. Although it had been his formal role to keep case notes of patients he had not done so during the experiment, when it was part of the policy to drop all bureaucratic procedures. He had not realized at the time

The crisis

that this was not a matter ultimately of the medical director's responsibility, but a legal requirement of his own position as registrar. Knowing that he would be asked about this at the inquiry, and forced to clarify his loyalties, he informed the medical director on 23 July that he felt he could no longer work in the day hospital and was withdrawing his support. This was quite a crucial moment for the medical director, as it represented the first formal expression of dissent among his medical team and showed beyond a doubt that this staff member was not going to support him at the inquiry.

Following some informal inquiries and visits to the day hospital, the Area Health Authority decided to proceed with a formal investigation having as its terms of reference to

consider under the terms of HM (66)15 the management and the medical and allied practices relating to the selection, care and treatment of patients at the day hospital, to consider the Art Department as it impinges on the day hospital, and to report to the Authority.

(DHSS circular)

After consulting the Royal College of Psychiatrists and the Royal College of Nursing, the AHA drew up a team to undertake the inquiry, which included three external assessors. Although the medical director did not have the right to object to the constitution of the panel, the AHA replaced one specialist at his request because he believed him to be prejudiced against him personally.

The complete inquiry team consisted of the AHA chairman and vice-chairman, four AHA officers, the area medical officer, the area nursing officer, the area general administrator and a secretary, and the three external assessors – a consultant psychotherapist, a professor of psychiatry and a chief nursing officer, all currently working in psychiatric hospitals.

The inquiry was not a public one, neither would its findings be published; this was to allow the witnesses to feel completely free in giving their evidence. All members of staff were invited to do so, and all except three attended in person; some also submitted written evidence. One of the psychoanalysts decided against giving any evidence, and the clinical assistant confined herself to written evidence. All testimonies were treated confidentially.

The committee of inquiry heard evidence throughout the week of 19 July 1976. The medical director himself attended three times before refusing to attend unless the inquiry proceedings were transcribed for the patients' benefit. In this he again maintained his principle that all matters relating to the day hospital must be brought up there and treated as material for analytic interpretation.

Repercussions of the inquiry

Working their way through the complex maze of accumulated information and opinion, the committee took six weeks to complete its report. This essentially confirmed the legitimacy of the patients' complaint and made a number of recommendations, reinstating bureaucratic rules abandoned as part of the experiment. All the usual NHS hospital procedures regulating patient care and treatment were to be restored.

The news of the report further excited newspaper interest. The report itself contained a review of the day hospital's history, and showed how the medical director had diverged from the basic principles of most therapeutic communities – preventing staff and patient participation in decision-making by stopping business meetings; blurring staff roles by denying them the specialist skills of their own discipline and regarding them all as therapists and exacerbating this by depriving staff of the support from colleagues they might have obtained from separate staff meetings; increasing permissiveness in the matter of alcohol consumption on the premises; and regulating behaviour solely through psychoanalytic interpretation, which had become the single therapeutic tool after all other learning situations had been discontinued and which considered all matters, practical and pathological, in terms of their unconscious meaning.

The popular press, which had managed to obtain a copy of the confidential report, focused on the main problem it raised – the difficulty of deciding the degree of clinical freedom hospital consultants should be allowed. Attempts to curb that freedom,

The crisis

for instance by peer reviews, had proved unsuccessful because of doctors' militancy. *New Society* was sceptical of the experiment, stating that the day hospital methods were 'rather euphemistically dubbed "treatment", for no better reason, it would seem, than it occurs within a "hospital".' The periodical criticized the medical director for having 'refused to observe even the most basic of research requirements in the course of his work'. It agreed that such innovations as the abandonment of selection procedures, record-keeping and other usual facilities were 'progressive' and 'refreshingly abrasive', but said that unless such a policy were carefully explained not only to the patients but also to their relatives and the staff, it could only result in a 'muddle, bitterness and breakdown'.

The committee of inquiry had decided to examine the medical director's deliberate divergence from usual therapeutic-community practice (as characterized by the earlier regime at the day hospital) to see whether this had been executed with 'due regard to the welfare of patients and staff and whether this was acceptable under the National Health Service'. In the event, it particularly criticized the way he had reduced the variety of potential therapeutic methods to the one therapeutic tool of the 'correct interpretation' of patients' verbalizations in terms of infantile wishes, which he regarded as valid for all patients. They found this idea old-fashioned, but conceded that he 'is free as a clinician to use this technique . . . It cannot be said to . . . constitute bad practice.' However, although the members agreed there was 'room for experiments', and that it was possible that the medical director's approach may have helped some patients, they felt that the 'present situation' was 'a cause for grave concern'. The regime had not been set up carefully as an experiment to be evaluated at regular stages, and may actually have harmed patients: 'Some of his omissions verge on the unprofessional and should not be tolerated in an NHS Unit.' Commenting on the way in which the staff felt their professional expertise had been 'denigrated', the committee pointed out the conflict staff members had felt as they tried to reconcile the director's approach with their professional consciences. Furthermore, they had had to practise psycho-

227

therapy exclusively, although they had received no formal therapeutic training.

Commenting on one of the most crucial issues, that of the administrative/clinical distinction, the inquiry report stated that 'where clinical and administrative considerations overlap, chaos has resulted'. The way the medical director had regarded administrative matters, such as cleaning, meals and fares, as questions requiring clinical judgements rather than administrative decisions had made it extremely difficult for the administration to take action, as these problems involved 'major principles related to the boundaries of clinical freedom and the duty of the managing Authority towards its patients and staff'.

Nevertheless, the report took a clear stand on the issue of clinical judgement. While regarding therapeutic techniques (such as the 'correct interpretation' and the 'blank-screen' non-involved therapist's role) as matters concerning professional judgement, it maintained that the administrative structure must be allowed to continue in its own right, and that it has a specific function and area of authority. It declared:

We do not believe that the principle of clinical independence should be regarded as precluding the Authority from taking action in defence of the interests of patients and other staff.

In other words, the panel were confirming Parsons' (1956) view that the 'technical' (therapeutic) and 'managerial' (administrative) sub-systems have different functions and separate areas of authority, neither being reducible to the other; and that despite the technicians' technical expertise which justifies some form of tenure and a degree of autonomy, ultimately the managerial/administrative level is hierarchically superior to the technical sub-system.

Given its stand on the relative autonomy of these two sub-systems, the committee's main recommendation was that although the medical director was free to choose which therapeutic technique to employ in his work, there were certain administrative regulations with which he must comply. He would therefore have to reinstate procedures concerned with patient diagnosis and selection, admission and discharge, and

228

The crisis

keep records and case notes. He should 'actively encourage occupational and socially supportive activities', and provide a 'caring and supportive attitude' to patients. As far as decisions about cleaning, meals and fares were concerned, this was to be arranged between the medical director and senior nursing and administrative staff. Contrary to the medical director's own view, the committee felt that the PSC was indeed a suitable place for discussing matters relating to the day hospital. If the medical director was going to continue his experiment, he should discuss it with the PSC, plan it more carefully and allow for systematic evaluation. In order for it to work, he should consider his staff's training more carefully.

This meant that the inquiry committee rejected the core innovation of the experiment – the re-definition of every aspect of life in psychological terms which robbed organizational activities of practical meaning and value – and made it clear where it saw the boundaries of clinical freedom: the medical director could employ his chosen therapeutic techniques, but he could not be so generous in his definition of the area over which he had clinical autonomy as to include practical and organizational matters. The NHS had certain responsibilities towards patients, and these included the provision of an administrative structure. The report, therefore, put organizational matters back into their original place as the background to therapy.

Despite this attempt to clarify the situation and the inquiry committee's willingness to 'grasp the nettle', the question of clinical authority continued unresolved. The medical director firmly persisted in his view that he himself could legitimately define the area over which his authority extended. It was some time before steps were taken to counteract his position. In fact it took a second inquiry, concerned with disciplinary measures, to curb the consultant's rights. But even then, rather than re-examine the concept of clinical freedom in depth, the AHA confined itself to stopping an individual instance where this freedom was being abused by charging malpractice and negligence.

Obviously case notes, record-keeping, admission procedures and so on, are only common-sense and necessary back-up for clinical practice. It is less clear to what extent the administration

229

can insist also (as the report did) that 'emotionally and socially supportive activities' be brought back. These are less obviously administrative necessities and could be interpreted as questions of clinical decision. However, when complaints arise over such activities (or the lack of them), the consultant might be expected to modify his programme automatically in the light of his patients' feelings and advice from colleagues. Given the medical director's views, the administration had no option but to reinstate such supportive activities itself – eventually instituting further inquiry proceedings about the consultant's clinical practice.

The medical director's public reaction to the report was one of apparent delight: the report was so bad, he said, that

they're serving it to me on a plate . . . it's so easy to demonstrate its illogicalities. It's so crazy . . . the report demonstrates the irrationality of the patients, of the PSC and of the inquiry committee. We should show its illogicalities and its contradictions and bring it into the open and get the back-up of law and public opinion.

His two supporters on the staff team also received the report with scepticism. In any case, the inquiry and the report had thoroughly clarified everybody's position and, despite their previous ambivalence, all the staff except these two decided to implement the recommendations.

It soon became clear to others in the institute that the medical director himself was not complying with these recommendations. He denied the right of the PSC to ask what he was doing about putting the directives into practice, and when PSC members tried to liaise with the patients for communication and social work purposes (as required by the report), the medical director angrily condemned their 'interference' in the day hospital's affairs. This reaction was reported through the Cogwheel committee to the AHA and, by the time the report had been out two months, the AHA asked the medical director for a commitment to its recommendations. In response, he informed the AHA that he was now operating two types of treatment in the day hospital:

The crisis

Category A, or 'mixed treatment methods', would

take advantage of existing facilities as required by staff and patients electing for this treatment method; to develop new facilities as required in conjunction, if necessary, with other centre staff or outside agencies in keeping with the recommendations of the Area Health Authority, Division of Psychiatry, and the Professional Staff Committee.

Appropriate records would be kept and the registrar would make daily reports to the consultant in charge, who would have overall responsibility.

Category B, 'psychoanalytic therapy', would take place in the library, which would be 'out of bounds' to category A patients and staff. 'Patients electing for this treatment are to agree to refrain from using any other facilities offered by the day hospital or the [institute].' Here the medical director would be directly responsible for treatment.

All patients and staff were free to choose which method they preferred, and although they could reverse their decision they would not be able to use more than one method at a time. In this way the medical director was hoping to avoid contradicting the views of the report on administrative autonomy, while attempting to continue working in his own preferred manner. As he felt that any compromise within his own treatment situation between his idiosyncratic approach and the inquiry report requirements would be tantamount to accepting its explicit and implicit criticisms, by instituting two separate treatment regimes he could let others compromise for him in one context, while in the second he continued his own regime untainted by any changes.

The PSC had hoped that, with the report having clarified issues and assuming the medical director's cooperation, they might now settle back into an ordinary routine. Yet once again they were confronted with the same problem, but now the medical director had lost every shred of support, which he had once had from them, for his clinical freedom and his actions were regarded as plainly recalcitrant. The PSC members' previously painful ambivalence gave way to outright condem-

231

nation for wasting the chance he had been given. Only one occupational therapist and one clinical assistant continued to support the medical director; the rest of the staff worked with category A patients.

Meanwhile the patients had managed to obtain a copy of the confidential report by setting off the fire alarm and taking a copy from the empty staffroom during the ensuing fire drill. They were divided in their reaction to the report and, though most patients wanted to work in category A, some attended the category B sessions with the medical director.

In fact, the patients experienced a new conflict of loyalties. Many had felt attracted to the charismatic element in the medical director's personality, but realized that the report rejected much of what he stood for. To identify with him meant allying themselves with a self-declared rebel whose methods were disapproved of by the AHA, and who demanded self-denial in respect of convenience and useful facilities. On the other hand, to opt for category A meant working with a group of shaky staff all on their own without their leading light. In the period leading up to the inquiry report there had already been two suicide attempts and now the conflict deepened.

Towards the end of September 1976, one of the clinical assistants decided to stop working in the day hospital and at the PSC meeting at which this was discussed the medical director also made his views of the report clear:

The report contradicts itself, therefore it is irrational. It is based on an irrational argument . . . My job is to put rational thought in the place of irrationality . . . I would fail in my duty if I didn't discuss the report, but I can't go along with the PSC if it unreservedly accepts it . . .

When asked whether by this he meant he would not implement the recommendations, he declared, 'I cannot implement irrational recommendations.' He added that as the inquiry committee had accepted the principles of his approach (that is the psychoanalytic interpretative aspect), their recommendations concerning the reinstatement of bureaucratic rules had not been logical.

The crisis

Many of the PSC members felt that their concern over the day hospital had been vindicated by the report's acceptance of the PSC's right to make decisions influencing the hospital's daily life. The medical director, on the other hand, could accept the PSC only as a forum for discussion – 'those not intimately concerned cannot make decisions . . . the PSC can't tell me what to do in my own clinical patch.' So saying, he left the meeting early, leaving his two main supporters from the staff to argue his case for him.

The inquiry had brought changes in the role of the PSC. Previously, as the 'board' of the institute, it had not been concerned with day-to-day decisions, but the inquiry panel had charged its members with ensuring that the report's recommendations were duly implemented. This caused the PSC members a new role conflict: while in their therapeutic work they were colleagues of the medical director and his staff, they had now been invested with managerial authority *vis-à-vis* the day hospital.

After a week of publicity – with the medical director speaking on the local radio and *The Guardian* reporting on the inquiry – the medical director announced that Henry Ezriel was in full agreement with him and supported his theory and practice. In response to PSC members' attempts to liaise with patients to implement the recommendations, the medical director, refusing to 'modify' his experiment, forbade any PSC member from communicating with his patients. None the less, on 19 October PSC representatives had a meeting with patients in the day hospital, as a result of which a liaison committee was set up to facilitate communication between them.

From the moment the medical director openly showed his contempt for the 'irrational' report of the committee of inquiry, opinion hardened against him. The PSC contented itself with merely ignoring his assertion that it had no right to interfere in his 'clinical patch', but the AHA replied (on 19 October 1976) to his formal proposal to run two types of treatment with not only a refusal but a demand that he state by 27 October whether he would comply with the inquiry recommendations or not. (While staff in the day hospital had in fact begun to keep clinical records, they had not been very successful in view of the uncooperative attitude of the other staff. Any attempts to meet the recommendations were ridiculed and interpreted psychoanalytically.)

The medical director withdraws

On 20 October 1976 the medical director announced that he had 'withdrawn his labour' from the hospital as he could not put up with interference in his work. He had heard about the PSC/day hospital liaison committee and described this as 'disobeying my rule'. As he would no longer be clinically responsible for his patients, the institute's consultants decided at the PSC meeting the same day to share clinical responsibility for the patients among themselves.

When the PSC chairman pressed the medical director to say whether his withdrawal from the day hospital meant he was resigning, he refused to commit himself. It appears that his announcement was a deliberate form of protest, something resembling a strike, but it rebounded on him when the PSC chairman suggested a resignation under pressure. The medical director left the meeting after only one hour, even though the discussions were far from being concluded. In his absence the PSC, having raised the issue earlier in the session, decided to write to the AHA proposing that the medical director be asked to resign, or at least suspended to 'prevent his presence in the Centre', which they regarded as harmful to patients.

Realizing what a shaky position he had created for himself, the medical director resumed his clinical responsibility for the day hospital and continued to work the two-category system, ignoring its rejection by the AHA. On 28 October the AHA wrote to him, saying that it was still unclear whether or not he was implementing the recommendations for all patients at the day hospital. He was advised that if by 4 November he had not unambiguously committed himself, he would be suspended and new inquiry proceedings instigated to consider his future employment – with the possibility that this 'could lead to the termination of your employment by the Authority'. The very next day two AHA officers and the chairman of the Cogwheel committee arranged an urgent meeting with the medical director to ascertain his position. The latter still insisted on the need for two types of treatment, and declared that the inquiry report was hostile to psychoanalysis. No immediate decision was taken, and at the PSC meeting the situation in the day hospital was described as 'fairly total confusion': the patients were beginning to talk of creating a third category of treatment.

Since the medical director had failed to 'unequivocally accept' the principal recommendations of the inquiry report, he was suspended on full pay on 4 November 1976. He was no longer allowed to set foot in the institute without written permission. The AHA was setting up another inquiry, this time into whether the medical director should receive disciplinary sanction and be dismissed from his post as AHA consultant.

For two months the day hospital was in the charge of a locum (temporary) consultant psychiatrist, until a more long-term locum was appointed in January 1977. During this period, the former medical director's two main supporters on the staff continued to promote his approach under the category B system, instead of joining the rest of the staff in trying to help the patients over the trauma of the preceding months. These two were an occupational therapist and a clinical assistant (who was both a qualified psychiatrist and a psychotherapist). The latter was surprised when, as a consequence of her continued rebellious stance, the question of renewing her contract was brought up at a PSC meeting; previously, the contract had always been renewed automatically. By way of warning her against her persistent non-cooperation with the inquiry recommendations, or at least to demonstrate their right to control her work, the PSC renewed the contract provisionally for three months. Eventually, in September 1977, both she and the occupational therapist were 'eased out' of their positions. When the occupational therapist, who was no longer allowed to practise under the NHS, took the AHA to a tribunal to challenge the decision, it found she had neither been treated badly nor dismissed unfairly.

The new locum took up his appointment in January 1977. He and the PSC immediately concerned themselves with implementing the inquiry recommendations, reinstating most of the bureaucratic procedures and 'supportive' approaches. The new locum also drew up a declaration of 'understandings' at the day hospital which amounted to a formal statement of an informal commitment or contract for patients as members of the therapeutic community.

In addition to being assessed and formally admitted, the patients were given to understand that each had certain obligations to the day hospital – emphasizing the idea of community membership. As well as being enjoined to contribute fully to the patients' side of the therapeutic contract by describing feelings and experiences to provide the material for therapy, patients were told they must attend at the times required and share in 'chores, recreational or occupational activity and community work'. In this way the former medical director's one-dimensional system, which had reduced all treatment and aspects of community life to purely analytic interpretation, was being replaced not only by as rounded a treatment experience as possible, including group therapy work, but also in its practical, recreational and occupational aspects. Moreover, whereas the earlier medical director had cut himself off from other departments and outside agencies, the new locum wanted to forge links with them and to integrate the day hospital and adult departments.

The second inquiry

By 7 March 1977, the terms of reference of the new committee of inquiry had been set up. The AHA stated that it was to

> inquire into the running of the day hospital and the failure of [the medical director] to comply with the recommendations of the committee of inquiry contained in its report dated September 1976 by the Area Health Authority (Teaching), and to make recommendations.

The three people on the committee were a recorder of the Crown Court, a consultant psychiatrist and a lay member. The medical director on the one hand, and the five consultants and doctors on the other, would be represented by Queen's Counsels who would cross-examine witnesses giving evidence. This

236

second inquiry was very much more serious than the first, as it followed a procedure laid down for 'serious disciplinary cases involving doctors or dentists'. It was no longer a question of curbing the excesses of an overzealous therapy programme but a disciplinary issue involving the possible sacking of a doctor from the AHA. This kind of case is rare, and usually considered only in instances of gross misdemeanour (such as sexual activity with a patient) or negligence, since doctors hold tenured jobs as a result of their expertise and the particular nature of their relationship with their patients.

Aside from two preliminary meetings, the committee sat for sixty-one days between 30 May and 10 November 1977, and it was not until January 1978 – one year and three months after the suspension of the medical director – that its findings were completed. Its report was kept strictly confidential.

In general terms, the second inquiry had been examining the validity of the earlier inquiry's recommendations. If they were found to be justified, then the medical director's behaviour in failing to comply with them was not; if they were found wanting, then his actions would be legitimate. The second inquiry was in no doubt: the recommendations had been reasonable and the medical director at fault. He had not met the required standards of care expected of a consultant in the NHS, he had failed in his responsibilities and he was not suitable to work as a consultant. He was not struck off the professional register of doctors, as it was felt that with guidance he could continue to function according to his qualifications; while he should not be allowed to continue as a clinically independent consultant, he could be managed by a senior consultant. In consequence, he was demoted to the level of registrar or clinical assistant.

The report criticized a number of specific aspects of the day hospital experiment:

(a) The idea of running a large-group therapy session all day was impossible, and against psychoanalytic practice.
(b) Ezrielian interpretations were difficult to make and needed a degree of training found lacking in most of the staff.
(c) The experiment had been neither planned nor supervised.
(d) As only one type of treatment had been allowed, the staff

had lost morale and felt de-skilled through not having been able to practise the expertise gained in their original training (for example nursing, occupational therapy).

(e) The committee did not accept the idea of applying one form of treatment for all patients, especially given that the patients had not been selected for that treatment or indeed selected at all.

(f) The day hospital was not being used properly during the whole day as a result of the treatment perspective.

(g) The standard of care was not sufficient, and stopping of the provision of meals unethical.

(h) The medical director had ignored the administration and NHS requirements, and by his lack of care for the patients and the rejection of their needs while pursuing his regime had made excessive demands on his staff; his conduct could be described as 'unprofessional'.

In other words, although the report was highly critical of the medical director's methods and approach, it did not regard him guilty of malpractice. Because of his professional autonomy, a doctor may treat his patients as he sees fit as long as his activities do not constitute malpractice. The AHA may, as in this case, not agree with his experimental approach and may not want to go on employing him, but he is still free to work with some other AHA as long as no malpractice is proved against him.

The medical director was then summarily dismissed.

During the eighteen months following the second inquiry report (until June 1979), the locum and staff attempted to establish a selection policy, discharging patients they felt to be unsuitable for a therapeutic community. But the attempt to establish a flourishing new regime failed. Between April 1977 and December 1978, nine out of the twenty-eight patients who had been accepted out of 117 referrals did not attend and nine others were discharged. Day hospital attendances in 1978 totalled 2,170 (*SBH 112 Return of Mental Illness Facilities*, DHSS circular), which meant that allowing for public holidays during the year, only forty-three attended per week, or nine a day. (At the height of the experiment in 1974 and 1975 daily

The crisis

attendance was usually between twenty-five and thirty, although there were no records to substantiate these figures.)

A report by the AHA in June 1979 on the closure of the day hospital attributed this decline to a number of factors: the day hospital was set apart from the rest of the district's facilities for mental illness; it lacked clearly defined selection criteria; it had an 'isolationist' aspect; and in the past it had failed to keep adequate patient records and statistics. The report concluded: 'It would not be appropriate to allocate scarce resources to a facility of such limited scope and application in terms of services for the mentally ill generally.' Not only would closure not affect services adversely as compared with the closure of a medical or surgical ward, but it would also save £60,000 revenue per year.[5]

Following the AHA report, the day hospital was finally closed in August 1979 after alternative treatment had been found for all remaining patients. The staff went to work full-time in the adult department, and the premises stand empty and unused.

Concluding remarks

This review of the events of the crisis brings into sharper focus some of the issues raised in earlier chapters. Leaving a more extensive consideration of professional autonomy, psychoanalytic reductionism and questions of organizational structure to the final chapter, here I shall only examine a few issues brought up by the events related above. Why, for instance, did the patients organize themselves and make an official complaint rather than remain apathetic or simply leave the day hospital? And why did the NHS respond by instituting an inquiry rather than regard the patients as trouble-makers to be put down or ignored?

The patients' complaint

While their complaint forcused on their being ridiculed and deprived of facilities, the patients were indirectly criticizing the medical director for over-extending his psychoanalytic theory into controlling their behaviour and denying the role of the administration. They objected to being used as 'guinea pigs' and

239

spoke of 'subtle means of control', as well as being deprived of both participation in decision-making and facilities such as fares and, especially, meals.

But why did the patients make a formal complaint rather than leave? I would suggest that there were two main reasons. In the first place, the patients' leadership was articulate and politicized. There seemed to be a high level of intelligence and verbal facility in the patient body, perhaps as a result of the fact that even in the mid-1970s it was still just as fashionable to drop into an 'alternative' organization (such as a therapeutic community) as it was to drop out altogether. During the earlier crisis the day hospital had made itself quite a name for radicalism as a result of its much-publicized protest against conventional psychiatry. It attracted intelligent patients in need of help and eager to experience more 'democratic' and *avant-garde* treatment. In addition the earlier protest had generally politicized the organization, whose members were ready to define actions by outsiders in political terms and draw a sharp dividing line between 'us' and 'them'. Some of the patients who complained in 1976 had already been involved in the earlier protest, and those who were not felt they had inherited the political will of their predecessors.

On the other hand, many of the 'rank-and-file' patients felt they were at the end of the road. Some had been in prison, or committed to mental hospitals and treated with ECT and drugs, and they hoped that the day hospital would provide the one alternative left rather than what they feared might be a lifetime of repeating their earlier institutional experience. They hoped it would provide them with some kind of solution, if not outright salvation. At the same time they may have believed that their role in a therapeutic community was to attempt active participation in the institution. It is not difficult, therefore, to see why they took political action rather than leave the hospital.

Having seen why the patients complained, why did the AHA, from the point of view of the organization, not decide to ignore their letter? Since the patients had made a formal complaint, the AHA was bound to see whether there were grounds for this. Consequently it referred the matter initially to the only organizational body conversant with the day hospital, and asked

The crisis

the PSC whether its members thought the complaint did or did not constitute an unwarranted attack on the medical director.

Although the PSC regretted the necessity for an inquiry – many of its members had initially felt quite proud of the institute's 'therapeutic baby' – they were concerned for the patients. The latter had identified themselves by name when the medical director spurned their letter as anonymous, and they appeared perfectly serious about the complaint. Moreover, many PSC members had been privately worried about the day hospital because the patients often seemed unruly and the staff (particularly the medical director) recalcitrant when administrative personnel in the institute or the nursing hierarchy tried to play their proper roles. So when finally the staff rejected the PSC's right to query the day hospital approach, the PSC felt it necessary to press for an inquiry because members felt that the erosion of administrative authority had gone too far.

The first inquiry

The results of the first inquiry made it clear that the panel felt the medical director had become too extreme in his approach. The various recommendations put forward implied more or less the reconstruction of the day hospital to what it had been before the experiment began. But why were the results of the first inquiry so unsuccessful in righting the situation?

Most of the staff agreed with the medical director when he maintained that administrators could not dictate to medical men, whose responsibility was solely to their patients. By so doing he was calling on that sanctified institution, the doctor–patient relationship, on the basis of which patients have a right to confidentiality which, it is held, cannot be respected if the doctor's work is being monitored. As representatives of the medical director's employer, the Regional Health Authority had the option to decide not to employ him, but it could not manage his work.

The situation became even more unacceptable to the medical director (whose authority rested on professional autonomy), when the PSC, on AHA instructions, tried to introduce a monitoring system whereby senior PSC members, medical and non-

241

medical, were formally required to check on a particular aspect of the medical director's work to see whether he was meeting the inquiry recommendations. When he himself admitted that he would not, the AHA on behalf of the Regional Health Authority suspended the medical director, pending the findings of a second inquiry.

The second inquiry

Although the medical director was dismissed by the AHA as a result of the second inquiry recommendations, it was not because he was found to be negligent, to have committed malpractice or to have failed to honour his contract (by, for example, not working the required number of sessions). It was rather that the inquiry committee decreed that his approach constituted 'wrong' practice (not *mal*practice). Such a theory-based professional judgement is usually – as in this case – judged by a peer group. The outcome of its assessment of the medical director's work meant that although he could no longer work as an employee of the AHA he could, since he had not committed malpractice, work elsewhere in the NHS. He was not, in other words, regarded as a threat to patients.

The detailed history I have recounted in these pages gives, I believe for the first time, a study of a system in which a theoretical approach was elaborated into an institutional form in such a way that it concretely illustrates the politics and ideology of de-institutionalization in the post-anti-psychiatry period. It shows how democracy can be used as an empty slogan when it masks manipulation and social control, and proves that freedom from rules is no guarantee of liberty. Indeed, in this case 'democracy' allowed a tyranny of the therapeutic to emerge until once more rules were imposed and the experiment deemed a failure.

8

The tyranny of the therapeutic

The day hospital's unique approach to treatment – the use of psychoanalysis in a highly flexible community context – developed as a result of a number of influences: in particular the psychotherapeutic orientation of the staff in the institute in which the hospital was based; and the history of the day hospital's earlier crisis when it had had to fight to protect its therapeutic role against a return to its previous traditional out-patient function.

Far from returning to its earlier role, the day hospital developed into an unconventional therapeutic community. Although it shared the principles of permissiveness, democracy, role-blurring and reality confrontation of other therapeutic communities both therapeutically and institutionally, it developed in a skewed and exaggerated way. Whereas its sister institutions believed in the democratic participation of patients in the running of the hospital and in a tolerant and supportive attitude to behaviour, which was primarily to be understood rather than controlled, at the day hospital this flexibility was taken to such an extreme that all vestiges of formal rules were abandoned. Similarly, whereas therapy based on an understanding of the individual's role in the community replaced neurochemical treatment in most therapeutic communities, at the day hospital there was an exclusive concern for unconscious processes.

The resulting approach, which combined aspects of community treatment with psychoanalysis, was unique and had important unintended consequences. In a situation in which rules and roles had been abandoned, the force that emerged to fill the vacuum left by the removal of these formal controls was psychoanalysis itself. Given the lack of formal means to set limits to behaviour and the fear of contradicting the ideology that rules were not only unnecessary but authoritarian, the only means at hand was the – albeit unconscious – use of the therapy itself. The automatic statement that unacceptable behaviour had arisen because of unconscious drives each time a dissenting voice was heard or deviant behaviour exhibited meant that control was secured by consistently reducing all behaviour or verbal contributions to evidence of pathology – the action or statement of the patient was regarded as illegitimate. The reductive use of psychoanalysis replaced the formal controls that had been abandoned as part of the day hospital's rejection of traditional psychiatry. This manipulative use of psychoanalysis occurred despite its originally altruistic adoption as part of a 'new order' in psychiatry.

For the day hospital's unique approach to treatment was a combination of two treatment methods that rejected traditional psychiatry: psychoanalysis and the community perspective. The rejection of the 'authoritarian' methods of psychiatry arose out of a dislike of the degradation imposed on patients by highly bureaucratized rules and the passivity demanded of them. It is ironical, then, that the hospital's exaggerated use of psychoanalysis in a context uncontrolled by bureaucratic rules can itself be said to have led to social control and self-degradation.

Despite its radical image the day hospital exemplified the process by which, through a regime of therapy, the progress of patients was defined by staff in terms of psychiatric health or illness, progress and regression. Therapy in these terms can be seen as a kind of 'degradation therapy' (Goffman, 1968), whereby the patient has to take on the staff's version of himself as a condition of treatment: namely that his actions, attitudes and statements are governed solely by his pathology.

Although it might be an exaggeration to describe the day hospital therapy entirely as a process of Goffman-type self-degradation, none the less the combination of a reductive use of psychoanalysis and a debureaucratized context did lead to more or less subtle attacks on the self. Contrary to Goffman's damning indictment of the role of formal rules in the process of self-degradation, I would argue that rules could actually have

244

set limits on the claims the institute made on the patients. In the day hospital they were being impelled to see all expressions of their personalities in daily life exclusively in terms of pathology. To my mind the imposition of a negative definition of self is potentially more destructive than the requirement to obey externally applied rules, particularly because in the context of a psychiatric hospital the individual's sense of self has already been weakened by the loss of status experienced by becoming a 'patient', through the stigma attached to his role and the actual experience of his mental condition.

I would argue, therefore, that an all-embracing ideology is as pernicious as the strictures of an over-regulated institution. As Goffman himself has amply shown, where there are rules, people always find ways of gaining elbow room. By finding a private space for private activities and the personal face, the patient can survive precisely because rules can be bent or at least rebelled against.

At the day hospital the medical director adopted the anarchists' argument that all rules are by their very nature constraining and life-destroying and that a lack of rules is automatically life-enhancing and freeing. But such a position ignores the fact that rules themselves can be both freeing and/or constraining, as Giddens puts it in *The Constitution of Society*:

> . . . *rules have two aspects to them . . . [they] relate on the one hand to the constitution of* meaning *and on the other to the* sanctioning *of modes of social conduct.*
> *(1984, p. 18)*

According to Giddens, when we obey rules we are being constrained by social forces as well as being participants in the reproduction of the social world, and are therefore acting on the world as much as being constrained by it. For instance, when we learn a language we are both constrained by the grammatical rules we must use and enabled by them to communicate. For Giddens society therefore has a dual nature whereby structure, made up of rules and resources, is both experienced as outside actors and also embodied in their actions. In this way structure is both constraining and enabling, even

245

though stretched over time and space it is beyond the control of individual actors.

However, it is doubtless true that the impact of the institution is far greater where the identity of the rebel is ruled out by the apparent lack of rules. A structureless organization leaves the individual feeling vulnerable, as the lack of parameters makes it hard for him to know how to behave. Indeed, at the day hospital the staff explicitly wanted patients to sense this vacuum to prevent them falling back on old roles as a way of avoiding feeling insecure. In such a fluid context the presence of a totalistic ideology was doubly powerful. Consequently, the individual grasped at whatever was thrown his way and all too rapidly developed a view of himself as pathologically motivated rather than as an individual possessing individual tastes and ideas, as well as problems.

I would argue from the evidence of my case study that it is this lack of structure that prevents a counter-culture from developing. The latter would, I believe, have provided the patients with an alternative system of values, definitions of reality and the self that would have counteracted the official psychoanalytical version of their condition and status. However strong or intrusive the official framework may be, patients or inmates always find a loophole, a way of bending rules or of dodging strictures: in prisons, for example, where no monetary economy is permitted, tobacco becomes the currency and is used to purchase goods or services from others, and these 'illegal' processes provide another social world of social meanings, roles and statuses that can be used to counter the official world.

Because the day hospital lacked a formal structure, the groupings the patients made informally (see Chapter 6) tended to be almost accidental groups of individual reactions and did not represent any kind of coherent patient view. For example, those who individually sought refuge from their problems through drink tended to congregate in the 'library' to share bottles of cider on a purely social basis. It was only when the staff as a group actually wrote down a rule for the first time (concerning the ending of the provision of meals and travel expenses) that the patients responded as a coherent group. It was only then that a real patient culture can be said to have developed. The self-defined role of patient from that time on provided these individuals, previously isolated from each other, with a common point of reference: that they were being controlled by the staff whose previous democratic proclamations were now considered fraudulent. The staff's explanations and definitions of reality in terms of the patients' pathology were now regarded as suspect and a social explanation for their problem posited in their place.

When an institution (residential or non-residential) employing a totalist ideology has jurisdiction not merely over a fifty-minute session but over the whole day environment of the therapy, the impact of an interpretation based on pathology is far-reaching indeed. By making the whole day hospital the equivalent of the psychoanalyst's consulting room, the day hospital was reversing the more usual attempt by analysts to exclude external reality and in this way it became a totalizing environment. As Coser (1979) argues, therapy can be defined as totalitarian where one and the same therapist both provides therapy and exercises a policing function. In a context that lacks rules, roles and boundaries, the lack of formal authority necessarily collapses into the therapy because the latter remains the only available tool of control. Thus where patients in therapy are admonished by their therapists freely to associate about anything that comes into their minds – fantastic, illegal or murderous – and at the same time must be controlled (however covertly) for acting violently or illegally, then a totalitarian system of therapy has indeed evolved.

The questions about the nature of psychiatric treatment and its relationship to social control that are raised by the story of the day hospital must be seen in the broader context of the different treatment methods available. I would argue that in the context of traditional, more 'authoritarian' methods of treatment the day hospital's approach represented a new – and in some ways more ruthless – tyranny, emerging as it did under the guise of 'democracy'. Whereas Goffman (1968) outlined the manipulation and degradation of traditional psychiatry I extend these ideas to show how more 'humane' treatment such as psychotherapy in a more democratic context can be even more manipulative. Although the day hospital was aware of the schizoid family mechanisms of collusions, the denied smiles and double-binds, it adopted these methods itself when faced with the vacuum formal rules and structures had left as a result of hospital policy. It identified with Szasz's (1961) belief that mental illness was a myth and yet simultaneously participated in a witch-hunt of those whose pathology was more evident in their behaviour. From all these aspects it could be argued that my work illustrates well Foucault's (1965) perception of the will to truth – a desire for power that emerges in the name of treatment in every age, particularly in the modern age as a result of more intrusive socialization processes and the development of the social sciences. Lest my case study seems to imply a seesaw movement from rules to anarchy and back to rules again, let me say that I premise my argument on what I see to be the essence of the psychoanalytic process.

The unique perspective of the day hospital developed, as I suggested earlier, from the two main strands of reaction against traditional psychiatric treatment – broadly speaking, the 'community' and the 'psychoanalytic' perspectives. Both express the renunciation of the perversity of the 'helping institutions' which strip people of their identity in the pursuit of individual pathology. Both accuse psychiatry of a tendency to reduce the complexity of mental disturbance to a simplistic concept of mental malfunction in the individual, but each has its own idea of what is lacking in conventional treatment. In schematic terms, the community critique sees both the creation and healing of mental illness as being dependent upon factors in the individual's social or familial context, while psychoanalysis emphasizes the complexity of the relationship between the conscious and unconscious self and the belief that insight into this relationship will provide the prerequisite for psychological integration and 'psychic health'. Let me spell out these two perspectives in slightly more detail.

The community perspective

Apart from the anti-psychiatry movement, which represented a vocal but small minority within the more mainstream psychiatric world, at about the same time a somewhat less radical but none the less important reaction against traditional psychiatry developed amongst those who in one form or another favoured 'community care' as an alternative to hospital incarceration and physical treatment.

Largely as a result of the changes produced by the introduction of psychotropic drugs which removed the need for long-term hospitalization of many patients, the last ten years in psychiatry have seen a general trend towards the speedy return of patients to the community. Consequently, the need for the massive Victorian hospitals that have always served as the main psychiatric treatment institutions in the UK has, it is felt, been largely removed and many are being closed down.

Community care has thus become a serious alternative to psychiatric hospital. However, with the economic recession of recent years and the fact that most governments have placed a low priority on psychiatry, the necessary funding to make community care a really viable alternative to conventional treatment has not been forthcoming. Consequently, just as the over-emphasis upon residential treatment led to far too many patients becoming 'institutionalized', so the attempt to rely exclusively on community care has also proved unsatisfactory, largely as a result of lack of supportive personnel and organization. And, as Andy Scull has shown, in *Decarceration* (1977), the American experience is not encouraging. According to Scull, the massive closure of residential hospitals in the US has not been matched by parallel care in the community, so that the state has saved money at the expense of the patients who, without sufficient support, have been allowed to deteriorate.

A somewhat similar story has occurred in Italy (for a comparison between Britain and Italy, see Rogers and Pilgrim, 1986), where acute cases are still hospitalized but only for the period of crisis and in a special ward in a general hospital. Although in many parts of the country support in the community is well-defined, well-funded and well-organized, resources are not evenly spread throughout the length and breadth of the country and in the poorer areas this has meant the destitution of many former patients – the *'abbandonati'*.[1] The experiences of both the US and Italy therefore have demonstrated that if the service is underfunded the rhetoric of decarceration can be used to underwrite a disregard for distress and a movement towards a situation where individuals and their families attempt to replace the welfare state and deal with their own distress unaided by public services. Paradoxically, community care becomes the individual's right to suffer distress in his own family, should he have one.

Psychoanalysis

Whereas the community perspective and treatment arose as a reaction against the traditional emphasis upon individual pathology, so psychoanalysis in its turn emerged to offer a more subtle and complex view of pathology. Its perspective implies the rejection of the idea that individual pathology is a disease, and adopts instead a relational and conflictual view of the nature of distress in both social and intrapsychic terms.

The family – and later society – becomes a social world for the enactment and integration of psychic conflict which cannot be reducible to medical aetiologies. When the particular childhood experience of an individual reflects too closely the inner phantasy world of the child in adulthood the individual often repeats, again and again the distorted family relationships that originally troubled him. In such situations the individual may resort to psychoanalytic treatment in the hope of being liberated from maladaptive behaviour by exploring, in the 'transference' relationship with the psychoanalyst, both the defences that are narrowing or distorting his life and the unconscious desires they mask. The idea is that in the process of the analysis the patient 'transfers' on to the analyst feelings and desires that he once felt for his parents or other 'love-objects'. It is the interpretation of these emotions, experienced in the 'here and now' of the analytic relationship in terms of what the analyst understands are the unconscious motives of the patient, that constitutes the treatment. In theory at least, once the defences are known and the unconscious desires understood, the patient is liberated from disabling patterns of thought and behaviour.[2]

Although the day hospital illustrates how psychoanalysis itself can lend itself to control, it would be simplistic to argue that psychoanalysis itself is an instrument of repression. Even if one accepts that at a more general level it is an important institution in a regime where knowledge is power (Foucault 1965), within this particular discourse it remains possible to differentiate between enabling or destructive applications of psychoanalysis. Similarly at the organizational level it is all too easy to argue that rules are either repressive or permit order. I would argue that they are both constraining and enabling. Our behaviour may be limited by rules, but freedom or creativity can be experienced both within their limits and in the way in which we can participate through rules in the construction of our world.

Beyond the issue of *provision* of care, including its political meaning and its consequences for people in distress, is the question of power that is the theme of this book. Just as Goffman's (1968) critique is important not because he addresses the problem of provision but because of his sustained display of the workings of power, so I rest my case on the sustained display of the workings of democratic tyranny. In my view Laing, Szasz and Foucault, as well as Goffman, have all pointed in this direction, but the social and political climate of the 1970s and 1980s was needed to set the stage for my study.

In the 1960s Laing showed how power was transmitted through the family; Szasz argued that treatment is more oppressive than punishment; Goffman described the impact of the institution on the patient in the treatment process and Foucault the role of the 'will to power'; a generation later my study displays the workings of power in the relationships between knowledge and power and shows how much more oppressive such tyrannies are when they are marked by an egalitarian rhetoric. For here 'the truth' was itself a weapon. Here was a degradation in pure form rather than the use of rituals to degrade. Here was the Laingian family in the guise of a helping institution; here was Szasz's myth of mental illness embodied in the social construction of badness; here was Foucault's will to power in raw form. I would argue that, in such a context, the invasion of the inner core of the individual is far greater than that described by Goffman,[3] which arises as a result of the assignation of roles and detailed rules, or indeed the stigma attached to the individual under labelling theory. I would even go as far as to maintain that the potency of the power in the day hospital that lay hidden beneath Goffman's rules or the interactionist's deviant labels is matched only in the more totalitarian situation of brainwashing. Because the control was masked by an ideology that pretended to be democratic and therapeutic the invasion of the self was far more far-reaching than was dreamt of in the world of *Asylums*. By constantly reducing all statements to pathological motivation, the patients came to see themselves as possessed by their pathology and lacking other more adult aspects of their personalities. In the process their sense of self was actively eroded, whilst the expert's was enhanced.

The day hospital as an instance of a control process must make us rethink many of our ideas of power. There was no active coercion, no formal rules, no visible sanctions or rewards, and yet the subjugation of one group by another was profound.

Notes

Chapter 1

1. The day hospital became quite famous because of an earlier protest. See Chapter 2.
2. This became a prevalent view in the late 1960s. See, for example, Szasz (1961).
3. There is another and important criticism of Goffman that must be made. What Goffman did was to expose the mental hospital to us in such a way that we could identify with those undergoing its rigours. Although it must sometimes happen that relatively well people are hospitalized through mis-diagnosis, it must not be forgotten that the treatment at and the organization of the traditional mental hospital are designed for those who are, by and large psychotically ill. Goffman is quite right to point out those aspects of the organization that have more to do with organization requirements than patients' needs (for example to cope with the exigencies of organizing the daily life of large numbers of individuals etc.) and the unintended consequences of the treatment (for example institutionalization) but he entirely ignores the extent to which patients may actually be helped by, for example, the structured nature of the day in a mental hospital. It cannot be assumed that all patients suffer from the totalistic nature of the mental hospital. We may throw up our hands in horror at the rule-bound life of an inmate, but this may be a far safer and reassuring context for someone whose own ego-boundaries have become unstable.

To the mature person concerned with his individuality and the development of his sense of self, the rules of a mental hospital deprive him of the possibility of choice and growth. The psychotic or deluded person who has lost his sense of self and of freedom may well gain relief from a situation where the room for choice is narrowed. Between these two extremes is the therapeutic community which, like psycho-

253

analysis, encourages within certain limits the exercise of freedom and choice.

4. More recently, the literature on therapeutic communities has increased, but most of it is still written by practitioners in the field rather than by sociologists.

5. Apart from the intrinsic problems of creating hypotheses and carrying through a sophisticated quantitative analysis, I did not see how such an approach would be particularly appropriate in view of the theoretical attitude of the day hospital and the small number of staff and patients.

6. See the 'bring it to the group' syndrome (Chapter 4), where decisions by participants in authority (staff) were avoided and action legitimated by the matter having been brought to the large group, which was the 'democratic' body tacitly recognized as having a certain authority.

Chapter 2

1. See Chapter 3.

2. I am indebted to a day hospital member of staff for much of the following information. It was also corroborated by the report of the first committee of inquiry in 1976.

3. Cogwheel committee of the Division of Psychiatry: the representative body for consultants, dealing with questions of policy.

4. Psychotherapy may be defined as more concerned with inter- and intrapersonal tensions, while sociotherapy focuses on inter- and intra-group tensions.

5. At the Henderson Hospital in Surrey, sanctions of discharge and probation for discharge were used most successfully against violence and other rule-breaking in the community. Perhaps the success was due in part to the Henderson's residential nature and the fact that patients might have found it difficult to find other accommodation and the kind of social network the hospital provided; in the day hospital, on the other hand, the patients were not in a total institution and had to look after themselves in most ways.

6. Revolving-door patients tend to return to hospital again and again as soon as they are discharged.

7. Unfortunately the lack of any selection policy and the staff's refusal to give any individual assessment interviews meant that it was impossible to match treatment to needs, or indeed to know what individual needs were. It is likely that at that time (about 1974) there was a variety of different kinds of patient at different stages, in need of

Notes

different types and degrees of support. In fact, it was argued at the inquiry in 1976 that this lack of selection had contributed to the failure of the experiment, as such an unusual approach to treatment would be expected to require very careful selection of patients for the new venture to stand a chance of success.

Chapter 3

1. The way in which the day hospital was seen by some to be part of a social movement which was breaking with organic psychiatry is shown in the following extract from a discussion with a staff member:

Staff member: Organic psychiatry is dying, but it will fight to the end. It may close down the day hospital because of the threat psychodynamic therapy represents to organic psychiatry. It can make inquiries and write letters, but it will lose in the end because the social climate is changing. But fighting from only *inside* the hospital is not enough. In 1972 [when the day hospital was threatened with closure] we needed the organizations, doctors and pressure groups to help the place survive.

With *One Flew Over the Cuckoo's Nest* people laughed. They realized that this could just as easily be one of themselves. Everybody has a fear of madness. This is why for the most part mental patients are shunned, drugged and locked away. We don't want to see what reminds us of ourselves, and also we're afraid. But if people begin to understand, through films etc., they will begin to lose their fear and stop being so punitive. Take myself: I feared madness, so I studied it to understand and lose that fear. But the whole social structure must be changed, too, to really change everyone's attitude – like the family, and usual conceptions of normality and success.

2. The term 'avoided relationship' refers to the relationship the patient tries to adopt with the therapist, a relationship which is slightly less difficult for him to cope with than his underlying fear hidden in the unconscious, which it is the task of the therapist to uncover and bring to the conscious mind. See Ezriel (1959).
3. This is the well-known transference symptom whereby the patient transfers to the therapist feelings which stem from his relationship with his parents and other authority figures in his earlier years.
4. Ezriel's technique was also applied in a hospital in Israel by

255

Asylum to Anarchy

A. C. R. Skynner, but without such psychoanalytic reductionism. See Skynner (1974).

5. In the institute's child guidance clinic for example, it was relatively clear that the principal social worker was employed as an independent therapist by the social services department (or the Area Health Authority), working as a colleague of the consultant, providing a personalized service (the referral would be to a named therapist) as well as managing junior social workers. Below this, junior or trainee social workers were seconded or attached to a medically qualified consultant colleague, or to the principal social worker by the medically qualified consultant. Despite the fact that organizationally the consultants carried the greater weight of authority (see Freidson, 1970) the therapists did work in a multidisciplinary fashion, liaising with rather than controlling each other. In the case of a complaint from the consultant about work done by another therapist, the problem would usually be taken up first with the individual concerned, then with the senior professional of the same discipline within the institute, then possibly by the Professional Staff Committee, followed by the Area Health Authority or another appropriate external body.

6. Douglas (1973) argues that when rules are hidden they may be even more effective because of this, since it is easier to oppose and fight what is known and/or seen.

7. Pieces of information, as with all knowledge, can be used as 'counters' in a power struggle between patients and staff. So Roth (1973) argues that in tuberculosis hospitals doctors would avoid asking patients for information, even where it would help the treatment, for fear that by placing the patient in a quasi-colleagial position they might lose their medical authority over them. Patients for their part would withhold information to meet their own interests.

8. The term 'borderline' describes those patients who are regarded as being on the border between neurosis and psychosis (see Rycroft 1968). Although the day hospital had abandoned diagnostic labels, when I first arrived there this was the term most frequently used for formally describing (for example at a conference) the majority of the patients.

9. The reaction to the proposal to close down the day hospital in 1972 shows how Britain had not yet followed the American decarceration trend in which hospitals were emptied and patients placed in the community.

Notes

Chapter 4

1. In practice, few patients were turned down. The selection process had already been achieved before the patient reached this 'democratic' filter.

2. In Goffman (1968) this label was used retrospectively to refer to individuals who through some action broke the final straw of people's toleration and were committed to hospital. Here the idea of 'pre-patient' is more literally used, in the sense that until they were actually admitted they were not defined as patients and could, in fact, choose whether or not to become a patient.

3. In this way, the process of becoming a patient was more akin to joining a club.

4. Family therapy is psychotherapy which regards the family, not the individual patient, as the therapeutic object. (See Rycroft, 1968.)

5. Unfortunately, there are no clear records as evidence that it was deliberate policy not to keep clinical or bureaucratic accounts of any kind during this period.

6. Lacking formal admission procedures, some new patients often seemed overwhelmed by the lack of structure and withdrew into themselves, starting to speak only weeks later. Different patients responded differently. 'Neurotic' patients felt threatened by the lack of any structure for constraining them; more psychotic patients could cope more easily, since the lack of boundaries in the social context echoed their inner lack of boundaries. (Psychotic here implies lack of insight, according to psychiatry; or a failure in reality testing, that is, an inability to distinguish between mental images and phantasies and external reality, in the psychoanalytic definition.)

7. Even outside the NHS, no register of psychotherapists has as yet been drawn up and there is therefore no recognized standard. Until the NHS creates its own training programme, or officially recognizes other training bodies, NHS psychotherapy (except at the Tavistock Clinic, where training is carefully designed) will remain a crude instrument as workers in allied disciplines proceed merely by imitation of others and lack both theoretical training and personal analysis. As a result, many of the day hospital staff experienced uncertainty in terms of their qualifications and role.

8. It is possible that respect for Ezriel's thought and person contributed to the staff's loyalty to the experiment. For throughout the conflict over the medical director's modification of Ezriel's theory not one word of criticism of Ezriel was expressed by anyone, not even those who finally were in the greatest opposition to the medical

257

director. It was only that certain doubts were aired as to the applicability of Ezriel's theory to large groups, as opposed to small-group therapy. Since the day hospital staff had been initiated into psychotherapy mainly through the medical director's teachings and those of his mentor, it is hardly surprising that they should have found it hard at first to take a detached look at the methods employed in the hospital.

9. Freidson (1970) argues that egalitarianism in therapeutic communities cannot but remain utopian, because although differences in power can be flattened by agreement and differences in bureaucratic authority by abolishing the formal position, there always remains the authority of expertise since it is only through expertise that the organization can attain its stated goal. As long as the aim of the hospital is the therapeutic care of patients, then – even if formal roles have been dissolved – it has need of the doctor's expertise and remains dependent on his services.

This was borne out exactly by the example of the day hospital: despite the fact that the hierarchy had deliberately been flattened in so far as all members were supposed to have equal authority, a new structure of hierarchical authority appeared based on degrees of expertise. In this, the patients were at the bottom of the pyramid and in a helpless position as the result of their relative ignorance in the realm of therapeutic expertise and their concomitant need to benefit from that expertise to learn how to cope with their everyday lives.

Moreover, apart from technical expertise as reflected in professional qualifications, staff and patients were also differentiated by their personal experience of psychoanalysis. Only five staff members had undergone psychoanalysis themselves and, in a situation where the ability to understand unconscious drives was the only recognized skill, this was bound to create a hierarchy of enlightenment.

10. After some months away from the day hospital, I heard that a few weeks after this incident the patient concerned left, and some months later it was reported that she had committed suicide. The organization had not been flexible enough to help her by trying to meet her needs sufficiently (if indeed they could be met). The incident is a painful reminder of the kind of personal conflict involved when one disagrees with a very powerful ideology yet lacks the resources to defy it.

11. According to the theory, however, through 'successful' analysis a patient begins to have a sense of these things. If he has understood his own 'authentic' (that is, not disguised by defences) and 'inauthentic' thinking, feeling, acting, he can begin to discern the same in others. Until, however, he has reached this point of understanding (through

258

Notes

witnessing the influence of his own unconscious mind on his actions and thoughts), he sometimes remains in more doubt about it than he was before he started analysis. In its very nature, therefore, psychoanalysis is a more involving and confusing ideology than most.

12. To 'collude' implies giving into or accepting the pathological phantasies of the patient, rather than showing them to be based not on fact but fiction, and hence trying to see why the patient has developed a need for them. In other words, the term implies a siding or identification with the patient's neurotic defences.

13. Some staff members may, of course, have been suspicious of openly committing themselves in my presence, as they were unclear about my own, necessarily unstated, position.

14. Colleagues in the psychoanalytical world tend not to take seriously, or act upon, what a patient says about his psychotherapist, as it is generally assumed that feelings aroused in the transference relationship have clouded his objectivity.

15. Smith (1955) argues that the emphasis in nursing on specialist skills implies the development of the idea of charismatic authority in parallel with the specialist skills which give doctors the right to charismatic authority.

16. The overlap of medical and administrative authority need not automatically result in disagreement and interprofessional conflict, because usually the areas of authority are quite distinct for each aspect of the treatment and hence require separate skills. So the physiothera- · pist teaches the stroke victim how to walk again, while the coronary specialist monitors his blood pressure and brainwaves. Where the work relates more closely to medical work – for example nursing care – there is a less clearly demarcated area of skill and authority. Ultimately, however, all nursing or paramedical specialties have so far been regarded as encompassed by medical work, on the basis that the scope and depth of the theoretical underpinning of medicine does include nursing, occupational therapy, physiotherapy, and so on. Where there are conflicting opinions between members of separate disciplines, the doctor has ultimate responsibility for the patient. When the disagreement is at ward level, or in small units where the work is mainly technical rather than administrative, the conflicting views are usually negotiated. Where, however, they are between a doctor at his technical level and nursing or paramedical staff at District or Area Health Authority administrative level (who are the other managers of the doctor's nursing and paramedical staff), the matter is less easily resolved because the latter are part of the employing authority with overall managerial control (see Freidson, 1970).

17. Coser (1979) draws a parallel between the overlap of value systems in a totalitarian institution and the 'schizophrenic' mother frequently found in modern Western society. In the typical Jewish family the father's area of responsibility lies with the child's inner disposition and his development into a 'good Jew', and the mother is concerned with the immediate consequences of behaviour. Coser sees this division of labour – where the mother exercises behavioural control by rewards and punishments and the father takes the longer term view of the attitudinal development of the child – as providing a role clarity which contributes to healthy psychological development.

The differentiation here is not merely one of simple distribution of authority, but a matter of what type of authority is shared out to each parent. With his father concerned with personality development and his mother with behavioural conformity, the child learns that his parents have different expectations of him; by learning what the different demands on him are he develops a certain freedom and psychological space as he orders these expectations into a particular role vis-à-vis his respective parents.

The typical modern middle-class mother, on the other hand, is frequently concerned with the psychological development of her child at the same time as she is fulfilling a supervisory role. This being so, she may well be depriving the child of his mental space, or distance from her expectations, by placing him in a double-bind of simultaneous and mutually contradictory demands. For example, if he spills food when helping to clear the table, she may find this initiative laudable and at the same time scold him for being careless. In consequence, the child will be baffled as to what exactly is expected of him.

18. Although Etizoni (1964), argues that the supportive (that is thera-peutic) leader in such a triad should have priority, I would agree with Coser (1979), who warns that, as I witnessed in the day hospital, this would lead to an imbalance between the three parties – the patient, the therapist and the administrator. In any case, where the therapist is medically trained and thus has overall responsibility for the patient, and where the administrator is not a doctor (as is the case in Britain), such an imbalance of authority exists already. In consequence it is not only difficult to control or limit the authority of the therapist, but at the day hospital it was also difficult for the administrator, as well as senior nursing and occupational therapy staff, to exercise properly their legitimate area of authority.

Even where both staff members are medically qualified, as at the O'Brien Hospital, the difference in functions between the therapist and the administrator did constitute some degree of role conflict for

Notes

the patient in the triadic relationship. This, however, was ameliorated by the fact that the contact between the two doctors was kept to a minimum, thereby reducing the possibility of contradictory demands being made simultaneously. Gradually the patient could learn the appropriate behaviour for the two separate contexts in which he had to function.

Chapter 5

1. For an example of an in-patient psychoanalytic setting in which the everyday reality and the unconscious were dealt with together, see the account of the work of the Cassel Hospital (Kennedy *et al.*, 1987).
2. This is not to argue that silence cannot be a legitimate response from a therapist. There may be occasions when it is better to give the patient time to think about the interpretation, or silence may be a response to the assumption that the patient is trying to manipulate the therapist. If, however, silence is used every time an uncomfortable question or a direct expression of feeling is voiced, it appears not so much sensitive help for the patient as self-protection for the therapist.
3. The use of scatological and sexual language was acceptable throughout the institute because of the emphasis in psychotherapy on the preoccupations and desires of the infant as represented in the adult's unconscious.
4. See Chapter 3 for a brief summary of the work of H. Ezriel, who developed the concept of 'non-interpretative intervention'.
5. Emerson (1969) argues that jokes usually convey a covert message about a taboo subject.
6. The difficulties of working in the day hospital should, of course, be appreciated. The patients were always unpredictable and occasionally violent, and during the experiment both staff and patients lacked formal structures to reduce stress as well as any normal procedures for dealing with emergency situations.
7. My interlocutor left after twelve months.
8. It was only later that this theory of psychological development was linked to a more metaphysical theory of knowledge invoking reincarnation (see Wilson, 1970).
9. For example 'loading the person', and 'doctrine over person'; see Lifton (1961).
10. All educational, psychological, religious and political agents of change rely on four general approaches in their endeavours to change people: coercion, exhortation, therapy, and realization. Thought reform emphasizes the first two, while psychiatry tends to emphasize

the last three and does not employ coercion except the coercion of shame. Exhortation signifies a moral imperative to change which, as pointed out, is held in common by both psychiatry and religious sects. Therapy and realization both emphasize the individual's ability to change if only he will, with the help of others; in therapy the mode is to relieve pain; whereas realization may cause pain.

Chapter 6

1. See comments on mockery in Chapter 5, referring to Coser's analysis of humour (Coser, 1960).
2. See, later in this chapter, the extended example of the encounter-group therapist, where this patient reiterates the absent medical director's approach to delegation of authority.
3. See Bruno Bettelheim, (1960) for a description of similar differences between groups in respect of emotional reactions to adversity.
4. The magazine is also called *People not Psychiatry*.
5. According to one member of staff, before the experiment, in the 1960s and early 1970s and during the protest of 1971–2, many of the patients were highly literate, well-educated and full of initiative. She argues that at that time, becoming a member of a therapeutic community was as fashionable as 'dropping out' and the two were very similar phenomena, stemming from peer-group rebelliousness.
6. K. Kesey's *One Flew over the Cuckoo's Nest* uncompromisingly depicts group therapy as social control.
7. Although this patient was part of the social-club group, he was rather disturbed at this time and rarely allied himself with any group. He was the patient who was 'discharged' by a small number of staff for attacking a visiting ex-patient in the day hospital.

Chapter 7

1. 'Screws' is prison slang for prison officers.
2. No records were kept during this period to verify this impression.
3. Contradictions such as these may in fact add to the mystique of a charismatic leader. See Chapter 5 for the parallels between the day hospital ideology and that of religious sects.
4. See Chapter 2, where the history of the Professional Staff Committee and its relationship to the medical committee is examined.
5. A little over a third of this sum could at the time have provided individual private analysis in five sessions a week at £10 a session for

each of the nine patients attending regularly. However, such treatment may not have been suitable for all patients.

Chapter 8

1. In Italy, fortunately, there does remain the recognition of the role of the asylum – or haven – which some patients seem to need at certain acute stages of mental pain or confusion to contain them when they themselves can no longer control their impulses.

2. Although the reductionism of the day hospital and the non-repressive use of psychoanalysis represent two quite different uses of the same theory, perhaps the seeds of the 'reductive' problem do none the less lie within psychoanalytic theory, specifically in Freud's use of the concept of 'over-determination'. According to psychoanalytic theory, action can have more than one cause. So, for instance, if I am at a dinner party and someone who has just won a literary prize is rude to me, my angry retort can be seen as a reaction to his or her bad manners as well as a response to my own feelings of envy at the other person's success. An analyst is more likely to see my action in terms of the motivation of my unconscious envy, whilst I may insist that I was merely reacting to insolent behaviour. The problem is that because Freud talked in terms of determination or cause, we are inclined to think in terms of a *single* cause for an action, perhaps because in the physical sciences over-determination does not exist as a concept: physical events can have only one cause. Freud's emphasis on the concept of cause may have occurred because he felt he had to show how 'scientific' psychoanalysis was in order to be accepted by the establishment. Today, with the establishment of psychoanalysis, it might be possible to talk once more in terms of actions having more than one meaning (rather than *cause*), this being closer to what Freud in fact meant when he talked about over-determination.

As it stands, however, psychoanalytic theory does leave the way open for insecure psychoanalysts to be reductive and controlling in their interpretations. However, it is probably not sufficient merely to replace cause with 'meaning', as I have suggested; it would be necessary to elaborate concepts in the theory in order to develop ways of preventing practitioners from the error of reductionism. Instead of the vacuum in the theory which guides practice, where good nature or good sense should prevail to prevent deliberate or unconscious reductionism, practitioners would then have to contend with actual concepts in the theory. Furthermore the lack of concepts to delineate the boundaries of practice is, I believe, what lies behind the question:

'what constitutes a good analyst?', that is implied in the perennial search for a 'good' analyst. If such concepts were developed to prevent crude reductionism, then the singular importance of finding a 'good' analyst (of course, it will remain preferable to have an intelligent and good-natured one), who is aware of the reductive mistake, would lessen.

3. Goffman has been criticized for over-extending his theory of total institutions to include even boarding schools and ships. Mouzelis (1971) points out that not all total institutions exploit the negative characteristics usually associated with them and therefore they should not, as Goffman implies, be built into the definition of a total institution. Mouzelis quotes the examples of expensive finishing schools and luxurious clinics, in both of which the power relationship between staff and inmates is mediated by the clients' money. Secondly, he argues that even if mortification processes do exist they do not always have a destructive or degrading effect on the self.

Mouzelis argues that the concrete acts of depersonalization vary with culture. Because the concept of family honour has far greater value for the Greek peasant, a recruit undergoing the rigours of army national service training is much more likely to feel humiliated by attacks on his family name than on his sense of individuality. The head-shaving and humiliatingly meaningless tasks and exercises designed to break his will thus – compared with his Western counterpart – have little effect on his sense of self, which is much more tied up with his sense of family identity. From this perspective, Mouzelis suggests, Goffman is wrong to argue that self-degradation automatically arises from the mortification processes experienced by inmates in total institutions.

Appendix
THE CRISIS – A DIARY OF EVENTS

8 January 1976
The day hospital staff issue a letter to the patients terminating the provision of daily lunches and restitution of transport fares.

11 January 1976
The patients send a letter (signed 'The Day Patients') to the district administrator, with copies to the Minister of Health and the chairman of the institute's PSC, to complain about conditions and treatment in the day hospital. They demand an inquiry.

14 January 1976
The district administrator writes to ask the medical director for his comments on the patients' letter, and in another letter he asks the PSC's views of the patients' complaint, also referring to a letter (dated 22 December 1975) he has received from the chief environmental officer and giving a detailed report of the 'filthy' conditions of the day hospital.

16 January 1976
The medical director replies to the district administrator, arguing he cannot 'engage in piecemeal discussion of complaints with reference . . . [to] the total situation', as only those 'intimately concerned and directly involved can know the intricacies'.

The day hospital patients, in a letter signed by sixteen of them, request permission to attend the PSC meeting on 21 January 1976 to participate in the discussion of practical arrangements in the day hospital, because day hospital staff consistently fail to consult them on decisions affecting them.

19 January 1976
The medical director sends a letter to the PSC chairman, suggesting

265

Asylum to Anarchy

that patients attend the PSC meeting to discuss their complaint, 'in order to avoid colluding with anonymous blackmail'.

The PSC chairman writes to the medical director that he sees 'no point' in inviting the patients to this meeting, since the medical director has 'maintained . . . with rigorous consistency' that all treatment and responsibility for day hospital patients lie with him alone.

The PSC chairman writes to the 'day patients who signed the letter of 16 January 1976', assuring them that their letters are 'being taken with the utmost seriousness' by the PSC, which cannot, however, invite them to its meeting on 21 January as it will not be making decisions then about the 'practical arrangements' to which they had referred.

21 January 1976

The patients write to the PSC chairman (eighteen signed the letter), suggesting they attend the next PSC meeting, that is on that day.

The PSC chairman proposes by letter that the patients attend the meeting on 28 January – one week hence.

The PSC chairman writes to the district administrator, informing him that at a PSC meeting with the day hospital patients on 28 January it will be decided whether 'there is a *prima facie* case for urgent inspection and subsequent inquiry'.

At the meeting, the PSC dissociates itself from the day hospital and agrees to invite patients to the next meeting.

22 January 1976

The medical director writes to the district administrator that he would 'welcome an inquiry, an open forum to assess our work here', because 'unhelpful interference could be guarded against in the future'.

28 January 1976

The day hospital patients attend the PSC meeting.

29 January 1976

The PSC chairman sends the minutes of the PSC meeting to the district administrator, and informs him that the patients claimed that lack of admission and discharge procedures meant that 'dossers' were using the day hospital.

31 January 1976

The medical director sends a letter to the district administrator,

266

Appendix

claiming that the patients' accusation (at the PSC meeting on 28 January) that 'dossers' were using the day hospital was not a reality but part of a 'mechanism of defence called "projection" '.

In the large group, the medical director complains he cannot do therapy when the boundaries of the place have been pushed so wide as to allow 'upstairs' (that is the institute's adult out-patients' department), the Department of Health and Social Security and the NHS to be involved.

6 February 1976
A patient makes an individual complaint to the district administrator that children are using the day hospital and that some patients are attempting to make a profit by recouping excess money on fares.

26 February 1976
The rumour goes around the day hospital that the medical director may abdicate.

21 April 1976
The medical director writes to the area medical officer stating that 'the provision of food, fares, medical certificates, telephones etc. for the patients are superfluous complications and should be withdrawn.'

4 May 1976
Two male patients attack an ex-patient (female) in the day hospital. Two members of staff are hit when trying to separate them.

5 May 1976
The PSC meeting discusses the violent incident, and blames the medical director for it.

The violent patient is discharged by some of the day hospital staff.

The medical director states that he is against this discharge, but even one of his strongest supporters declares: 'We all have our limits of toleration.'

6 May 1976
The PSC chairman writes to the district administrator, the district nursing officer, the Area Health Authority, the Division of Psychiatry, a consultant psychiatrist at Horton Hospital (who had been the first medical director of the day hospital) and the medical director, expressing his concern at the way a violent patient was dealt with in

the day hospital and saying that 'staff and patients are being exposed to unnecessary risks'.

12 May 1976
The PSC discusses its authority and the possible change of chairman.

4 June 1976
The nursing hierarchy ask for information on the nurses' work in the day hospital.

9 June 1976
The second burglary in ten days. Day hospital patients are suspected.

15 June 1976
The day hospital's clinical assistant asks the inquiry committee to visit the day hospital, as her evidence 'can only be meaningful if it is heard in the context of staff and patients in the hospital'. (The committee subsequently refuses her request.)

16 June 1976
Interim recommendations are sent from the Area Health Authority, pending the results of the official inquiry into the patients' complaint.

17 June 1976
One of the external assessors of the inquiry panel visits the day hospital at 9.30 a.m. He talks to twelve patients, but no staff arrive until 10.45 a.m.

28 June 1976
A member of the 'drinking group' is caught breaking into the day hospital at the weekend. Staff think that the 'gangster group' is behind the attempt.

5 July 1976
The clinical assistant asks the inquiry committee to hear her evidence in the presence of day hospital staff and patients in the committee room, as a 're-creation of the large group'.

19 July 1976
Two advisers to the inquiry panel visit the day hospital for a day.

Appendix

23 July 1976
The registrar resigns from the day hospital.

27 July 1976
The medical director writes to the Regional Health Authority to ask for an 'inquiry into the inquiry', because 'they keep changing the rules as they go along'.

A further member of the inquiry panel visits the day hospital.

A secretary who, under instruction from the medical director, was typing a transcript of the inquiry evidence is told by the administrator to stop transcribing.

28 July 1976
The registrar's resignation from the day hospital is accepted by the PSC.

The registrar writes to the medical director, asking him to confirm his withdrawal from the day hospital.

The patients ask for permission to attend a PSC meeting.

29 July 1976
On the second occasion of his giving evidence, the medical director leaves the inquiry committee room when the panel declines permission for him to report the inquiry discussion back to the day hospital.

The clinical assistant suggests that the inquiry visit the hospital, instead of her attending the inquiry.

30 July 1976
The PSC chairman writes to the medical director, saying the PSC acknowledges the registrar's withdrawal from the day hospital and re-confirming that the medical director has medical responsibility during the holidays.

The PSC chairman writes to the day hospital patients that the decision about their attending the PSC meeting will be 'held over'.

The medical director contacts *The Guardian*, saying that lay members of the inquiry panel could easily be persuaded by a specialist adviser that he (the medical director) is ill.

The medical director decides to take his holiday the following week, but says he will not go away and will 'drop in on the day hospital'.

269

Asylum to Anarchy

3 August 1976
The medical director 'visits' the day hospital while on leave.

4 August 1976
The area nursing officer phones the day hospital's nursing officer, concerned because she has heard the day hospital has 'no medical cover' during the holidays.

5 August 1976
The nursing officer phones the district nursing officer about the lack of medical cover.

During July and August: Suicide attempts by two 'activist' patients.

September 1976
The inquiry report is released.The medical director acknowledges receipt of the report.

22 September 1976
Under the terms of the inquiry, the patients are not allowed to see the inquiry report. Many PSC members feel that this is a mistake.

The PSC is worried that the medical director may countermand PSC attempts to set the recommendations contained in the inquiry report in motion.

29 September 1976
First PSC discussion of the inquiry recommendations.

One clinical assistant decides to stop his sessions at the day hospital.

The PSC fails to convince the medical director of its right to make decisions influencing the day hospital, as the medical director calls on his prerogative of professional autonomy. Having refused to accept the inquiry report on the grounds that its recommendations contradict the inquiry team's acceptance of his principles, the medical director leaves the meeting early.

5 October 1976
The patients give a spurious fire alarm and steal a copy of the inquiry report while the staff do fire drill.

The medical director gives an interview on LBC radio.

The medical director reports that H. Ezriel supports his position.

Appendix

The Guardian publishes an article about the day hospital inquiry.

6 October 1976
The PSC decide that day hospital patients should meet the PSC to open up communication between them.

12 October 1976
The medical director sends a letter to the area administrator, outlining a proposal to have two types of treatment in the day hospital: category A to provide non-analytical psychotherapy, social-learning activities etc; category B for Ezrielian analytical psychotherapy for patients who would pledge themselves not to use other facilities in the day hospital. The director would accept clinical responsibility for category B patients and share responsibility for A patients with consultants from the institute.

13 October 1976
The PSC discusses day hospital implementation of the recommendations of the inquiry report.

The medical director refuses to 'modify his experiment' and 'forbids' any PSC member to communicate with day hospital patients.

19 October 1976
PSC representatives have a meeting with day hospital patients in the day hospital. A liaison committee is set up to facilitate communication between them.

The area general administrator writes in reply to the medical director that the latter's proposal for two types of treatment cannot be accepted. The medical director must state by 27 October 1976 whether he will accept to follow the inquiry recommendations or not.

20 October 1976
The medical director informs the Area Health Authority (AHA) that he has withdrawn his labour from the day hospital.

The PSC decides that medical responsibility for the day hospital will be held jointly by the institute's consultants.

The PSC requests the AHA to ask the medical director for his resignation, or to suspend him 'to prevent his presence in the centre', which members regard as 'harmful to patients'.

In answer to a PSC request for a copy of the inquiry report to be

271

given to the day hospital patients officially, the AHA reply that this is impossible.

Having rethought his 'withdrawal' from the day clinic, the medical director proposes to day hospital staff and patients that there be a separate large group run on his lines 'with no interferences', which would operate in parallel with the rest of the hospital.

From 21 October
The medical director resides in the library 'for those who want to drop material provisions'. The rest of staff and patients (category A) work in the large-group room.

27 October 1976
Medical responsibility for day hospital patients reverts to the medical director.

28 October 1976
The AHA write to the PSC that it is unclear whether the medical director is implementing the inquiry recommendations and warn that if he fails to do so by 4 November 1976 they will suspend him and begin an inquiry about his 'further employment', which could lead to an end of his employment with the AHA.

29 October 1976
Two AHA officers and the chairman of the Cogwheel committee of the Division of Psychiatry meet the medical director to ascertain his position. The latter maintains his category A and B distinction, and declares the inquiry report to be antagonistic towards psychoanalysts.

4 November 1976
The medical director fails to meet the AHA deadline for giving his acceptance of the inquiry recommendations and is suspended on full pay, pending the results of an inquiry into the question of his employment, and whether the AHA should 'discipline' him by taking away his position as consultant.

8 December 1976
The day hospital clinical assistant has her contract renewed for three months (instead of the usual twelve).

1 January 1977
A locum is appointed as temporary medical director of the day hospital.

Appendix

24 January 1977
The locum draws up a charter of 'understandings at the day hospital' in which it reverts to a traditional structure and a renewed interest in individual and external reality.

October 1977
The medical director is dismissed by the AHA and no longer allowed to work as a consultant under the NHS.

1977 to 1978
Of the medical director's strongest supporters, one failed to have her contract renewed and another was dismissed.

During 1979
The day hospital is gradually wound down. There are no new admissions, and alternative treatment is sought for the remaining patients.

August 1979
The day hospital is closed down.

Further Reading

All books are published in London unless otherwise stated.

BECKER, H. S. (1961) *Boys in White*. Chicago: University of Chicago Press.

——(1964) 'Personal change in adult life', *Sociometry*, vol. 27, no. 1.

BILLIS, D. (1984) *Welfare Bureaucracies*. Heinemann.

BLUMER, H. (1965–1966) 'Social implications of G. H. Mead', *American Journal of Sociology* 7.

BROWN, G. (1973) 'Some thoughts on Grounded Theory', *Sociology* 7.

CIOFFI, F. and BORGER, R., eds (1970) 'Freud and the idea of a pseudo science', in *Explanations in the Behavioural Sciences*. Cambridge: Cambridge University Press.

COULTER, J. (1973) *Approaches to Insanity: A Philosophical and Sociological Study*, Oxford: Martin Robertson.

——(1979) *The Social Construction of Mind: Studies in Ethnomethodology and Linguistic Philosophy*. Macmillan.

COX, C., and MEAD, A., eds (1975) *A Sociology of Medical Practice*. Collier-Macmillan.

DAVIS, A. and HOROBIN, G., eds (1977) *Medical Encounters: The Experience of Illness and Treatment*. Croom Helm.

DITTON, J., ed. (1980) *The View from Goffman*. Macmillan.

ELLIS, T., McWHIRTER, J., McCOLGAN, D. and HADDON, B., (1976) *William Tyndale: The Teacher's Story*. Anchor.

ERIKSON, K. T. (1957) 'Patient role and social unrest: a dilemma of the mentally ill', *Psychiatry* 20.

——(1979) *In the Wake of the Flood*. Allen & Unwin.

ETIZONI, A. (1960) 'Interpersonal and structural factors in the study of mental hospitals', *Psychiatry* 23.

FARRELL, B. A. (1981) *The Standing of Psychoanalysis*. Oxford: Oxford University Press.

Further reading

FREEMAN, L., ed. (1983) *Social Movements of the Sixties and Seventies*. Longman.

FREIDSON, E. (1963) *The Hospital in Modern Society*. Glencoe, IL: Free Press.

GABRIEL, Y. (1983) *Freud and Society*. Routledge & Kegan Paul.

GLASER, B. and STRAUSS, A. (1968) *The Discovery of Grounded Theory: Strategies for Qualitative Research*. Weidenfeld & Nicolson.

GOODE, W. J. (1960) 'Encroachment, charlatanism and the emerging profession: psychology, medicine and sociology', *American Sociological Review* 25.

HALMOS, P. (1969) *The Faith of the Counsellors*. Constable.

HUGHES, E. C. (1959) *Men and their Work*. Glencoe, IL: Free Press.

INGLEBY, D., ed. (1981) *Critical Psychiatry: The Politics of Mental Health*. Harmondsworth: Penguin.

KENNEDY, I. (1981) *The Unmasking of Medicine*. Allen & Unwin.

NEILL, A. S. (1962) *Summerhill: A Radical Approach to Education*. Gollancz.

RAWLINGS, W. B. (1980) 'Everyday therapy: a study of routine practices in a therapeutic community', unpublished PhD thesis, University of Manchester.

ROCK, P. (1973) *Deviant Behaviour*. Hutchinson.

——(1973) 'Phenomenalism and essentialism in the sociology of deviance', *Sociology* 7.

SARTRE, J.-P. (1969) *Being and Nothingness*. University Paperbacks.

SEDGWICK, P., ed. (1982) *Psychopolitics*. Pluto.

STRAUSS, A. (1959) *Mirrors and Masks: The Search for Identity*. Glencoe, IL: Free Press.

SZASZ, T. (1974) *Ideology and Insanity: Essays on the Psychiatric Dehumanization of Man*. Harmondsworth: Penguin.

TREACHER, A. and BARUCH, G. (1981) 'Towards a critical history of the psychiatric profession', in Ingleby, ed. (1981).

WOLF, A. and SCHWARTZ, E. (1962) *Psychoanalysis in Groups*. New York: Grune and Stratton.

WOOTON, A. (1975) *Dilemmas of Discourse: Controversies about the Sociological Interpretation of Language*. Allen & Unwin.

Bibliography

All books are published in London unless otherwise stated.

BARNES, M. and BERKE, J. (1973) *Mary Barnes.* Harmondsworth: Penguin.

BENNET, E. A. (1966) *What Jung Really Said.* Macdonald.

BERGER, P. and LUCKMANN, T. (1966) *The Social Construction of Reality.* Harmondsworth: Penguin.

BETTELHEIM, B. (1960) *The Informed Heart: Autonomy in a Mass Age.* Glencoe, IL: Free Press.

BLOOR, M. J. (1981) 'Therapeutic paradox – the patient culture and the formal treatment programme in a therapeutic community', *BJM Psychology.* 54, pp. 359–69.

COOPER, D., ed. (1968) *The Dialectics of Liberation.* Harmondsworth: Penguin.

COSER, R. L. (1960) 'Laughter among colleagues', *Psychiatry* 23: 81–95.

——(1979) *Training in Ambiguity: Learning through Doing in a Mental Hospital.* Glencoe, IL: Free Press.

CUMMINGS, E. (1969) 'Therapeutic community and milieu therapy strategies can be distinguished', *International Journal of Psychiatry*, pp. 49–59.

DOUGLAS, M. (1973) *Rules and Meaning: The Anthropology of Everyday Knowledge.* Harmondsworth: Penguin.

EMERSON, J. P. (1969) 'Negotiating the serious import of humour', *Sociometry*, vol. 32, no. 2.

ETIZONI, A. (1964) *Modern Organizations.* Englewood Cliffs, NJ: Prentice Hall.

EZRIEL, H. (1959) 'The role of transference in psychoanalysis and other approaches to group treatment', *Acta Psychotherapeutica, Supplement*, vol. 7, pp. 35–46.

FAIRBAIRN, W. R. D. (1952) *Psychoanalytic Studies of the*

276

Bibliography

Personality. Tavistock Publications.

FOUCAULT, M. (1965) *Madness and Civilization: A History of Insanity in the Age of Reason*. New York: Pantheon.

——(1972) *The Archaeology of Knowledge*, A. M. Sheridan Smith, trans. New York: Harper Colophon.

——(1977) *Discipline and Punish: The Birth of the Prison*. Allen Lane.

FREIDSON, E. (1963) 'The hospital – historical sociology of a community institution', in E. Freidson, ed. *The Hospital in Modern Society*, Glencoe, IL: Free Press, pp. 1–36.

——(1970) *The Profession of Medicine: A Study of the Sociology of Applied Knowledge*. New York: Dodd, Mead & Co.

FREUD, A. (1937) *The Ego and the Mechanisms of Defence*. Hogarth.

FREUD, S. (1923) *The Ego and the Id*, in James Strachey, ed. *The Standard Edition of the Complete Psychological Works of Sigmund Freud*, 24 vols. Hogarth, 1953–1973. vol. 19.

——(1950) 'Humour', *Collected Papers 5*. Hogarth, pp. 215–21.

——(1962) *Two Short Accounts of Psychoanalysis*. Pelican.

GARFINKEL, H. (1967) *Essays in Ethnomethodology*. Englewood Cliffs, NJ: Prentice Hall.

GIDDENS, A. (1984) *The Constitution of Society*. Cambridge: Polity Press.

GLOVER, J. (1970) *Responsibility*. Routledge & Kegan Paul.

GOFFMAN, E. (1959) *The Presentation of Self in Everyday Life*. Harmondsworth: Penguin.

——(1961) 'Role distance', in E. Goffman, ed., *Encounters*. New York: Bobbs Merrill and Indiana Publications.

——(1968) *Asylums: Essays on the Social Situation of Mental Patients and Other Inmates*. Harmondsworth: Penguin.

——(1975) *Frame Analysis*. Harmondsworth: Penguin.

GREGORY, B.A.J.C. (1967) 'The day hospital as a therapeutic community', *Group Analysis*, vol. 1, no. 2, pp. 71–3.

HARTMANN, H. (1937) *Ego Psychology and the Problem of Adaptation*. Imago, 1958 (English translation).

HINSHELWOOD, R. D. and MANNING, N., eds (1979) *Therapeutic Communities: Reflections and Progress*. Routledge & Kegan Paul.

HOBSON, H. (1971) 'The therapeutic community disease' (unpublished paper).

JONES, M. (1962) *Social Psychiatry in the Community, in Hospitals and in Prisons*. Chicago: Thomas.

KENNEDY, R., HEYMANS, A. and TISCHLER, L. (1987) *The Family as In-Patient: Families and Adolescents at the Cassel Hospital.* Free Association Books.

KESEY, K. (1966) *One Flew Over the Cuckoo's Nest.* Methuen.

KREEGER, L., ed. (1975) *The Large Group: Dynamics and Therapy.* Constable.

——(1981) 'Commentary', Group Analysis, vol. 19, no. 3.

LAING, R. D. (1960) *The Divided Self.* Tavistock Publications.

——(1967) *The Politics of Experience.* Harmondsworth: Penguin.

LAING, R. D. and ESTERSON, A. (1964) *Sanity, Madness and the Family.* Harmondsworth: Penguin.

LEMLIJ, M., MULVANY, S. and NAGLE, C. J. (1981) 'A therapeutic community is terminated', *Group Analysis*, vol. 19, no. 3. pp. 216–19.

LIFTON, R. J. (1961) *Thought Reform and the Psychology of Totalism: A Study of Brainwashing in China.* New York: Norton.

MAY, R. (1967) *Psychology and the Human Dilemma.* Princeton, NJ: Van Nostrand.

MERTON, R. K. and BARBER, E. (1976) 'Sociological ambivalence', in R. K. Merton, ed. *Sociological Ambivalence and Other Essays.* Glencoe, IL: Free Press, pp. 3–31.

MORRICE, J. K. W. (1979) 'Basic concepts', in R. D. Hinshelwood and N. Manning, eds (1979) pp. 49–58.

MOUZELIS, N. (1967) *Organization and Bureaucracy.* Macmillan.

——(1971) 'On total institutions', *Sociology*, vol. 5, no. 1.

'Papers from Italy', (1987) *International Journal of Therapeutic Communities*, vol. 7, no. 1, pp. 1–55.

PARSONS, T. (1954) 'A sociologist looks at the legal profession', in T. Parsons, *Essays in Sociological Theory*, revised edition. Glencoe, IL: Free Press, pp. 37–85.

——(1956) 'A sociological approach to the theory of organizations, 1 & II', *Administrative Science Quarterly*, 1, pp. 63–86 and 225–39.

PATEMAN, T. (1972) *Counter Course.* Harmondsworth: Penguin.

PUNCH, M. (1974) 'The sociology of the anti-institution', *British Journal of Sociology*, vol. 25, no. 3, pp. 38–52.

ROGERS, A. and PILGRIM, D. (1986) 'Mental health reforms: some contrasts between Britain and Italy', *Free Assns* 6: 65–79.

ROTH, G. and WITTICK, C., eds (1975) *Economy and Society.* Berkeley, CA: University of California Press.

ROTH, J. A. (1973) 'Information and control in tuberculosis hospitals', in E. Freidson, ed., (1963).

Bibliography

RYCROFT, C. (1968) *A Critical Dictionary of Psychoanalysis.*
Nelson.

SCHEFF, T. (1966) *Being Mentally Ill: A Sociological Theory.*
Weidenfeld and Nicolson.

——ed. (1967) *Mental Illness and Social Processes.* New York:
Harper & Row.

SCHUTZ, A. (1962) *Collected Papers.* The Hague: Nijhoff.

SCULL, A. T. (1977) *Decarceration: Community Treatment and the
Deviant: A Radical View.* Englewood Cliffs, NJ: Prentice Hall.

SEGAL, H. (1964) *Introduction to the Work of Melanie Klein.*
Heinemann Medical Books.

SHARP, V. (1975) *Social Control in a Therapeutic Community.*
Farnborough, Hants.

SKYNNER, A. C. R. (1974) 'Group therapy', in V. Varma, ed.
Psychotherapy Today. Constable, 1979.

——(1975) 'The large group in training', in L. Kreeger, ed. (1975)
pp. 233–50.

SMITH, H. L. (1955) 'Two lines of authority', *Modern Care.* March
1955.

STANTON, A. M. and SCHWARTZ, M. S. (1954) *The Mental
Hospital: A Study of Institutional Participation in Psychiatric
Illness and Treatment.* New York: Basic.

STRAUSS, A. (1981) *Psychiatric Ideologies and Institutions.* Glencoe,
IL: Free Press.

SZASZ, T. (1961) *The Myth of Mental Illness.* Harper & Row.

——(1973) *The Manufacture of Madness.* Paladin.

WHITELY, S. (1981) 'Commentary', *Group Analysis,* vol. 19, no. 3.

WILSON, B. (1970) *Religious Sects.* World University Library.

WINNICOTT, D. W. (1958) *Collected Papers.* Tavistock
Publications.

WOOLEY, P. and HIRST, P. (1982) *Social Relations and Human
Attributes.* Tavistock Publications.

WOOTON, A. (1977) 'Sharing: some notes on the organization of
talk in a therapeutic community', *Sociology,* vol. 2, no. 2, pp. 38–
48.

ZEITLIN, I. M. (1973) *Rethinking Sociology: A Critique of
Contemporary Theory.* New York: Meredith Corporation.

Index

280

Index

Index

Index

Index

Index

object relationships, *see* transference
O'Brien Hospital (USA) 106–8
'oceanic feeling' (Skynner) 63
Oneida community 133–4
ontology 25
organic psychiatry, breakdown of
    255
organization, *see* administration
outside, contact with 34–5, 42
    abandoned 42–3, 46
    see also encounter-group
        therapist, National Health
        Service, nurses
'over-determination' (Freud) 263

Parsons, T. 107, 213, 228
participant observation 2–4, 16, 19,
    84, 89, 91
patients
    complaint by, *see under* crisis
        (major)
    control of, *see* control strategies,
        psychoanalytic reductionism and
        control
    mystification 65–6, 118–19
    strategies by, *see under* reality,
        struggle for definition of
    see also new patients, subgroups
People not Psychiatry 161
personal space 148, 245; *see also*
    under reality, struggle for
    definition of
phantasy and reality in
    psychoanalysis 218–20
phenomenology of power/control
    174–9
Pilgrim, D. 249
polarization 207–12
politeness, social, lack of 116–17
power/control 84, 251
    hidden 4–7, 16–20, 24, 57–9,
        66–7, 256; *see also*
        psychoanalytic reductionism
        and control
    of doctors 31–2

and knowledge 5–6, 248, 251
phenomenology of 174–9
and violence 101–8
see also 'democracy', control
    strategies
'power-knowledge' concept
    (Foucault) 5–6
practical problems, *see*
    administration
pre-natal impressions 134
'pre-patient' 86, 257
'primary ontological security' (Laing)
    25
private psychotherapy 1, 13, 74
private space, *see* personal space
Professional Staff Committee (PSC)
    34–5
    and crisis 94, 157, 184, 189–93,
        202–6, 212–18, 229–35, 241,
        265–8, 270–2
    lack of constitution or authority 56
    origins of 29–32
    seen as outsiders 92
projection 205
protests, *see* crisis
PSC, *see* Professional Staff
    Committee
'pseudo-mutuality' (Lemlij *et al.*) 75
psychoanalysis 24–6; *see also*
    therapeutic community
psychoanalytic reductionism and
    control 5, 7, 18–20, 40, 46, 64–70,
    244, 263
    and Ezriel's theory and practice
        50–8
    see also control strategies,
        debureaucratization, large
        group, power/control
psychotherapy, *see* day hospital,
    groups, psychoanalytic
    reductionism and control
Psychotherapy Institute, *see*
    institute
Punch, M. 58, 176

qualifications, lack of, *see under* staff

Index

reality
  levels of 85
  outer and inner 8, 46; *see also*
    administration,
    debureaucratization
  phantasy and, in psychoanalysis
    218–20
  strategies 246
  testing 53
reality, struggle for definition of 15,
  109–10, 143–79, 245–6
  and interaction 162–74
  and patient subculture 159–62
  and phenomenology of power
    174–9
  see also subgroups
realization 261–2
reductionism, *see* psychoanalytic
  reductionism and control
Regional Health Authority 269
rehabilitation aim 33
reincarnation 261
required relationships 53
resistance, *see under* reality, struggle
  for definition of
'retreatists' (patients' subgroup) 160–1
'revolving-door patients' 39, 254
ridicule, *see* mockery/humour
'ritualists' (patients' subgroup) 160–1
Rogers, A. 249
role
  conflict 37, 83–4, 96–101, 123,
    194–9, 260
  in groups 51–2
  multiplicity 178
  of parents 260
Roth, G. 75–6
Roth, J. A. 256
rules 37–8, 245
  dispensed with 5, 16, 40, 44, 114,
    204–7, 244–7, 256
  hidden, *see under* power/control
  in mental hospitals 12, 15, 253
  need for 244–6
  see also administration,
    debureaucratization, National

Health Service
Rycroft, C. 131, 256, 257

sanction, negative assessment as 38,
  254
scapegoat position 51–2, 146
'schizophrenic mother' (Coser) 260
Schutz, A. 175
Schwartz, M. S. 69–70
Scientology 134
Scull, A. T. 16, 249
selection, *see* admission groups
self-realization 33, 40–1, 45; *see also*
  identity, individual
self-selection 45–6, 86–7, 257
sharing in small groups 64–5
Sharp, V. 147, 149–50, 158–9, 178
shoplifting, *see* gangsters
silence 63
  beneficial 261
  see also non-response
Skynner, A. C. R. 63, 67, 256
small groups 35–7, 41, 43, 45, 49, 60,
  196–7
  abolished 42, 43–5, 46, 49, 93, 112,
    163, 197
  sharing in 64–5
  see also subgroups
Smith, H. L. 259
smoking/tobacco 61
  as currency 15
  as expression of freedom 12
social
  'adaptation' 40–1
  changes 25–6
  context of day hospital 24–7
  politeness, lack of 116–17
social-club group 149–50, 151, 161,
  262
sociotherapy 35
'splitting transference' 112
staff
  control through interpretation
    89–96; *see also* control
    strategies, psychoanalytic
    reductionism and control

286

Index

meetings and their abolition 37–8, 42–3, 71

qualifications, inappropriate 33, 39, 46, 86, 88–9, 91, 198

reactions to subgroups 146, 151–2, 154–5

see also role (conflict)

Stanton, A. M. 69–70

status, 'equal'
and jokes 119–20
see also egalitarianism as utopian ideal

strategic interaction, *see* control strategies, debureaucratization, reality, struggle for definition of

subgroups, patients' 149–59, 246
activists 131, 147, 156–9, 160, 270
conformist/elite 147–8
drinking 150–2, 153, 159, 270
gangsters 151, 152–6, 268
isolates 147, 149, 160–1, 162
social-club 149–50, 151, 161, 262

Szasz, T. 161, 248

taboo subjects 65–6; *see also* non-response

Tavistock Institute 24, 25, 49

theoretical and ideological background 24–7, 48–79, 255–6
administrative authority diminished 72–4
charisma 74–9
'democracy' and psychoanalytic control 57–9
'democracy' and therapeutic community 64–72
everyday routine 59–60
Ezriel's theory and application 50–7
large-group session 60–3

therapeutic context, *see* asylum, historical background, tyranny of therapeutic

therapeutic community
'disease' (Hobson) 75
movement 1, 4, 12–13, 26

see also day hospital

'therapeutic hegemony' (Sharp) 147

therapy 261–2
groups 35–6; *see also* groups, asylum

thought reform 136, 138–41

tobacco, *see* smoking

totalism, ideological 135–41, 195

totalitarianism 108, 260

'totalizing discourses' (Foucault) 6

tranquillizers, *see* drugs and ECT

transference
countertransference 114
'rebellion' 70
relationships 50, 51, 164, 173, 250, 255, 259
'splitting' 112

travel vouchers, *see* administration

tyranny of therapeutic 243–52, 263–4
community perspective 248–50
psychoanalysis 250–1

unaddressed recipient 124

unconscious motivation, *see* psychoanalytic reductionism and control

understanding, lack of, *see* mystification

United States
decarceration in 249
mental hospitals in 106–8

utopianism, *see* egalitarianism as utopian ideal, Oneida community

violence 261
and control 101–8
'vocabulary of motive' 145

Weber, M. 75–6, 77

Whitely, S. 45

Wilson, B. 133, 261

Winnicott, D. W. 25

Wittick, C. 75–6

Wooton, A. 64–5

work groups 35

287

This first edition of
Asylum to Anarchy
was finished in October 1987.

It was phototypeset in Caledonia
on a Linotron 202 and printed by
a Miller TP41 offset press on 80 g/m^2
vol. 18 Supreme Antique Wove.

The book was commissioned by Robert M. Young,
edited by Karl Figlio,
copy-edited by Frances Fawkes and Gillian Beaumont,
designed by Sonia Alexis, indexed by Ann Hall
and produced by David Williams and Selina O'Grady
for Free Association Books.